DEVELOPING A
DIVORCE RECOVERY MINISTRY

A HOW-TO MANUAL
Includes A Complete Divorce Recovery Workshop.

BILL FLANAGAN

NAVPRESS

A MINISTRY OF THE NAVIGATORS
P.O.BOX 35001, COLORADO SPRINGS, CO 80935

The Navigators is an international Christian organization. Jesus Christ gave His followers the Great Commission to go and make disciples (Matthew 28:19). The aim of The Navigators is to help fulfill that commission by multiplying laborers for Christ in every nation.

NavPress is the publishing ministry of The Navigators. NavPress publications are tools to help Christians grow. Although publications alone cannot make disciples or change lives, they can help believers learn biblical discipleship, and apply what they learn to their lives and ministries.

Library of Congress Catalog Card Number: 90-64260
ISBN 08910-93818

Cover illustration: Tim Lewis

Printed in the United States of America

CONTENTS

LIST OF LETTERS, FORMS, AND OTHER SAMPLES

ACKNOWLEDGMENTS

No book is ever written in complete isolation and independence. It has taken many years and many people to develop the resource you hold in your hands.

I am deeply grateful for the privilege of becoming involved in the lives of hundreds of men and women working through the pain and tragedy of divorce. Each one of them, in their own way, has been my teacher.

I am sincerely appreciative of two wonderful congregations of Christ's people: The First Presbyterian Church of Colorado Springs, Colorado; and St. Andrew's Presbyterian Church of Newport Beach, California. They have risked and adventured with me in providing this ministry of healing and wholeness. My two senior minister colleagues, John Stevens and John Huffman, have been a source of important support.

My heartfelt thanks to Jim Smoke, who has been an encourager, collaborator, and close friend. Jim generously contributed from his own files a significant portion of the material included in the workshop lectures.

I am indebted to Fuller Theological Seminary's doctor of ministry program and the National Association of Single Adult Leaders (NSL), who encouraged me to put this material into written form. Jerry Jones, publisher of the *Single Adult Ministries Journal*, and Doug Fagerstrom, executive director of the NSL, initially encouraged me to get this material into the hands of pastors and church leaders. Along with the NSL board, they have worked diligently to strengthen the ministry of divorce recovery among the thousands of men and women undergoing the tragedy of a failed marriage.

Along the way, many individuals have provided the necessary support and skills that I do not possess. Many thanks to Fran Fleck, my secretary and administrative assistant, who has spent hours typing this material, as well as providing administrative direction to the divorce recovery ministry at St. Andrew's.

The men and women who have been discussion leaders and coordinators in the workshops have given me my greatest joy in over twenty-five years as a pastor. Through these people I have been privileged to watch the miracle of healing. My thanks, appreciation, and gratitude to them knows no bounds.

Also, I extend my sincere thanks to two of my friends and colleagues on the St. Andrew's staff: Candy Baylis, the director of children's ministries, has developed a wonderfully creative workshop for children; and Steve Murray, our minister of youth, coordinates an excellent program for teenagers that has deeply touched the lives of hundreds of adolescents. Thanks so much, Candy and Steve.

Finally, my love goes to Christy, my life partner of twenty-eight years, and our daughter, Julie. They have not only encouraged me in this ministry, but have spent many days and nights alone while I have been counseling, traveling, writing, and speaking to the needs of divorced and separated persons. Their support and encouragement has kept me going and given my life joy and purpose. Such fulfillment is possible only when you are surrounded by people who love you, and when you have peace in the knowledge that you are doing exactly what God has called you to do.

INTRODUCTION

Since 1971, it has been my privilege to specialize in single adult ministry and to develop an outreach to people who are struggling with the tragic finality of a failed marriage and a broken relationship. I have never been divorced and do not feel that this experience is a necessary qualification for leading a divorce recovery ministry. This is true for the same reason that one does not have to be a professional athlete to be a coach, give birth to a child to be a children's doctor, or be an alcoholic or a drug addict to help people with those problems.

For many years I thought that the best way to help the divorced was to fill my schedule with counseling appointments. But eventually I, as one concerned pastor, realized that one-on-one counseling would do little to address the growing need in my church and community.

In 1977, while attending a workshop led by Jim Smoke at the Crystal Cathedral, I came across his book *Growing Through Divorce*. I knew then that God was prompting me to expand and utilize this tool to reach a larger number of people. Fortunately, our congregation had the vision, resources, and willingness to take the risk and to venture into this new and exciting ministry.

I spent the summer of 1977 equipping twelve of our divorced single men and women in group dynamics; they, in turn, helped me become more sensitive to realities and issues about which I, not having been divorced, could only surmise and conjecture. Conducting our first divorce recovery workshop in my own living room was a tremendous experience and a tremendous watershed time in my ministry.

We had hoped for about seventy-five people to come to our initial workshop at the church. However, after getting the word out through both church and community advertising, more than 150 people came. It was overwhelming to see what happened and how God used this seminar in each of our lives to draw us into a fellowship of healing and closeness beyond our wildest imaginings.

Since that first night, I have tried to achieve three goals in my workshops:

1. To extend a hand of care and concern, representing the love of Jesus Christ and His restoring forgiveness.
2. To create meaningful, authentic friendships that can last far beyond the end of the workshop itself (see chapter 13, page 157).

3. To promote in the participants a better self-understanding and a desire for continued growth and adjustment.

Over the years I have received several calls or letters each week from Christian leaders asking one or more of the following questions:

◆ I've heard you lead a divorce recovery workshop. What do you do?
◆ How does your program work?
◆ What materials do you use?
◆ Are there resources available that provide a workable understanding of what the Bible teaches about marriage, divorce, and remarriage?
◆ I'm not divorced. Can I have anything meaningful or credible to say to these hurting people?
◆ Will you come and help us lead a seminar?

This book is an attempt to answer these and many other questions. This was originally compiled in 1986 as a dissertation for my doctor of ministry degree at Fuller Theological Seminary. It was published by the National Association of Single Adult Leaders (NSL). The proceeds from its publication benefited the development of their networking and training ministry with single adult leaders across the nation. This book includes new information from the divorce recovery curriculum in current use in our workshops.

Pastors and church leaders today are overwhelmed with the magnitude of the divorce problem. It can affect key people in their churches, the marriages of their children or close relatives, or even their own marriage. Leaders have been forced to take a long look at deeply and firmly held convictions, and many hard-line attitudes have softened. Thankfully, the number of churches that actually pressure divorcing men and women to withdraw from fellowship are much fewer than in the past.

I am not applauding a loosening of standards or a lowering of our view of biblical authority. I *am* suggesting that, because of the tidal-wave proportions of these issues, congregations can no longer just talk about the tragedy of divorce. We have to take some decisive and creative action.

Pastors are painfully aware of the vast number of Christians and nonChristians alike who need a loving, caring, and healing divorce recovery ministry. Much has been written in recent years that either analyzes divorce as a sociological phenomenon or addresses psychological principles for the person going through this tragedy. Little has been provided for the Christian leaders who want to develop skills and sensitivity in conducting this kind of ministry. I hope that my involvement with divorce recovery ministry will be of some practical help in filling this need.

Even though I'm doing a lot of the same things over and over, the divorce recovery ministry is never boring. There is always a new group of people who desperately need the touch of Christ in their lives. It's thrilling to watch these people come alive, become whole, and see themselves through redemptive eyes.

Another reason I'm still involved is the quality of the people I am privileged to minister to. Divorced people are the most honest, transparent, open, affirming, caring people I know. I recently taught a class of married people for the first time in quite a while. Their masks were more securely in place. The transparency wasn't there, nor did they demonstrate the same enthusiasm to learn and grow. Single adults who are going through major transitional times in their lives seem to be especially open—to the gospel, to growth, and to serving. I find that inspiring and challenging.

Divorced people often come to the church to ask really searching questions:

- ◆ Can I ever be whole again?
- ◆ Is there life after divorce?
- ◆ Is there any hope for me?
- ◆ Will I ever laugh again?
- ◆ Can I be useful to God again?

I thank God that I've been allowed to share in the restoration and forgiveness process and to help people realize that God doesn't reject them; that they are valuable human beings, created in His image; and that they can stand with anyone else in the Body of Christ as redeemed, loved, and gifted people.

Having the opportunity of watching people in the healing process and seeing them come alive has been one of my greatest joys. I have been privileged to watch them discover and use their spiritual gifts and find a place in the church where they can grow in maturity, where they become the people God wants them to be. I haven't found anything in the church that compares to this ministry. It offers a cutting-edge outreach to a segment of society so in need of God's touch.

It is my prayer that this material will provide some tools and resources to help bring rays of hope, encouragement, and healing into many lives. I also pray that all the divorce recovery ministries being launched in the church today will not only heal many deep wounds, but will ultimately assist in addressing the root causes of our divorce epidemic, and will help restore God's divine intentions to the institution of marriage.

PART ONE

CONSIDERING A DIVORCE RECOVERY WORKSHOP

CHAPTER ONE

THE DIVORCE RECOVERY MINISTRY

God hates divorce. That is the clear biblical affirmation of Malachi 2:16: " 'I hate divorce,' says the LORD God of Israel." But it is necessary to be just as clear that God still loves divorced people.

Divorce destroys a divine ideal. It tears asunder the fabric of God's divine intentions for marriage and disrupts a relationship that He designed, in the words of the traditional marriage ceremony, "for the welfare and happiness of all humankind."

God hates divorce because of what it does to the people involved. Because our Lord desires our wholeness and happiness, it grieves Him deeply when things in our lives are shredded and ripped apart. It breaks *God's* heart when anything breaks *our* hearts.

In the history of His dealings with humankind, God has established three great institutions: the church, human government, and marriage. Each of these was created for a particular mission and purpose. And inherent in their creation was God's desire for them to characterize unity, harmony, and oneness. His divine intentions were that each of these institutions would declare His glory, His creative design for humanity, and His will and purpose in the world. Unfortunately, both biblical and church history teach us that none of these three has been the perfect witness God intended.

But for some reason, we as Christians seem to have been more judgmental regarding failure in the institution of marriage than regarding failure in the broader context of the church. Many congregations will ask the recovered alcoholic, the ex-convict, and the converted drug addict to give testimonies as to how God has redeemed and released them from their bondage. But not so with the divorced person. According to so many communities of faith, divorced people have committed the "unforgivable sin" and are stereotyped as being sexually promiscuous or emotionally unstable. I have talked with literally hundreds of separated and divorced persons who have told me how their church made it clear, either verbally or nonverbally, that they were no longer welcome in the church family.

The epidemic number of persons experiencing divorce is causing many within the Christian community to reevaluate their thinking and to develop ministries that touch the need of those caught up in this tragedy. The numbers are, indeed, alarming:

- ◆ Approximately one-half of all first marriages fail.
- ◆ More than 80 percent of divorced people remarry within three years and 65

percent of them will fail again. Those who remarry a third time have a failure rate of 75 percent.

◆ More than a million children a year are involved in divorce cases. Currently some thirteen million children under age eighteen have one or both parents missing.

◆ Single parent families are growing at twenty times the rate of two parent families.[1]

Recently, sociologist Constance Ahrons of the University of Southern California used the term "binuclear family" to explain the new family created by divorce and remarriage. For the '90s this may be the most accurate term to describe people touched by divorce. There are now more than eleven million "blended families" incorporating children from former marriages into a new household. But these families are by no means like the glamorous "yours, mine, and ours" families depicted in television situation comedies. Few of these real-life blended families experience success.

Thankfully, churches across the nation are beginning to move beyond the traditional condemnation of divorced people to ask what they can do for the individuals and families involved in divorce. Churches that are reaching out to divorced people are discovering a most fertile mission field.

A recent study by opinion researcher George Gallup seems to indicate that the divorce experience often draws people closer to God while at the same time driving them *further away from* the church. Gallup found that, while 73 percent of divorced people would claim that "prayer is an important part of my daily life," only 54 percent are members of a church. By contrast, 64 percent of never-married singles say that prayer is important to them, and a more comparable 60 percent are also church members. Gallup comments that, "Those who are separated or divorced often feel alienated from their church, complaining that the churches focus on the needs of intact families and often reject the divorced."[2]

THE NEEDS OF THE DIVORCED PERSON

People going through divorce feel a sense of alienation, a loss of self-esteem, and a monumental sense of guilt, failure, and rejection. They are accustomed to feelings of burnout as they assume added responsibilities in the area of personal finances, children, and other household disruptions.

Separated and divorced people most often feel an overwhelming sense of loneliness, as if they are the only one going through this crisis and no one else is able to understand what is happening to them or how they are feeling.

Divorced people seek to meet their own needs in three basic ways (as we will explore more fully in the first lecture):

They Internalize.
Divorced persons are very good at throwing "pity parties" for themselves. They very often will withdraw into themselves and their homes and become reclusive—rejecting all attempts of others to reach out to them. It is not uncommon to watch people in the shock of rejection build a wall around themselves and shut out the rest of the world.

They Externalize.
Others going through divorce may opt for the so-called "swinging singles" scene in order to run away from the issues and problems that surround them. "I can escape my problems if I run fast enough." They think that, if they change their geographical location, they can start out fresh and the reality of what is going on in their life will disappear. They soon discover, of course, that there really is nowhere to run.

They Actualize.
This third possibility is the most difficult and requires a painful acknowledgment of the reality of their situation. To "actualize," the divorced person must come to the place of being able to look into the mirror and say, "I am divorced. I am single. I am alone. I don't like it. I don't feel good about it. I wish this wasn't happening to me, but it is. I must begin to put the pieces together. I must understand that I have to start, not where I would like to be, but where I am."

THREE STAGES OF DIVORCE

The first chapter of Jim Smoke's book *Growing Through Divorce* discusses the three stages of the divorce experience:[3]

Shock
This describes that numbness, that aimless wandering, that zombied state where the divorcee is unable to respond normally, simply because of the tragic magnitude of the situation. People who are in shock cannot think or act clearly or with objectivity. The caring concern of others can minimize the length of the shock period.

Adjustment
People going through divorce begin to adjust when they are able to admit where they are and who they are. Recognizing the fact that they have to reevaluate and readjust to a totally different lifestyle and setting new goals for their lives means they are beginning to adjust.

Growth
Ideally the divorce will turn into an opportunity for growth. Jim Smoke clarifies the distinction between *going* through a divorce and *growing* through it. That such adjustment (*actualizing*) and growth can occur is ultimately the aim of the divorce recovery ministry.

THE DIVORCE RECOVERY WORKSHOP: WHAT IT IS NOT

When considering a divorce recovery workshop, it is important to ask: Who is this workshop for and why am I considering it? One way to help understand the purpose of the workshop is to look at what it is *not*.

A Marriage Reconciliation Workshop
In the first session, attendees are encouraged to seriously consider reconciling their marriages; guidelines for taking that course of action are provided. We tell them that, in order for a reconciled marriage to take place, four realities need to be present:

◆ A willing man
◆ A willing woman
◆ An emotionally neutral professional counselor
◆ A faith and trust in God

These four realities help people assess the prognosis of their relationship and the hope for its survival. If the individual is still hoping but cannot say yes to all four necessary realities, then, for all practical purposes, the likelihood of reconciliation is not good. It doesn't matter whether the person is only separated or actually divorced; the marriage is probably over, no matter how a person feels or what his or her spiritual convictions might be. When one party says it's over, it's over. That is the painful, awful truth.

As Christians, we never want to close the door on a marriage relationship. The lecture on the first night explains that divorce is the hard, not the easy, way out. It also suggests that, if there is any way for reconciliation to occur, it should by all means be pursued. Up front, attendees are encouraged to come to the point of saying either, "Yes, I belong in this workshop because my marriage has failed," or, "No, I don't belong here because I think I can do more to try to save my marriage." The workshop is not the place for those who have a realistic opportunity and a desire for reconciliation. (For those who see reconciliation as a possibility, we have a counseling referral program.)

But at the same time, it is critical for those coping with the finality of a broken marriage to have a place to begin the healing process. We can't go both directions, simultaneously healing marriages and binding up the brokenhearted. The workshop is clearly, and intentionally, focused on addressing the needs of those who are adjusting to the finality of a broken marriage.

A "Broken Dating Relationship" or "Loss of Mate by Death" Workshop

I've had people say, "I'm not divorced but I've had a painful relationship; can I come to the workshop?" I tell them no. The minute someone in the group says, "I have never been divorced, but I'm going through this relationship problem," that person has trivialized the basic reason all the other people are there. Being divorced is not the same as having a bad relationship. The upheaval, pain, and rejection are unique to the divorce experience. This is especially true when children are involved. Consequently, I have tried to keep the workshop undiluted and focused. It is not for widows or relationship breakups; it is for the divorced.

This is not meant to belittle the pain of those other life experiences. Workshops addressing needs such as grief recovery and mending broken relationships are very worthwhile. There are helpful books for such groups, such as Terry Hershey's *Beginning Again: Life After a Relationship Ends* (see Bibliography, page 251). But it is not the purpose of the divorce recovery workshop to meet those needs.

An Exploitation of Vulnerable People in the Name of Christ

I'm a bit nervous about those who see the divorce recovery workshop as nothing more than an evangelistic ploy or *just* an opportunity to get divorced people into a place where they can witness to them for Christ. I feel very strongly that our ministry must not exploit the vulnerability of anyone. And the divorced person can be one of the most vulnerable of all people. People walk through our doors who haven't darkened the door of a church in years.

They are scared to death and they are hurting. When divorce recovery ministries lose their perspective and see this only as a golden evangelistic opportunity, they will also lose their opportunities to reach out to pain-filled people looking for someone they can trust.

That is our first mission: to gain their trust. I've seen some workshops where people have left confused. They have gone away saying, "These people don't really care about helping me get over my divorce; all they want to do is get me into their church." We lose our integrity and their confidence when this happens.

In my lectures it is clear that Jesus Christ is at the very core of what I teach and believe. A biblical foundation is apparent; the gospel of love is pervasive. But I am not there to exploit or manipulate. I've watched many of our people come to Christ. But it has not been because of some heavy-handed witness. Rather, it has been because they have found us to be a loving, caring community and they want to know why.

I realize this is a tough issue for some. There is always the question of how Christian we need to be when we are speaking to so many nonChristians. What can we do to not turn people off but at the same time not compromise who we are?

Over the years I have come to this opinion: Since a divorce recovery ministry is such a powerful way to reach nonChristians in the community, I will bend over backwards not to offend them or lose their trust. I intend to keep them coming long enough to earn the right to be heard. That means walking a tightrope between not exploiting their vulnerability at a very critical time in their lives and yet not losing the opportunity to share the love of Jesus Christ with them.

In actual practice, this sharing of Christ's love takes place not so much from the platform during the lectures, but rather in a relational way in the small groups and the longer-term relationships that grow out of them. Our leaders are expected to be able to share the reason for the hope that is within them. No evangelistic literature is offered; no public opportunities for commitment are given. And yet participants have often wanted to investigate further why we are extending ourselves so vigorously and authentically, and many are drawn to the Lord because of this.

While avoiding overt evangelism, sometimes during the lectures I will use biblical illustrations, particularly New Testament stories like the prodigal son, the woman taken in adultery, or the paralytic by the pool of Bethesda. The issues raised by these texts have proven extremely relevant as a way to introduce the Lord as well as the Bible as a viable resource for truth and healing. This strategy has brought many men and women to an initial commitment or recommitment of their lives to Jesus Christ. No apology is made for the fact that ultimate healing comes from the One who gave us life to begin with and who has a purpose and a design for us to follow.

The divorce recovery ministry has taught me so much about ascertaining the feelings and moods of people as the gospel addresses itself to the questions of our day, particularly the issues surrounding a broken marriage. David Watson reminds us:

> It is not enough for the Gospel to "be relevant"; it must be "seen" to be relevant before there can be any effective communication. William Temple once caricatured theologians as "men who spend blameless lives giving entirely orthodox answers to questions no one is asking." . . . Christ has entrusted us with the ministry of reconciliation and this demands keeping very closely in touch with both the world and with God. Jesus not only spoke with great authority, which astonished His hearers;

He was also utterly relevant to the daily needs of ordinary people which is why, initially at least, He was so popular with the "tax collectors and sinners" who were ostracized by the hypocritical piety of religious leaders. His message got through and it was powerful and authentic communication.[4]

The Goal or Climax of Your Church's Outreach to Divorced People

If at the end of the workshop you simply breathe a sigh of relief, close up shop, and move on to the next project, you've missed the point. The workshop is designed to be a beginning, not an end. I trust that, as you read this book, you'll catch a glimpse of the joy and satisfaction I've found in this ministry to a very needy but also very spiritually receptive group of people. But a word of caution: Unless your coworkers and the people in your church catch this vision, unless you can instill in them a commitment to an ongoing ministry to the divorced, then your efforts in putting on the workshop will probably bear little lasting fruit.

THE DIVORCE RECOVERY WORKSHOP: WHAT IT *IS*

Now that we have looked at what the workshop is not, let's explore some of what it is.

A Workshop to Help People Heal from—
and Grow Through—the Devastation and Pain of Divorce

It is our primary purpose to provide a healing ministry where people can grow, to provide an atmosphere where they can move beyond the devastation and pain that now surrounds them.

A Caring Community of Small Groups

Although the teaching and content in the large-group time is valuable, the most important thing you can do is recruit and train a supportive, loving team of small-group leaders. The most lasting ministry takes place in the small groups when wounded healers care for one another. Care, not content, is the essential ingredient.

A Bridge from the Community to the Church

A divorce recovery workshop creates an entry point from the community into the church. It gives people not normally involved in a church the opportunity to "come home." As we will see, this goal is best achieved when the workshop is held in a church building, rather than on neutral ground.

A Place to Be Heard

I've already said it, but it bears repeating: An effective, ongoing divorce recovery ministry is a marvelous opportunity to reach nonChristians. Many of them are suspicious of the church and will arrive with their defenses high. One of your primary objectives will be to earn their trust so that they can begin to see Christ in you and be drawn to Him.

An Opportunity to Integrate Single Adults into the Church

One of the greatest joys for me is to see how people have come through our workshop, gotten involved in the life of our church, and are now contributing in significant ways.

I am reminded of this often. Just the other day I was talking with two people who had recently become members of our church. I had almost forgotten (someone had to jog my memory) that they both first became involved in our church through the divorce recovery workshop. And when one of our key elders recently gave a report at a church meeting, I recalled that he was in our workshop in 1981. In fact, he met his present wife in his small group. Now, many years later, he is one of our most respected elders. Every time I see this kind of thing I have a deep sense of pride, humility, joy, and thankfulness to God.

If one of our attendees is already plugged into a church, great. We hope their involvement in the workshop will cause them to get involved even more significantly. And if they were not involved in a church before coming to the workshop, then my prayer and goal is that, through their new relationships and the love and care received, they will be drawn to the Body of Christ. Ultimately, that is what this workshop is all about—helping people realize their need for having the Lord at the center of their lives.

CHAPTER TWO

QUESTIONS YOU SHOULD ASK BEFORE SPONSORING A DIVORCE RECOVERY WORKSHOP

Before we look at the specifics of building a divorce recovery ministry in your church, I must alert you to some of the issues you may face. Thinking through these questions beforehand will help you be more effective in planning a successful ministry.

Do you have these two important qualifications: compassion and sensitivity?
I have discovered in leading workshops that my personal compassion and sensitivity is very much on trial, particularly since I am not a divorced person and thus have to win the right to be heard. For example, if, on the very first night, you talk about divorce being a sin, as I did early in this ministry, you are not displaying the kind of discernment and sensitivity that is necessary ultimately to reach people and be a healing factor in their lives. Nor is a lecture that is simply content-oriented going to make much of a difference. I want people who are sitting in my workshops to feel that I really care about their situations; that I can identify with them (to the best of my ability); and that I can address the issues and hurts in their lives with tact, wisdom, and compassion.

Are you able to live with the tension between upholding marriage and ministering to the divorced?
Christian leaders should be prepared for some suspicion and controversy on the part of some people in the church. I remember so well, a few years ago, a woman commented at the door on Sunday morning, "Reverend Flanagan, it is such a wonderful thing that you are doing for 'those' people."

It can be tension-building for a church to uphold a high biblical view of the sanctity and divine purpose of marriage while actively including in the church those who have failed in those areas.

It is necessary for the pastor, as well as any church that undertakes this ministry, to have a clear understanding of biblical teaching regarding marriage, divorce, and particularly remarriage. This has been an extremely difficult biblical struggle in my own ministry. Naturally, different Christians and congregations will come to varying positions on this matter. The church that holds a strict viewpoint regarding remarriage should consider very carefully whether they should develop a divorce recovery ministry. For some, their theology will simply be incompatible with a healthy divorce recovery ministry.

(You should be aware at the outset that I take the position that remarriage may be permitted for divorced people, after careful counseling. If that is not your own understanding, it may affect the way you implement various aspects of my proposed workshop format.)

Do you have an ongoing ministry to single adults in your church?

If you do not now have a general ministry for single adults, it will be necessary for you to develop a strategy and program for continuing to meet the needs of people who "graduate" from the workshop. As I'll stress in chapter 13, the goal should be to build relationships in the small groups that will continue beyond the workshop's end. Hopefully, many of these relationships will involve people becoming a part of your church family.[1] It is extremely important to insure that single people entering your larger fellowship out of the workshop don't feel they're wearing a tag marked "divorced" as they participate in various church functions.

Are you willing to allow and encourage the divorced person to hold leadership positions in the church?

A commitment by church leaders to include divorced people in the decision-making process and leadership of the church needs to be clearly in place before a successful divorce recovery ministry can be undertaken. Certainly such people should meet all the qualifications for leadership that anyone else would have to meet. I'm not calling for any kind of preferential treatment. But if the door to leadership opportunity is closed to the divorced, then you are sending them the message that they are second class, and you will not have an effective divorce recovery ministry.

Are you prepared to deal with other divorce and single-parent family issues?

It is important to understand that when the church opens its doors to the divorced, other issues will present themselves.

Actively including the divorced in church fellowships. Consider the impact this will have in the overall events in the life of the church. For example, are single parents welcome at church-wide potluck suppers, and will they feel comfortable with married couples and their children?

Ministering to single parent children in Sunday school. The implications for the children of single adults enrolled in the Sunday school also need to be carefully considered. Many Sunday school teachers are ill-prepared for the inconsistent attendance of children who are with different parents on different weekends and for how this can impact the continuity of a Sunday school class.

Blended families. Couples who remarry and experience all the financial, emotional, and blended-family issues have their own particular needs. We have established several groups and classes at our church targeting the special needs of remarried couples. As result, they are appreciating the fellowship, contact, and mutual encouragement that such groups afford.

Is your senior pastor one hundred percent committed to a divorce recovery ministry?

Last, but certainly not least, the total support and cooperation of the head of staff (senior pastor) and church board is fundamental. I have known several people on church staffs who have launched divorce recovery workshops without their senior pastor's permission and then realized they didn't have the underlying foundation of support that they needed so very much. If there are any complaints about your workshop, they will be directed to your senior pastor, not to you. Without his prior support, the whole ministry will fall like a jolted house of cards. The entire church staff must be together in seeking the Lord's will before the workshop begins.

SOME PRACTICAL QUESTIONS

As you contemplate a divorce recovery ministry, you may have dozens of very practical questions churning in your mind. Perhaps some of the following questions (from my "most asked" file) will echo your own concerns.

Is our church large enough to sponsor a workshop?
Perhaps you are thinking that your church is too small to ever sponsor a divorce recovery workshop. First, let me say that I don't think it's a matter of congregational size, but rather a matter of the willingness of the church and its leaders to give the resources and support needed to make a workshop happen. Having said that, I should add that it would probably be unrealistic for a church with less than 200 or 300 in attendance to accomplish an effective workshop. One alternative for the smaller church would be to use my six-part video series *Divorce Recovery: Rebuilding the Castle That Has Come Down,* which is available through Gospel Films.[2] The video is not as effective for larger groups, but it works well for the smaller church or group with limited resources and facilities.

What kind of commitment will our church have to make in order to have a divorce recovery workshop?
Unless you and your church are serious about making a long-term commitment to your divorce recovery ministry—both during the actual workshops and in the lives of your workshop graduates—I would encourage you not to begin. It is not a ministry for the short sprinter.

On the other hand, sponsoring a successful divorce recovery ministry year after year is one of the best ways to build integrity for your ministry in your community. Because we have been consistent and steady with our workshop at St. Andrew's Presbyterian since 1981, we now get referrals from judges, family law and domestic relations attorneys, counseling centers, plus other churches. Our long-running track record has gained us credibility.

One of the best ways to illustrate the value of a long-term commitment is that 70 percent of the people who come to our workshop come because they were personally invited. That pattern has become an effective part of our divorce recovery program. We have an alumni list of nearly 7,000 in Orange County alone. That's a lot of people. Many others just call the church and say, "I've heard about your divorce ministry; can you give me some information?" We get literally hundreds of calls like that.

Who attends a divorce recovery workshop?
Our brochure clearly states that this workshop is for any divorced or separated person of any age. Below is an overview of those who actually attend our workshops. Your workshop may vary slightly from this pattern, but this composite is pretty typical of what you can expect:

Separated: The majority (50 to 65 percent) of those who attend a divorce recovery workshop are separated but not yet legally divorced. This may be a surprise to some.

The reality is that the painful adjustment process usually occurs before or simultaneously with the legal process. In most cases, one of the parties has decided the marriage is over long before the actual separation occurs. Consequently, the person seeking divorce recovery often begins to do so before the legal process is completed (which means the legal divorce often follows the workshop experience).

Most of these people have been separated from their spouses for several months. Those who have been separated for only a short time are usually too fragile to participate in the workshop. Sometimes they will attend the first one or two sessions, but they usually don't come back. They realize they are not yet ready to deal with the issues. Although we do not ask them to leave, neither do we encourage them to stay.

Divorced: Approximately 35 to 50 percent are legally divorced, most of them recently. Usually, a few have been divorced five to seven years or longer and have recognized that they still need to work through some issues and find healing.

Single parents: Approximately 60 to 75 percent of the separated or divorced people who attend have dependent children at home, while 20 to 25 percent have grown children. Only 10 to 15 percent are from childless marriages.

More females: At 65 to 70 percent, the women who attend our workshops far outnumber the men, although recently the number of men has been increasing.

NonChristians: Close to half of our attendees are what I would consider nonChristians. This high percentage of unbelievers underscores how a divorce recovery workshop can serve as an entry point into the church.

Alumni: About 20 percent of those attending any given workshop are doing so for the second or third time. We used to separate these alumni into enrichment groups. But on the advice of my leaders, we have now begun to integrate them into small groups with those who are taking the workshop for the first time. The alumni have added a depth and maturity that has been very beneficial.

Will a divorce recovery workshop be financially feasible for our church?

When anyone tells me their church cannot afford to host a divorce recovery workshop, I tell them they can't afford *not* to have one. Assuming that your church exceeds the 200 to 300 attendance minimum suggested earlier, it would be hard to lose your financial investment in a divorce recovery ministry.

We never intended to make a profit from our workshops, but because of the numbers now attending, a substantial profit is realized just from the very modest registration fees for each workshop (see chapter 10, page 127 for more financial information). Beyond this initial profit, participants often make special contributions to our church just to express their appreciation for the workshop.

As a number of your workshop alumni become integrated into your larger church ministry, they will bring with them a new vitality, financially as well as spiritually. Forty to 45 percent of our new adult church members are single people, many of them from our workshops. Although we don't keep track of what each person gives, I am confident that our single adult members bring considerably more dollars into the church than we are spending on all our combined ministries to them. Just the loose change offering we take up in our three singles classes covers three-fourths of the total singles' budget.

The bottom line is that people will support ministries they appreciate. Although increased church income should never be the reason for establishing a ministry, a healthy, long-term outreach to divorced people will more than pay its own way, especially after the second or third year.

Why are there only six sessions?

A six-session workshop, regardless of how well it is presented, is not adequate for complete divorce recovery. Some pastors as well as participants have suggested lengthening the workshop to nine, ten, or twelve sessions. I have not found that to be a workable option for this reason: The biggest challenge in conducting a successful workshop is to recruit and train a committed, solid leadership team. One of the requirements is that leaders attend every workshop session as well as two leadership training classes. That means we are requiring at least an eight-week commitment from our leaders.

Since our church provides the workshop twice each year, we are asking our leaders for a total yearly commitment of sixteen weeks. This is above and beyond anything else they may be doing in our church's ministry.

Our goal is to have two leaders for each small group. I look for the highest quality leaders I can find, many of whom are already busy people. Based on our experience, sixteen weeks a year seems to be about the maximum commitment to ask for and still maintain top-quality leadership. Furthermore, the longer your workshop runs, the more likely you will have no-shows and attrition among your leadership team. This can have a negative impact on the quality of ministry you are able to provide.

Availability of church facilities is another concern. It is best to have access to every meeting room in your church so that each small group can have as much privacy as possible. Will this tax your facility and other church schedules if you run longer than six weeks?

Before lengthening your workshop beyond six weeks, count the costs and be realistic about what you are able to do. And keep in mind that the bottom line in a successful divorce recovery workshop is not content (the amount of information you impart to the participants) but the quality of care and support you provide. Ideally, when the workshop ends, the participants are not saying, "I wish I could learn more." What they mourn at the end is the loss of community—because their small group has come to mean so much to them. This healthy feeling of attachment can be achieved just as well in six weeks as in ten or twelve weeks. (And of course, in many cases, the community whose loss is being mourned actually does survive well beyond the workshop's end.)

Why is each session just two hours long?

I'm quite rigid about sticking to a two-hour time limit for each workshop session. In fact, when the two hours are up, I and my two coordinators go around to all the groups and warmly but firmly remind people that it is time to call it quits. (For those who want to continue the conversation, there is an optional restaurant fellowship time after each session.) This two-hour time limit is important for at least three reasons:

1. We've heard the old saying, "The mind can only absorb what the seat can endure." This is especially true at a divorce recovery workshop. People are dealing with some pretty intense issues and feelings. Two hours is about the

maximum time people can perform the dual tasks of absorbing new information and sharing their lives in a very personal way. To extend beyond two hours is quickly to hit a point of diminishing returns.

2. Many of the participants are single parents who have baby-sitters or children in the nursery. Some parents have children who need to get up for school the next day. And some people may have an hour drive to get home. It is essential to remain sensitive to these areas of responsibility that go beyond the workshop itself.

3. By being consistent in when you begin and end, you are making it easier for participants to return each week. They know they can depend on you. They know they can arrange their schedule with certainty. And those going through a divorce situation will deeply appreciate the qualities of dependability and consistency.

How many workshops can you have in a year?
This will vary from church to church, depending on the size of your ministry, staff, and community outreach. You'll probably want to begin with just one a year. We currently offer two a year and find that to be about the maximum we can handle and still have time to adequately recruit and train our leaders.

What times of year are best for a workshop?
The best time of year for your community and church may differ from what works best for us. We have found the best time to be in February-March and September-October. This seems to fit the church calendar best. It also is designed to take into consideration holidays, school vacations, and other times when people are likely to be out of town. In other words, we simply try to schedule our workshops when we think we'll draw the largest crowds. (But don't schedule your February-March workshop to include the week before Easter.)

Can the workshop be condensed to one weekend?
Yes it can be—and has been many times! See chapter 3 for suggestions about condensing the workshop to a weekend seminar or retreat format.

Is there divorce recovery material suitable for children and youth?
I strongly encourage you to provide a divorce recovery workshop for children and teens in conjunction with the adult workshop. Divorce affects the children too. There are several benefits to running the children, teen, and adult sessions simultaneously:

♦ You are providing healing and ministry for the entire family unit.
♦ It is easier for the single parent to attend the workshop when there is something being offered for children during the same time period. (Of course, even if you do not have a separate workshop for children, it is imperative that you at least provide adequate child care.)
♦ It facilitates making the potluck dinner on the sixth night a truly family experience.

In our workshops, the children and adolescent sessions are only scheduled for the last three weeks of the workshop. We invite third- through sixth-graders to participate in a children's experience conducted by former workshop leaders and members of our children's ministry staff. Concurrent with that is a program for junior and senior high young people, conducted by our youth staff and a clinical psychologist.

These separate experiences have enabled us as a church to provide a total opportunity for the family unit. As they share together in expressing and growing through the issues that they are encountering, they help each other establish new, positive patterns for their lives. It gives children and young people a chance to express some of the needs they have and, along with the parents, to create an environment for working through important issues in their family lives.

This phase of our workshop has been extremely well received. An excellent resource is *Divorce Recovery for Teenagers*[3] by one of my pastoral colleagues, Steve Murray (see Bibliography, page 253).

(See chapter 12, page 153, for a diagram showing the correlation between children, adolescent, and adult workshops.)

PART TWO

PREPARING FOR THE DIVORCE RECOVERY WORKSHOP

PREFACE TO PARTS TWO AND THREE

Parts 2 and 3 of this book include all the tools, resources, hand-outs, and guidelines you and your staff will need to conduct an adult divorce recovery workshop. They are written with the assumption that you are the workshop leader/teacher. You have permission to reproduce all the pages in these two sections *for exclusive use in your local church ministry*.

The following chapters of parts 2 and 3 should be made available to these staff members:

Staff Member	Chapters to Make Available
Coordinator	Parts 2 and 3 in their entirety
Secretary	Chapters 3, 5, 9, 10, 11, 12
Group leaders	Chapters 3, 7, 12
Other staff	Chapters 3, 12, plus their job descriptions from chapter 5

If the workshop leader or main teacher is someone other than yourself, you will want that person to review the entire contents of this book. (Since various workshop personnel will have access to only portions of this book, some material will of necessity be covered more than once.)

CHAPTER THREE

A BASIC OVERVIEW
OF THE WORKSHOP

Before exploring in detail the various aspects of a divorce recovery workshop, let's take a brief overview of all that's involved.

The basic divorce recovery workshops that I have conducted consist of six weekly sessions from 7:30 to 9:30 p.m. The schedule for each session, including leadership meetings before each session, is as follows:

Before the Workshop Begins
6:45-7:30   Greeting, registration, refreshments (concurrently with leaders' prayer time)
7:00-7:20   Prayer with leaders

During the Workshop
7:20-7:30   Refreshments, leaders greet registrants
7:30-7:40   Welcome/announcements
7:40-8:25   Lecture
8:25-8:30   Testimony
8:30-8:40   Refreshments (on the way to small groups)
8:45-9:30   Small-group discussion

After the Workshop
Fellowship at nearby restaurant (optional)

One-time Activities
6:00-7:30   Catered dinner (fifth night, leaders only)
6:00-7:30   Potluck (final night, all participants and children)

LESSON CONTENT

Here is a brief synopsis of what is taught and discussed in small groups during each session of the workshop:

Session 1: Is This Really Happening to Me?

What are some of the myths, as well as the facts, of going through the painful process of a broken marriage? This session looks at the three stages of shock, adjustment, and growth. The premise is that you can either "go" through divorce or "grow" through it.

Session 2: Coping with Your Ex-Spouse

How does a person handle a relationship that in one sense has ceased to exist and yet in another sense goes on for life? How do you manage the frustration, anger, rejection, and hopelessness of relating to a person who has brought you so much pain?

Session 3: Assuming New Responsibilities

How do you plan for the future when the outlook may be very bleak? This session examines how to put new structures and disciplines into life and take advantage of new opportunities for personal development. The premise is that "you can't steer a parked car."

Session 4(a): Being a Single Parent

Divorce does not turn a whole parent into half a parent. This session show how to be a healthy family in a one-parent home or in a situation where custody is shared. It looks at both the advantages and disadvantages of single parenthood.

Session 4(b): Coping Skills for Worries, Dark Thoughts, and Down Days (Alternate Session for Nonparents)

Worry is frequently caused by the tendency to "catastrophize" situations. Down days and depression are usually caused by cognitive distortion. Recognizing patterns of cognitive distortion can help in changing thought patterns and in overcoming depression.

Session 5: Finding and Experiencing Forgiveness

Forgiveness is at the very core of healing from divorce. It has been defined as "surrendering my right to hurt back." This session looks at the principles of experiencing forgiveness from God and from ourselves, and, ultimately, of seeking the forgiveness of an ex-spouse.

Session 6: Thinking About New Relationships

The great majority of divorced persons marry again, but the failure rate for subsequent marriages increases rather than decreases. This session looks at the principles for building relationships that last.

Session 7: Thinking About Remarriage (Optional)

Divorced people often marry again quickly, and these second marriages usually fail. There are many things that must be resolved *before* the marriage, not after. The Bible holds up a high ideal for marriage and has some very serious things to say about divorce and remarriage. But both God's law and His grace must be taken into account.

THE WEEKEND WORKSHOP (OR RETREAT)

Many churches, either because of time constraints or because they were unsure of making a more long-term commitment, have condensed our basic workshop into a single weekend.

This schedule can provide a wonderfully intense and enriching experience. The disadvantage is that you don't have the six weeks passage of time for absorbing the material and, more importantly, for allowing relationships to develop. By far the most important result of divorce recovery workshops is the positive new relationships that can come into a broken life. One intense weekend does not necessarily give birth to such relationships.

If you follow a retreat format (Friday night, Saturday, Sunday morning), you should be able to fit in all six lectures. With a Friday night-Saturday format, you will have to eliminate one lecture. I usually elect to omit the parenting session, since this will not apply to all participants. In either format, I usually drop the group discussion following lecture 6 ("Thinking about New Relationships") and instead have a time of open questions with the entire group.

It's important to remember that, even for a brief weekend of discussing divorce recovery, you'll need to provide adequate leader training. This should be included in the schedule even if your main teacher is coming in from out of town just for the weekend.

A detailed schedule for weekend workshops can be found in chapter 12, see pages 154-155.

LEADERSHIP

One of the most important ingredients of a successful divorce recovery workshop is the leadership team you recruit and train. If you are getting ready to conduct your first workshop, you may not be able to start out with every leadership position fully functioning. You may need to begin with the Chevy version instead of the Cadillac. In the ideal scenario, you will have each of the following staff positions filled and trained for each workshop:

- ◆ *Teacher(s):* A pastor or lay leader who has a heartfelt desire for this ministry and the ability to communicate effectively to the larger group. (You may prefer to have more than one teacher—a pastor and a Christian psychologist, for instance.)
- ◆ *Coordinators:* Two people—a man and a woman—who provide the primary leadership, oversee the many details, and conduct the interviewing and training of small-group leaders.
- ◆ *Small-group leaders:* Two leaders—one male and one female—for each small group. Each group should be no more than eight to ten people, including the two leaders.
- ◆ *Secretary:* A person who is responsible for the registration table, name badges, money, book sales, signs, and assignment of people to their small groups (under supervision of the coordinators).
- ◆ *Telephone resource person:* A person who will help the church secretary field phone calls pertaining to the workshop during the weeks prior to its beginning.
- ◆ *Greeters:* At least one or two warm, hospitable people for every fifty people you expect to attend. They help welcome people at the door (and possibly on the sidewalk and even in the parking lot, depending on the size and layout of your church).
- ◆ *Refreshments chairperson:* An individual who coordinates the shopping for, and serving of, light refreshments before and during the first five sessions of the workshop.

◆ *Potluck chairperson:* Someone who is responsible for organizing the potluck dinner prior to the sixth and final workshop session. (Although not ideal, if you are short of staff, this person could be the same as the refreshments chairperson.)

Keep in mind that the above list of leaders is only for your *adult* divorce recovery workshop. If your church is planning a concurrent workshop for children and teens, additional leaders for each group will be required.

BE PREPARED AS THE TEACHER

Obviously the many how-to suggestions offered by this book are not sufficient in preparing you effectively to teach a divorce recovery workshop. The how-to's are presented first because of my desired practical focus. But in another sense your preparation will begin with the material in the Appendix and the Bibliography. The Bibliography lists many good resources relating to both doctrinal and practical issues. The Appendix contains transcripts of my workshop lectures (plus one lecture by Dr. John Fry). By reading these you will see what kinds of subject matter we have found most helpful in our workshops.

In chapter 8 you'll find outlines of these lectures. The outlines could be useful as a starting point as you organize your own presentation. The better you are able to personalize and internalize your lecture material, the more effective you will be as a teacher. The workshop will be most successful when you develop a good rapport and dialogue with your attendees, rather than simply reading from a canned script. Use the lecture material and the outlines as a launch pad for your personalized preparation.

Foundational to your ministry, of course, is your understanding of the Bible's teaching on marriage, divorce, and remarriage. If you have been in the ministry for any length of time, you have probably wrestled with this question several times over. Although a detailed study of Scripture is beyond the scope of this book, my lecture on "Thinking about Remarriage" will show you how I present my own understanding of this issue to a typical workshop audience. While I feel most of our workshop attendees are not ready to hear a detailed doctrinal study of divorce and remarriage, I do try to show them clearly the importance of both honoring God's law and accepting His grace when they are thinking about these issues.

WHY I USE *GROWING THROUGH DIVORCE* AS THE STUDENT STUDY BOOK

Jim Smoke's *Growing Through Divorce* is the book I recommend to all those who attend our divorce recovery workshops. In fact, a copy of the book is included with our workshop registration fee and my lectures are structured to follow its outline. There are, of course, many other helpful products on the market that you may want to consider (see Bibliography, page 251). But when I started doing divorce recovery workshops in 1977, Jim's book was about the only good material available. Although I have been impressed with several of the more recent books, I still believe his is the best for use in our workshops.

I have learned, however, that the most important consideration is not the book used. People don't come to a divorce recovery workshop with the purpose of amassing tons of new information. They come because they know they'll meet people who care for and love them, people who will help them move toward healing. In that sense, it doesn't matter what book you use.

A GUIDEBOOK . . . PLUS YOUR CREATIVE FREEDOM

This presentation is not the last word on how to conduct a divorce recovery ministry. It is simply what I have found to be most effective in my own ministry over the past fifteen years. You may find ways to adjust the suggested agendas and personalize the other materials to enhance your own workshop. Don't allow yourself to get so locked into my methodology that you are unable to find the best approach for your particular situation and abilities.

Chronologically, your first task in preparing for your workshop will be recruitment of your leadership team. The next chapter will explore that process in detail.

CHAPTER FOUR

LAYING THE FOUNDATION OF YOUR LEADERSHIP TEAM

One of the reasons we have experienced success in our divorce recovery ministry over the years is that I try to do as little of the work as possible. My role has primarily been to give the main lectures and train the small-group leaders. More and more, I seek to relinquish even this latter responsibility to my coordinators so that the overall ministry is not seen as my show.

My goal is to do everything possible to make this a cooperative adventure of a large number of people.

Back in 1977 my first twelve group leaders became like a growing amoeba, as they selected and trained ever-increasing circles of subsequent leaders. As a result, this participant-directed ministry has reached out a hand of hope and healing to nearly 8,000 individuals.

The greater the sense of ownership your leadership team experiences, the more likely it is that you will be able to recruit the necessary leaders year after year.

REQUIREMENTS FOR LEADERS

We don't have a long list of requirements for our leadership team. We want to minimize the number of hoops prospective leaders feel they have to jump through. Our essential requirements are as follows:

- ◆ They profess to be committed Christians.
- ◆ They have personally experienced the pain of divorce and have been participants in at least one previous workshop.
- ◆ They are active, participating members of a local church congregation (not necessarily our own), accountable to a pastor, and committed to distinctively Christian lifestyles.
- ◆ They see themselves fitting into a team of people cooperating as a whole for the purpose of reaching out to others. We are not looking for those who want to establish their own individual ministries, promote their own doctrinal beliefs, or be lone rangers in other ways.

Leaders Must Have Experienced a Divorce

I have a firm rule that every leader—with the exception of the teacher—must have personally experienced divorce. This is important in terms of credibility. The ministry that occurs in the small groups happens because the leaders are wounded healers. They have been there. They understand what the participants are going through. This is vital to the healing process.

The reason we make the one exception for the teacher is that, in many cases, this person may be a pastor or professional who has been charged with primary responsibility for the workshop and who may have much to contribute, even though he or she has not personally been through the divorce experience.

But because the teacher may not have been through a divorce, it is that much more imperative that the other leaders are able to relate personally with the divorced. Although I may have some helpful things to say as the teacher, those sitting in the audience know that I have not been through that experience myself. But when they get in their small group, they know they will be among those who have lived through those experiences. This is a vital ingredient to an effective divorce recovery workshop.

Using Leaders Who Do Not Attend Our Church

At St. Andrew's we found we could not sustain the workshop over the long run without recruiting leaders from other churches. The only exception we make to using leaders from other churches is our two coordinators. We consider them our top workshop leaders and require that they be active members of our church.

Using leaders who are members of other churches has not been a problem for us. Our requirements remain the same, regardless of what church the leaders may belong to. And every leader is personally interviewed by either myself or one of my coordinators. Our application and screening process helps us weed out any problem people and allows us to maintain a high caliber leadership team. (See pages 45-46 for the specifics on how to interview and screen your prospective leaders.)

Because we do have many people attending our workshop from other churches, we make a deliberate attempt not to be guilty of proselytizing. First, that reputation would hamper our effectiveness in the community. And second, that is not the purpose of our divorce recovery ministry. To protect our integrity in this area, we make it a clear policy with our leadership that there are to be *no commercials of any kind* given for our—or any other—church, either in the small groups or during the large group meeting. However, beginning with the third session, we set up a table with handout materials about our church ministries (as well as other approved ministries) for those who seek this information. I insist that our workshop is for the purpose of working through divorce-related questions and issues. We have no hidden agenda.

Theological Requirements for Leaders

It is not important to me that our leaders have any particular doctrinal or theological bent. The workshop does not deal with doctrinal issues other than in the broadest sense. Our leaders represent a wide variety of doctrinal viewpoints. My only requirement is that each leader be a professing, committed Christian. I'm not interested in leaders who are heavy-handed with their particular doctrinal beliefs. That is not the greatest need at this stage in the healing process. Rather, I'm looking for healing enablers.

At this juncture, the priority is to develop a caring community, not to burden the participants with theology and head-knowledge.

Behavioral Ground Rules

We have one main behavioral ground rule for our leaders: They are not to get involved in a dating relationship with any of the participants during the workshop. First, that may compromise their effectiveness as a leader. Second, it is not healthy for most of our participants to be involved in a new relationship at this stage of their recovery process. We cannot keep participants from dating on their own, but we will not allow our leaders to be personally involved in such a manner.

We also require that all leaders respect the rules of the church pertaining to smoking and alcoholic beverages on church property.

RECRUITING LEADERSHIP FOR YOUR FIRST WORKSHOP

Much of what I have discussed up to now about recruiting your leaders relies heavily on the assumption that there is a good source of alumni to draw from. This will not be the case for your first one or two workshops.

But rest assured: I have started divorce recovery ministries in two different churches. In neither situation did I find it overly difficult to begin developing the necessary leadership team. Here are some guidelines to consider.

Be Prepared to Do More Yourself the First Year or Two.

When I began both workshop ministries, I served as both the teacher and coordinator for the first two or three workshops. Initially, my vision and knowledge were needed to give the workshops shape and definition. But today they are much different from when I started them. They have been continually redefined and developed, not only by me but by the many people who have worked as my partners in this ministry.

It simply takes time to get a divorce recovery ministry up and rolling. Other leaders will come along to help you carry the load and provide leadership training, but you should be mentally and spiritually prepared to carry most of the responsibility in the beginning.

On the other hand, don't hold on so tightly that you are unable to let go as other leaders develop from within the ministry. It is important that leaders who develop from the ministry are able to *own* it. Today, my leaders do all the leadership recruiting, a great deal of the training, and most of the troubleshooting.

Use Your "Leadership Radar."

Keep on the alert for excellent leadership candidates in your church. Begin to work with at least two of them—one man and one woman—who have the potential to develop into your coordinators. Allow them to observe and participate in the first one or two workshops before giving them significant responsibility.

Handpick a Core of Small-Group Leaders.

Prior to doing my first divorce recovery workshop at First Presbyterian Church in Colorado Springs in 1977, I selected twelve divorced people—six men and six women—and invited them to my home for dessert and a time of discussion. These individuals came out of the singles ministry that was gaining momentum in our church.

I picked these particular individuals because of their sensitivity and desire to be part of a ministry. I selected them because of their leadership skills and their interest in helping others. They were good enablers, facilitators, listeners. And most of all, they understood the pain, the rejection, and the needs of the divorced.

Be a Leader/Learner.
After choosing the twelve group leaders, I sat under *their* teaching for the next several weeks. We discussed the needs of the divorced and where they sought answers and help. The focus of this time was for me not to teach, but to learn. Frankly, this is one of the primary reasons for my success: I have not been divorced, but I have listened. And I have let my coworkers know from the outset that I need to learn from them, that I don't have all the answers, and that I want to understand. To this day, those involved in my ministry see us working together as a partnership.

KEEPING A STEADY SUPPLY OF LEADERS

I've often been asked, "Do you have difficulty finding the number of quality leaders you need?" The answer is emphatically yes. The operative word here is *quality*. We can always find warm bodies willing to serve. But that is not good enough for a successful workshop. It is critical that we maintain the highest standards possible for our leadership team.

But let me hastily add that, although it is sometimes difficult to find the quality leaders required, we have never been unable to do so. Here are some reasons why I believe we have been able to maintain our leadership strength over the years:

The Alumni of Our Workshops Are Deeply Appreciative of the Ministry.
I have never been part of a ministry where the previous attendees are so enthusiastic and willing to help out. Getting a leader for a divorce recovery workshop is a lot different than putting a committee together to plan a picnic. Over and over again I've heard people say, "This ministry has been such a blessing in my life, and I want to give back to it in some way." I've heard that at least a thousand times. It is always music to my ears. Some alumni contribute money to this ministry. But many offer to help serve as leaders, with some staying with us for several years.

I believe this happens because it is such a fruit-bearing ministry. People who have been a part of the workshops have a sense of awe and wonder about the ministry because it has touched them in some of the deepest areas of their life when they were hurting the most. It is almost impossible for a divorced person to go through this workshop and not become a changed person, a person with a renewed sense of hope and purpose.

Because these people know that their time and effort counts, that they can make a radical difference in the life of someone else going through what they have gone through, we are able to recruit the quality people we need.

Two-Thirds of Our Leaders Have Led in Previous Workshops.
This formula of involving people who have previously led workshops helps us maintain a good workshop momentum. Furthermore, when we do come up short of leaders for any

given workshop, we can always find one of our capable alumni who will pinch hit for us in a leadership spot.

Our Current Leaders Recruit New Leaders.

We never ask for volunteer leaders from the floor. By asking for volunteers, you often get the neediest, least capable people. Rather, our current leaders are trained to discreetly give application forms to those they think would make good candidates for leadership. In baseball terms, this would be like scouting a farm team. To help remind them of the need for selectivity we say, "Please don't give an application to somebody that you wouldn't want to personally work with as a co-leader. If there's no one in your group who seems to meet our standards, then don't recruit anyone."

We Limit the Total Time Commitment to Eight Weeks, Including Two Weeks of Training.

As discussed earlier, the biggest barrier to getting good leadership is asking for too long a time commitment. It is not that the attendees couldn't benefit from more sessions; it's that the leadership will be weakened. When we ask for only eight weeks, most people can juggle their schedules to make that commitment. In fact, I have had executives and professionals significantly alter their business schedules so they can serve as leaders—a commitment that is almost unheard of in church ministries today.

The shorter time commitment allows the busier (and often more capable) people to serve as leaders. It also minimizes absenteeism and attrition among leaders due to weariness or schedule problems.

We Reward Our Leaders.

We publicly affirm them; we serve them a special leaders' dinner; we build a sense of family and *esprit de corps*. Our leaders are not used; instead, they are valued and appreciated. This keeps morale and interest high. Focus on your leadership team as if they were your own family. Care for them and love them. This will come back to you many times over.

RECRUITING SMALL-GROUP LEADERS

Small-group leaders represent the largest segment of your leadership team. And they play a vital role in the atmosphere and effectiveness of your workshop. Because of their importance, I am including a special section here with some specific suggestions and guidelines for recruiting these leaders.

Small-group leaders must be caring listeners. I do not look for people who have something to say. I tell my leaders that the people in their group are not primarily interested in their story. I also tell them that I can tell which of the small groups have the best discussion leaders: If I stand nearby and listen for five minutes and can't tell who the discussion leader is, then that group is being led by an excellent small-group leader!

Small-group leaders are only to facilitate, not teach. Nor are they to be healers or therapists. I do allow therapists and others from the healing professions to serve as leaders. But while they are in this leadership position, they are to take their professional hats off and leave them at the door.

APPLICATION FORM FOR SMALL-GROUP LEADERS

As mentioned earlier, we encourage our leaders discreetly to hand out application forms to those they observe to have good potential as small-group leaders. A sample form is found on pages 43-44.

APPLICATION: DIVORCE RECOVERY WORKSHOP DISCUSSION LEADER

Name _____

Address _____

Phone (Home) _____ (Work) _____

Occupation _____

Current marital status: ❑ Separated ❑ Divorced ❑ Remarried

Date your divorce was final: _____

Are you currently involved in a church? ❑ Yes ❑ No

If so, where? _____

Are you a member there? ❑ Yes ❑ No

Please indicate the prior Divorce Recovery Workshops in which you have participated:

Workshop(s): _____

Place: _____

Date: _____

Leaders' names: _____

Place: _____

Date: _____

Leaders' names: _____

Do you have children? ❑ Yes ❑ No ❑ Ages _____

Do your children live with you? ❑ Yes ❑ No

Are you currently active in any singles groups? ❑ Yes ❑ No

If so, where? _____

What offices or responsibilities do you have in those groups?

_____

Please answer the following questions briefly but clearly:

1. Describe in a few words what the Christian faith means to you.

2. Do you recall a specific time when God became real to you? Please explain.

3. What has helped you the most since your divorce; and how do you feel God has helped you in your life, especially as a single adult?

4. Have you had previous experience with small groups? Where, and what kind?

5. Have you ever led a small group? Where, and what kind?

6. Why do you want to be a sharing group leader, and what would you like to be able to do for the people in your group?

7. What kind of help or training do you feel you would need in order to become most effective as a discussion group leader?

8. Knowing the dates of the next workshop, will you be able to be present at all eight sessions (including two leader meetings and six workshop sessions)?

Following the submission of this application, you may be requested to have a personal interview with [name of teacher or coordinator].

Please return this application to: [name and address of church]

INTERVIEW GUIDELINES FOR SMALL-GROUP LEADER APPLICANTS

We go through six steps in interviewing potential small-group leaders:

Scheduling the Interviews
The coordinators schedule the interview time with the applicants. Applicants are interviewed for about forty-five minutes in groups of five or six. (We have found that group interviews are less stressful than individual interviews.) The church is usually the most convenient place to conduct these interviews.

The Interview
Interviews are conducted by the workshop coordinators, along with two other skilled, experienced, and sensitive small-group leaders. You may want to have a counseling professional on hand. Questions listed on page 46 are used in this stage of the interview.

The Role-Play
After the interview questions are completed, the applicants are asked to role-play as a group, with each of them portraying one of the problem traits described on pages 46 and 96. The purpose of the role-play is to see how each person might handle various situations that could occur in a small group. The applicants are asked to select a group leader for their role-play.

Discussion
After the role-play, a group discussion of the problems portrayed and various possible solutions concludes the interview.

Job Description
Coordinators discuss the Small-Group Leader's Job Description (see pages 51-52) with the applicants to see if they have any questions, problems, or concerns. Ask them if they would have any problem in accepting the responsibilities outlined in the description.

Evaluation
Applicants are thanked for coming and dismissed. Notes and evaluations, recorded during the first four stages, are discussed at this time by the coordinators and the two current group leaders. Applicants are told that they will be notified of the interview results shortly (see acceptance letter on page 47).

Seldom are applicants not accepted. First, only applicants that our leaders have personally recruited receive an application form. Second, if someone has taken the time to complete the application form, send it in, and come to the interview, they are quite serious about their possible leadership role. In most cases, the interview process is simply a jump-start on our leadership training.

ADDITIONAL RESOURCES FOR THE INTERVIEW

Areas to Be Covered in the Interview

- ◆ Personal history—past, present, and future plans.
- ◆ Applicant's goals for the workshop.

◆ Forgiveness—God, self, and others: What have been their experiences?
◆ Relationship with the Lord.
◆ Relationships with the opposite sex.
◆ Reasons for wanting to be a workshop leader.

Suggested Questions for Applicants

◆ How long has it been since your divorce?
◆ How are you processing your divorce?
◆ Do you feel you are growing through your divorce? If so, how?
◆ What do you feel is your responsibility in the group, and to the group?
◆ Do you feel it is your responsibility to have the right answer to every problem or question? Why or why not?
◆ How do you perceive the role of a facilitator (small-group leader)?
◆ How do you feel about being a team leader with a person of the opposite sex?
◆ How would you use good listening skills in your group?
◆ What frightens you most about being a leader?

Problems You Are Likely to Encounter in Workshop Small Groups

How would you handle some of these problem areas? (These questions are usually acted out in the role-play.)

◆ Overly talkative person.
◆ Quiet, withdrawn person.
◆ Personality conflicts between participants or between the participant and the leader.
◆ Person with all the "right" answers.
◆ Overly emotional person.
◆ Person who reveals too much.
◆ Overly negative person.
◆ Inappropriate expression of anger and hostility.

SAMPLE LETTER CONFIRMING LEADERS' SELECTION

Here is a sample copy of the letter our group at St. Andrew's has used to inform applicants that they have been accepted for small-group leadership. The letter alludes to leadership training sessions, which will be discussed more thoroughly in chapter 6.

SAMPLE LETTER CONFIRMING LEADER'S SELECTION

Dear [Name],

Thank you so much for your willingness to serve as a discussion leader in our fall divorce recovery workshop to be held on six Thursday evenings, September 27 through November 1, 1990. I know that God will significantly use your energy and time with people during the workshop to touch some real needs in the lives of folks who are going through the difficult process of divorce. I am looking forward with great expectation to working with a new group of leaders as well as with those who have previously served.

In regard to our preparation for September 27, I want to echo what you have already heard in a phone call from either _____ or _____, our workshop coordinators. We will have two leadership training events. Below are the details regarding these important meetings:

> Thursday, September 5 at 7:30 p.m. — New Leaders Only
> Bill and Christy Flanagan's
> [address]
> [phone]

This evening will be (a) an important introduction to the specifics of the workshop, (b) an opportunity to get better acquainted, and (c) a chance to explore the dynamics of leading a small-group discussion. *Please call the Single Adult Office, [phone number], if you cannot attend.*

> Thursday, September 12 at 6:30 p.m.
> All Workshop Leaders — Potluck Dinner
> Ralph Conn's
> [address]
> [phone]

Bring a hot dish, salad, or dessert to serve six to eight people. You will get acquainted with the partner who will share in group leadership with you, and we'll have a special presentation. *Please call the Single Adult Office, [phone number], if you cannot attend.*

If you have any particular problems or questions you would like to talk with me about, I will be happy to chat with you during the day in my office or by telephone [phone number]. I am thanking God for you and looking forward to working with you.

Faithfully in Christ,
[signature]

CHAPTER FIVE

JOB DESCRIPTIONS AND RESPONSIBILITIES

In this chapter we look closely at each leadership position you will need to fill, and we outline a specific job description for each. We begin with the teacher—the position you will most likely fill.

THE TEACHER

Description

I believe a good teacher must have several characteristics:

1. He or she should be a pastor, counselor, or qualified lay leader. But credentials are not the most important thing. What matters most is the person's compassion and deep desire to be used as an instrument of healing in the lives of the separated and divorced.
2. He or she should have a clear and dynamic speaking style. The content of the leader's teaching should be strong and meaningful to all who listen.
3. The teacher needs to be someone with the ability to communicate without relying heavily on the jargon of the church—someone who can command that kind of situation with skill, authority, and sensitivity and who can thereby earn the right to be heard. Keep in mind that a successful workshop has the potential for bringing large numbers of unchurched people in from the community.

For example, I do not address the issue of divorce as sin until the fifth night of the workshop. It is important for the issue of sin to be addressed, because true healing cannot happen without God's forgiveness and a repentant heart. But if I communicate that kind of message on the first night, I may lose half of the audience. They may simply tune me out and not return. The teacher must have the ability to see a person's life more from God's perspective and to enter the listener's heart with grace and mercy rather than with judgment and condemnation.

Responsibilities

You probably either will be the sole teacher or will share the teaching responsibilities with one or more other people. Depending on your strengths, abilities, and skills, you may be comfortable with and capable of all the teaching responsibilities.

Currently, the only night I bring in another speaker is for session 4. On that night I address single parent issues with the large group. In addition, since the workshops include a significant number of nonparent participants, I invite a counselor to speak to issues of particular interest to them in an alternative session. (See the supplemental lecture by John Fry, page 211.)

Several ministries I know of design the teaching responsibility to be shared by two or more people throughout the workshop. For example, you may personally feel most comfortable teaching sessions 1, 3, and 6, and may prefer to bring in another speaker who is more qualified to address sessions 2, 4, and 5. You may even want to divide up one speaking session among three speakers. I see no reason why these other approaches should not be considered. (If you do bring in an outside speaker, one who is not on your church staff, you will need to adjust your budget to cover honorarium costs.)

A case for only one teacher: The advantage to having one primary speaker throughout is a stronger sense of continuity. A single teacher can reemphasize an issue from one session to the next and can focus on a more comprehensive picture. With more than one teacher, the emphasis of the material leans more toward content than toward building a sense of community—of a healing, caring family unity.

Of course, continuity occurs primarily within the small groups rather than in the large teaching session. But the main speaker often creates the energy that fuels the small groups. A speaker who is especially effective and liked by the participants may help minimize the normal attrition and absenteeism throughout the six weeks.

A case for shared teaching: The advantage to having more than one speaker is that you are able to tap a wide breadth of expertise from very capable teachers in your church and community. Team-teaching might more effectively speak to the real-life issues of your attendees than when only one teacher is used.

The best approach for your particular ministry will depend on your own resources, gifts, and abilities as well as those of the other teachers who are able to participate.

WORKSHOP COORDINATORS

Description
Each divorce recovery workshop will have two coordinators: one man and one woman who have experienced at least one and preferably two prior workshops and indicate a high degree of commitment for this ministry. They need to be highly respected, organized "people persons" who can devote a significant amount of time over a twelve-week period, including the six to eight weeks immediately before the workshop begins.

A workshop coordinator should be a person who demonstrates Christian leadership by (a) a personal walk with Christ, and (b) a clear expression of His care for people. A workshop coordinator should also be a member of the sponsoring church.

Responsibilities
Workshop coordinators should carry out the following tasks:

1. Recruit all other necessary leaders.
2. Interview small-group leader candidates in consultation with the teacher (or

with the pastor/leader who ultimately has responsibility for the workshop).

3. Design and implement appropriate leader training in cooperation with the teacher.
4. Match up two leaders for each small group.
5. Set and control the budget. The secretary can assist in this. If the teacher is from your church, he or she can share in this responsibility as well.
6. Evaluate individual registration forms and make appropriate assignments to the various small groups.
7. Be available to buffer, troubleshoot, and clarify minor problems during the course of the workshop.
8. Assist secretary in promotion of the workshop as requested.
9. Lead twenty-minute pre-meeting for small-group leaders before each workshop session.
10. Assist teacher in selecting testimonial speakers.
11. Troubleshoot problems during workshop. During the first two sessions, this includes staying near the registration table in case problems with group assignments arise.
12. Arrange for substitute leaders for small groups when one of the regular leaders cannot attend.

SMALL-GROUP LEADERS

Small-group leaders should include two leaders—one male and one female—for each group of eight to ten people.

Description
The purpose of a small-group leader is to create an environment in which workshop participants feel comfortable and motivated to share their feelings, opinions, experiences, and needs. This facilitator's intention should be to assist group members in responding to, integrating, and absorbing what they have experienced in the context of their lives, their divorce, and the workshop.

Responsibilities
The small-group leaders' responsibilities are as follows:

1. Participate in the required leadership training prior to the beginning of the workshop.
2. Attend all six workshop sessions, unless there is a personal emergency.
3. Attend the weekly leaders' meeting prior to the workshop session.
4. Develop a confidential roster of small-group members, including their work and home phones (see sample on page 95).
5. Along with the co-leader, make a phone call to each group member each week (see guidelines for this, beginning on page 77).
6. Complete and turn in an attendance slip to the coordinators after each session.
7. Mingle and welcome people at the beginning of each session.

8. Study and become familiar with the Small-Group Leader Guidelines and other helpful materials found in chapter 7 (page 75).
9. Be primarily a listener and facilitator rather than a talker; be "actively passive." Recognize the weightiness of painful experience in people's lives; approach them with the gentler attitude of acceptance.
10. Refrain from acting as a trained therapist. Remember that each participant is responsible for getting what they need from the group experience. *The group leader's job is to facilitate, not fix.*
11. Work with the co-leader in helping maximize group discussion based on the information gained from the teacher, the discussion questions, and any particular needs and issues within the group.
12. Maintain strict confidence. Also remind the group of their responsibility to maintain this whenever confidential information is shared.
13. Do everything possible to develop an atmosphere of acceptance and love. This will help make it possible for group members to discuss openly the issues that block their adjustment to and acceptance of their divorce. The purpose of the small group is completed when each participant has been able to deal effectively with these issues.
14. Work toward building a nonjudgmental, ongoing Christian community.
15. Make the coordinators aware of problem issues as well as problem people, so that they can offer their counsel and, in some cases, give referrals to outside help.
16. Ask participants to fill out and turn in evaluation forms at the end of the workshop (see sample, page 94); fill out and turn in their own "leaders' evaluation forms" (see sample, pages 91-93).

SECRETARY

Description
The secretary helps free up coordinators so they can focus on relating to their leadership team and workshop participants. With the help of a capable secretary, coordinators don't have to worry about many of the administrative details.

Responsibilities
A workshop secretary should carry out the responsibilities listed below:

1. Recruit volunteer assistant secretaries. The secretary will need three to five people to assist with the various areas of responsibility outlined below.
2. Supervise preparation and distribution of promotional materials (see chapter 11, page 135).
3. Conduct workshop registration (nights 1 and 2 only). Registration involves collecting the fee (if it has not already been paid), giving registrants their study book, assisting the coordinator in assigning people to their small groups, and giving them their name tags. Here is a look at each step of the registration process:
   ◆ *Tables.* Arrange with the church office or custodian for the number of tables

you will need. Have the tables set up and ready ninety minutes prior to the beginning of the workshop on both nights.

♦ *Registration forms.* Have an adequate supply of registration forms printed and ready for use. As many as one-half of the attendees may register at the door. Most of these will not have filled out a preregistration form (see sample registration form on page 59).

♦ *Money box.* Arrange with the coordinators for the necessary amount of petty cash. The secretary will need to make change for those paying their registration fee as well as for those buying books.

♦ *Small-group assignments.* This is one of the most challenging and important aspects of registration. The secretary will be working closely with the coordinators to see that proper group assignments are made. Since many people register at the door, it will be necessary to make many assignment decisions in a very short time. (See page 57 for further directions on making group assignments.)

♦ *Name tag.* Purchase name tags and several marking pens. As people register, the secretary will need to put a number on the participants' name tags to let them know what small groups they are in.

Plastic, permanent tags with a Divorce Recovery Workshop logo should be given to leaders. These special name tags make the leaders more visible in the crowd. Leaders are to pick up their name tags at the leaders' meeting prior to the start of each workshop session. Also, paper stick-on tags should be provided for all participants. They will pick up a new one each evening as they come in.

4. Have large, easy-to-read signs made up in advance. (If possible, find a volunteer sign-maker with artistic ability.) Keep in mind that many of the people coming to a workshop may be in the church facilities for the very first time. Make it easy for all participants to find their way. Minimize the anxiety as much as possible. Use signs for such things as:

♦ *Parking lot.* If the facility where the workshop is being held is large, two or three signs should be put in visible places in the parking lot to direct people to the door nearest the workshop registration area.

♦ *Main entrance door.* Have signs pointing people to the registration area and the main workshop meeting room.

♦ *Registration.* Hang signs above the registration tables (preferably from the ceiling for visibility) for those pre-registered, those still needing to register, and so on. If a large number will be attending, have several registration lines, divided alphabetically.

♦ *Small-group locations.* Provide signs giving directions to each group's location. For example, the sign might read, "Groups 8-12 in the Youth Fellowship Hall," with an arrow pointing them in the right direction.

Again, remember to do everything possible to make it easy for people to find where they need to go. Don't give them an excuse to leave because they couldn't find their rooms. Also, be sure to provide the teacher, coordinators, and group leaders a map and/or list of where each group is located.

5. Make sure that ample copies of the study book, the cost of which is included in the registration fee, are in the registration area and ready for distribution as people enter. Have extra copies available for those wanting to purchase additional copies.

6. Materials table. Make sure that all materials being given away or sold have been approved by the teacher or coordinators and have these materials available on a materials table. Beginning on night 3, the registration tables will become the tables used for distributing free materials, for selling additional copies of the study book, and for selling workshop tapes (if sessions are taped).

GREETERS

Description

A greeter's function is to create an atmosphere of warmth and acceptance during the registration time. Greeters need to be specially trained to notice people who are alone or seem to feel lost. Plan to recruit at least two greeters for each fifty people you expect to attend.

Responsibilities

The greeters are usually needed only during the first two or three sessions. By that time, people pretty well know their way around and have made several acquaintances in the group.

1. Greeters need to circulate near the main entrance and (for larger churches) in the parking areas to help make sure people find their way in.

2. Greeters are not primarily responsible for mingling in the main meeting area, but for helping people *get to* that area. Small-group leaders and coordinators, once they are finished with their leadership meeting prior to each workshop, should be in the main meeting area helping everyone feel welcome.

TELEPHONE RESOURCE PERSON

Description and Responsibilities

There will probably be a lot of phone inquiries coming into your church office both before and during the course of the workshop. Unless your church secretary has time to train for and fulfill this function, it would be helpful to have someone on hand to field those calls. This person should be able to explain what the workshop is all about and help the callers decide whether or not they should attend.

REFRESHMENTS CHAIRPERSON

Description

A refreshments chairperson should be able to provide a warm and hospitable atmosphere for workshop participants. This person should shop for and serve light refreshments before and during the first five sessions of the workshop. (The potluck dinner chairperson will supervise the session 6 potluck.)

Responsibilities

1. Be prepared to serve the estimated number of people who are expected. Provide cookies, coffee, tea, punch, and other light finger foods that are easy to serve, eat, and clean up.
2. Since people arrive early, especially on the first night, arrive at the workshop location no later than 6:15 p.m. (one hour and fifteen minutes early) for the first evening. Arrive no later than 6:30 p.m. (one hour early) for sessions 2-5.
3. Arrange with the church office for the following items:
   ♦ Tables; covering and centerpiece for each table
   ♦ Coffee, hot water (for tea and decaffeinated coffee), creamer, sugar, tea bags, cups, stirrers, and napkins
   ♦ Lined baskets or trays for serving cookies
   ♦ Punch bowl and ladle for serving punch
   ♦ Extra cups and napkins
   ♦ Waste containers for small-group rooms/areas
4. The refreshments chairperson will:
   ♦ Cover the serving table(s) with table covering.
   ♦ Keep adequate supply of all food items on serving table.
   ♦ Prepare the punch and keep the punch bowl filled.
   ♦ Clean up at the end of the evening.

POTLUCK DINNER CHAIRPERSON

Description

The potluck dinner chairperson should provide a warm and hospitable atmosphere for the potluck dinner preceding the sixth session of the workshop.

Responsibilities

1. Make sure that the potluck is adequately publicized, in both the main teaching session and the small groups. Ask all participants to bring either a hot dish, vegetable, salad, or dessert to feed six to eight people. Carry-out food such as pizza, chicken, or pies is acceptable.
2. Estimate how many people will be attending the potluck. Base your estimate on average number attending nights 3 and 4.
3. Arrange with the church office for adequate number of chairs and tables to be set up.
4. Provide centerpieces for each table.
5. Recruit people to help you set tables and direct people as they arrive with their food.
6. Purchase place mats and napkins.
7. Arrive at the church by 4:00 p.m. (one hour early) to set tables so that everything will be ready as workshop participants begin to arrive between 5 and 5:30 p.m. The actual dinner will begin at 6:00.
8. Arrange with the church office (or the refreshments chairperson) for the necessary flatware, serving spoons, salt and pepper shakers, baskets, sugar bowls,

cream pitchers, packets of cream and sugar, table coverings, coffee, tea, hot water, and cups.

9. Clean up at the end of the evening. Recruit helpers as needed.

JOINT RESPONSIBILITIES

Joint Responsibility of Teacher and Coordinators: The Materials Table
When leading a divorce recovery workshop, important materials need to be readily available. On nights 3 through 6, the registration tables will be used for distributing free materials, for selling additional copies of the study book, and for selling copies of the workshop tapes (if sessions are taped).

The materials table will be the joint responsibility of the teacher and coordinators (and anyone else in a position of authority). The person or people with primary responsibility for the workshop will need to approve all materials to be offered; the coordinators, working with the secretary, will then see that all desired materials are made available.

Guidelines for your materials table. First, the teacher and coordinators should approve all materials offered. Many of those who come to the workshops are fragile people; there should be no attempts to exploit their vulnerability. Everything they might pick up during the workshop should have your "good housekeeping seal of approval."

Additionally, don't begin making materials available—not even information on your own church and singles ministry—until the third night of the workshop, for two reasons. First, your tables and space will be needed for registration on nights 1 and 2. Second, since many of these people have not been in a church for years, it is wise to help them get comfortable before inviting them to participate in any church activities other than the workshop itself.

During the course of the six weeks, many of our participants do ask for information regarding church programs. A good number also visit our singles ministry and worship services. But you must see that your displays reflect your focus, which is divorce recovery, not a church membership drive.

Materials to make available. You may want to include any or all of the following as part of the materials you will make available to your workshop participants:

- ◆ *A list of recommended counselors.* Since the workshop will no doubt involve a large number of people in need of personal counseling, it is necessary to have counseling referrals available. I refer people only to committed Christians whom I know personally and who have credentials as qualified and licensed counselors.
- ◆ *A list of recommended resources.* Put together a list of tapes (audio and video) and print resources. Of particular interest to workshop participants are materials regarding single parenting and how children need to adjust to a new family style (see page 253 for a bibliography of helpful resources).
- ◆ *Lawyer questionnaire.* Many workshop participants will ask for referrals to suitable attorneys to help them in their divorce process. I carefully avoid doing this, for ethical reasons as well as for the simple fact that I do not feel professionally qualified to recommend a lawyer. Instead, we utilize a lawyer questionnaire (see page 99). This is designed to help people determine whether a particular lawyer is suitable for their specific situation.

- *Cassette tapes.* We always tape the workshop lectures and make those tapes available (at our cost) to participants who want them either to review or to send to a friend who may benefit from the session.
- *Information on your church.* We are careful not to push our particular church to those who attend the workshop. But we do make materials available regarding its various ministries, especially the single adult ministry.

Joint Responsibilities of Coordinators and Secretary: Assigning People to Their Small Groups

Obviously an important part of the success of the small groups is having the right people in each group. Coordinators should begin making group assignments as soon as preregistrations start coming in. But remember that a large percentage of the people won't register until the first (and sometimes second) night of the workshop. As the coordinators and secretary work together at the registration tables during this short window of opportunity, you will need to have the following group assignment guidelines firmly in mind.

In making group assignments you will want to consider both diversity and similarity. People with common experiences can share helpful insights and offer an understanding ear; people from diverse backgrounds can bring fresh perspectives to bear on a problem. Some of the differentiating factors to consider are:

- Age
- Male/Female
- Separated/Divorced
- Length of time since the divorce
- Length of marriage prior to divorce
- Parent/Nonparent

You should be able to obtain all this information from the registration forms.

There is one important exception to our seeking diversity. As best we can, we put all parents together and all nonparents together. Single parents have unique issues to work through, many of which would simply not be relevant to nonparents.

When possible, we divide the parent groups by those with older children and those with younger children. This creates a challenge during registration, when time is so limited. Yet developing congenial groups is a vital part of a successful workshop. Those with adult children (who are probably not as much a factor in the divorce situation) can generally be placed in the nonparent groups.

On the following pages are samples of the small-group assignment sheets we have used. On these sheets, more slots are given for women than for men since, generally speaking, more women attend. If that is not the case in your situation, adjust accordingly.

Procedure for completing the group assignment sheets. Before the first evening of registration, assign everyone who has preregistered.

1. Put the names of the male and female group leaders at the top of each group's sheet. As much as possible, have parents leading parent groups and nonparents leading nonparent groups.

2. Divide the preregistration forms into two stacks:
   - Stack A: Parents with children at home.
   - Stack B: Nonparents, and parents of grown children.
3. Go through each stack and write the names of each person (male or female) in an appropriate slot in a parent or nonparent group. Once a group is filled, go on to the next group.

For on-site registration: As people register, write their names on an appropriate line on one of your sheets. This allows you immediately to assign them to their groups and to indicate the group number on their name tags.

You will want to be careful not to assign ex-spouses to the same group, and preferably not even to groups meeting in the same room. This can be a problem, especially if one or both of the ex-spouses doesn't register until the first night of the workshop. Usually, however, a registrant will take the initiative and let you know if his or her ex is in attendance.

A more sophisticated method of assigning group members. As your leadership team develops over time, they may want to increase the number of criteria used to make group member assignments. For example, they may want to assign parents by age of children and group members by how long they have been divorced or how long they were married before the divorce.

Some of my leaders have wanted to refine and assign our groups into even more categories, but I have been hesitant. I think it is best that everyone is not coming from precisely the same life situation.

When you decide to move to this more sophisticated level of assignment, it will be necessary to have some of your most experienced people running this phase of the registration process; or you may choose to assign groups by a computer program. As your ministry grows, you will discover the level of sophistication that is realistic, effective, and best for your situation.

DIVORCE RECOVERY WORKSHOP REGISTRATION

Fill out and mail with check or money order made payable to St. Andrew's Presbyterian Church, 600 St. Andrews Road, Newport Beach, California 92663. (714) 631-2885

- ❑ Workshop fee—$20.00
- ❑ Workshop fee without book—$15.00
- ❑ Second time through workshop—$5.00
- ❑ Book only—$6.00

Name _____

Address _____

City, State, Zip _____

Home Phone _____

Work Phone _____

Are you a parent? _____

Number of children aged: ❑ 0-5 yrs. ❑ 6-12 yrs. ❑ 13-19 yrs. ❑ 20+ yrs.

Childcare provided for infants through second grade, by reservation.
Supervised study for third- through sixth-graders April 4, 11, and 18 by reservation.

SMALL-GROUP ASSIGNMENT SHEET—PARENTS

[Yellow Paper]

Group # _____

1. Group Leader—Male _____

2. Group Leader—Female _____

3. Female _____

4. Male _____

5. Female _____

6. Female _____

7. Male _____

8. Female _____

9. Female _____

10. Male _____

SMALL-GROUP ASSIGNMENT SHEET—NONPARENTS

[Blue Paper]

Group # _____

1. Group Leader—Male _____

2. Group Leader—Female _____

3. Female _____

4. Male _____

5. Female _____

6. Female _____

7. Male _____

8. Female _____

9. Female _____

10. Male _____

CHAPTER SIX

LEADERSHIP TRAINING

In a very real sense, the magic of a divorce recovery workshop begins with the interaction among the leaders. Consequently, the leadership training sessions are of vital importance. At least two evenings of training should be planned:

- ◆ Session 1, two weeks before the workshop begins, is for the new leaders only. I always invite them to my home for this meeting.
- ◆ Session 2, one week before the workshop begins, is for both new and returning leaders. This is a combination potluck dinner and training session. I prefer to have this meeting in a home too. Meeting in homes seems to facilitate the sense of family and *esprit de corps* within our team.

You may feel you need three training sessions. If so, you should reserve the third session for fellowship and team-building. We have chosen to pursue this objective in our short meetings before each workshop session. These meetings include:

- ◆ A brief devotion (two to three minutes)
- ◆ Announcements
- ◆ Brief sharing (what's happening in groups and follow-up phone calls)
- ◆ Group prayer

Although the workshop schedule doesn't allow time for any additional individual interaction with group leaders, it is vitally important that the teacher and coordinators keep in touch with them informally throughout the workshop. (Because of their more compressed and intense schedule, I do schedule regular "debriefing" sessions during weekend workshops.) During my various times of interaction with group leaders, I try to impress upon them the three-fold purpose for their task.

1. The first purpose is to extend a hand of care and concern that represents the love of Jesus Christ and His restoring forgiveness. We try to help the leaders understand that they are not to come on too strong or to exploit the vulnerability of people at a very difficult time in their lives.
2. The second purpose is to create an environment for meaningful and authentic

friendships to begin. Friendship cannot be mandated, but the workshop is their opportunity to till the soil in which the beautiful reality of new relationships can germinate.
3. A third purpose of the workshop is the need to offer people relevant principles that have biblical grounding and practical application to their present situations in life.

We will now look at the objectives to be accomplished in each of the two training sessions, the agenda for each session, and a synopsis of the content to be covered.

LEADERSHIP TRAINING SESSION ONE

Session One: Objectives
In this first leader training session, we're interested in developing among the new leaders an *esprit de corps* as a team. Time will be spent simply getting to know each other. The two coordinators will set the tone for the session by telling about themselves and communicating why they are so excited about the workshop.

Additional Objectives
We will discuss guidelines for leading the small groups. Small-group leaders should be given a copy of chapter 7 of this book during this first session. Various parts of these guidelines will be discussed briefly, and the leaders will be encouraged to go over them on their own. The importance of these guidelines will be reemphasized during the second session.

As the group gets acquainted, the teacher and coordinators will be further assessing the potential of the various leaders. We especially will be trying to pick out the most likely candidates for giving testimonies during the main teaching sessions.

Session One: Agenda Overview
The two coordinators share the responsibility of leading this meeting. Usually, the teacher only makes the initial introductions and gives some closing comments. If this is your first workshop, you, the teacher, will carry the role of the coordinator.

I offer the following agenda for session 1 in leadership training.

7:00   Welcome
   ◆ Teacher welcomes participants and introduces coordinators.
7:10   Introductions
   ◆ Coordinators tell about themselves.
   ◆ New group leaders introduce themselves.
7:45   Responsibilities of Coordinators
   ◆ Coordinators share more in-depth about:
      a) their reasons for being involved;
      b) their enthusiasm about the workshop;
      c) how group leaders will work with them.
8:00   Importance of Weekly Leaders' Meetings
   ◆ Coordinators explain that the meetings should follow these guidelines:
      a) They should begin promptly at 7:00 p.m. before each workshop session.
      b) They should be considered very important and not optional.

　　　　c) They should allow time to get better acquainted.
　　　　d) They should include vital announcements.
　　　　e) If they can't attend, they must make sure their co-leader does.
8:10　Phone Calls
　　　◆ Leaders must call each member of their groups each week.
　　　◆ Phone calls are not optional.
8:20　Dress Code
　　　◆ Business casual dress is acceptable.
8:25　Alcohol Policy/Tobacco Policy
　　　◆ No alcohol is allowed before, during, or after the workshop.
　　　◆ Tobacco policies are set by the sponsoring church.
8:30　Questions
8:45　Information About Next Training Session (Potluck)
　　　◆ Arrange details for potluck dinner.
　　　◆ Purpose of the potluck is to allow leaders to meet returning (veteran) small-group leaders and to meet their small-group co-leader.
8:50　Study Books and Cost
　　　◆ Discuss study books and explain cost.
8:55　Discussion Group Guidelines
　　　◆ Distribute and discuss chapter 7 of this book.
9:20　Closing Prayer

Session One: Synopsis of Content

Introductions. One of the most important aspects of the leadership training is to build a sense of family and camaraderie. This begins by helping everyone get to know each other. Go around the circle and allow the leaders a brief time to talk about themselves. (The number of leaders you have will determine how long you can allow each person to talk.) You might ask them to share about their work, their children, how long they have been divorced, some personal trivia (like their favorite ice cream), and something particularly significant about former workshops in which they participated.

Responsibilities of the coordinators. Coordinators briefly go over their job description. Help your new leaders understand the vital role that the coordinators play in the workshop. Have the coordinators share what has motivated them to be on the leadership team and what their goals are for the upcoming workshop.

Several other matters should also be discussed:

◆ Leaders' meetings will be run primarily by the coordinators.
◆ The coordinators are the first ones to go to with problems (i.e., problems in your group, problems with your schedule, etc.). As a rule of thumb, women leaders should go to the female coordinator and men leaders should go to the male coordinator.
◆ Although group leaders are required to attend all workshop sessions, occasional emergencies or health problems arise. In these instances, leaders should notify a coordinator, with as much advance warning as possible, whenever a substitute is needed. They are not to find their own substitutes. (If the co-leader is experienced, a substitute may not be necessary.)

Importance of weekly leaders' meetings. Each evening prior to the workshop sessions, all leaders are to meet together. The leader meetings begin promptly at 7:00 p.m.

Let the new leaders know that these meetings are very important and not optional. These meetings are another way to build the sense of family and team with the leaders, which will carry over into the workshop as well. These meetings allow a brief opportunity to get a little better acquainted.

◆ These meetings are where important announcements are made, often pertaining to that evening's schedule.
◆ If, due to an emergency, one of the leaders is not able to be at the meeting, it is essential that their co-leader be present.
◆ Ask that those who have children not bring them to the leaders' meetings. (Start childcare at 6:45.)

Phone calls. Between the two of them, small-group leaders should call each member of their group each week. This, too, is not an optional activity. It is a vital part of the commitment each small-group leader makes.

◆ Faithfulness in making these calls can really make a significant difference in the success of a group. (Give examples of how the calls have made a difference).
◆ Making weekly phone calls to each small-group member is one of the best ways to let the people in your group know that you care.
◆ More guidelines and helps on phone calls are provided in the second training session.

Dress code. I ask all my leaders to dress in business casual style. Dress is not the most important part of what we do, but we must remember that we only have one chance to make a first impression.

Alcohol/tobacco policy. This policy will be guided by the policy of the church in which you meet. In most cases, that means no alcohol is allowed at any church-sponsored function. In addition, I recommend the following policy for all workshops:

◆ No consumption of alcoholic beverages before coming to a workshop session. One of the primary reasons for this is that we need to be very sensitive to those who have fought alcoholism in a marriage. It may even have been a major reason for the divorce.
◆ The optional restaurant time after the workshop is, in effect, an extension of our workshop. Thus, as leaders, the rule of abstinence would apply there as well.
◆ The tobacco policy, likewise, should coincide with the overall policy of the sponsoring church.

Dating policy. As discussed earlier, we absolutely forbid group leaders to date workshop participants, for two reasons: (1) It may compromise their effectiveness as leaders; (2) Most workshop participants should not be involved in a new relationship at this stage of their recovery process.

Questions. Allow ample time for the new leaders to ask any questions pertaining to the items discussed or to anything else related to the workshop.

Information on next training session (potluck). Ask for volunteers to provide the food items needed. Mention that it will be the first joint meeting of all leaders, both new and returning. Let leaders know that they will meet their co-leader at the upcoming potluck. The coordinators will need to finalize co-leader assignments during the next week.

Study books and cost. Urge them to read (or reread) the study book for the course (*Growing Through Divorce,* or whatever other book you have chosen), so that they will be better grounded in the overall subject matter and better prepared as discussion leaders. It is assumed that leaders already have a study book from when they previously participated in the workshop. Additional copies are made available to them at our discount cost.

Discussion group guidelines. The person leading this meeting should be thoroughly familiar with all the guidelines for leading a small group (chapter 7 of this book) and be prepared to discuss those guidelines during this session. Distribute copies of that chapter before beginning the discussion, and encourage the group leaders to study it on their own and to make sure any questions they might have get answered.

MATCHING UP YOUR CO-LEADERS:
BETWEEN LEADERSHIP TRAINING SESSIONS ONE AND TWO

Sometime between leadership training sessions 1 and 2 you will need to make final decisions concerning which co-leaders will be working together. The two coordinators, along with the teacher, are responsible for matching up these co-leader teams. By the time they get to the first leadership training session, the coordinators have had an opportunity to read all applications of the new leaders, to interview each of them, to talk with them once or twice on the phone, and perhaps to have met with them in person (other than in the interview).

The first training session is designed in part so that all the new leaders have an opportunity to share a little about themselves, thus giving the coordinators another chance to get to know them.

By this time, following the first leadership training session, the coordinators should be able to make their team assignments. In most cases the coordinators already know the returning leaders, so the focus is on getting to know the new leaders and determining which of the experienced leaders might match up best with each first-time leader.

The guidelines for pairing leaders are as follows:

◆ One man and one woman for each group (if possible).
◆ Each new leader paired with a returning leader. (About one-third to one-half of the discussion leaders in each of our workshops are new.)
◆ If one leader is a relatively new Christian, pair that person with someone more spiritually mature.
◆ Each half of the pair should represent a *different experience* of growing through a divorce (e.g., easy adjustment versus difficult adjustment) to provide as much variety as possible within the discussion group.
◆ Try to match parents with parents, and nonparents with nonparents.

The ideal is to achieve leader teams that best represent the life-situations of registrants. In reality, you'll simply need to be flexible in order to find the best mix possible. The better you can become acquainted with each leader, the easier it will be to find the right match-ups.

These pairings will be announced at the second training session.

LEADERSHIP TRAINING SESSION TWO

Session Two: Objectives

The second leader training session is a potluck dinner for all of the leaders, including veteran leaders, first-timers, and all other workshop personnel. It takes place one week before the workshop begins. This should be an evening of fun, fellowship, and team-building. It should include a strong challenge regarding the importance of the divorce recovery ministry and the centrality of the small-group experience to the overall ministry. It could also include some humorous role-playing about the do's and dont's of small-group dynamics.

Some more specific objectives include:

♦ Establishing initial rapport between the newly introduced co-leaders.
♦ Inviting input from past group leaders concerning methods that have worked for them.
♦ Providing informal training in group dynamics, possibly with an outside specialist—preferably someone experienced in divorce recovery ministry. (If there is substantial need for such training, a special session should be arranged.)
♦ Reemphasizing the importance of regular phone contact with group members.

Again, the emphasis of this meeting is on building enthusiasm and confidence and on team-bonding. The goal is to leave participants with a "can-do" attitude, rather than dwelling on potential problems.

Session Two: Agenda Overview

Once again, the coordinators share the responsibility for leading this meeting. The teacher usually only makes some initial introductions and welcoming remarks, then later gives some closing comments and a short devotional. If this is your first workshop, you, the teacher, will carry the role of the coordinators.

6:00   Potluck
    ♦ Check off names as group leaders arrive.
    ♦ Introduce each leader to his or her co-leader.
    ♦ Distribute name tags.
7:30   Introductions
    ♦ Introduce group leaders to all other workshop personnel.
7:35   Special Speaker (if any)
    ♦ If no special speaker is scheduled, adjust schedule to allow more time for other items.
7:50   Distribution of Folders
    ♦ Folders should include:

a) Leader guidelines
b) Publicity brochures
c) Discussion questions
d) List of group leaders—listed by group (pairings) and make-up of group (nonparent, etc.)
e) Names, addresses, and phone numbers of all group leaders, coordinators, and staff

7:55   Address/Phone Number Corrections
   ◆ Solicit corrections and additions.

8:00   Discussion Questions for Each Night
   ◆ Distribute questions for all six sessions and discuss their use.

8:10   Discussion Group Guidelines
   ◆ Review principles for good discussion groups.

8:15   Study Books
   ◆ Distribute extra copies to leaders who need them.

8:20   Coordinators' Goals for This Workshop
   ◆ Coordinators should express their excitement about being involved.
   ◆ Coordinators should also emphasize the importance of small-group leaders.

8:25   Leaders' Meetings
   ◆ Stress importance of these weekly meetings.

8:30   Testimonies
   ◆ Explain testimony policy. (No volunteers, please.)

8:35   Small-Group Assignments
   ◆ Explain how attendees are being assigned to groups.
   ◆ Stress that many more will sign up on the first night, so some poor assignments in each group may result initially.
   ◆ Explain reasons for co-leader pairings.
   ◆ Resolve any pairing problems immediately.

8:40   Hospitality
   ◆ Discuss the importance of mingling and making attendees feel welcome.
   Dress Code; Alcohol/Tobacco Policy; Dating Policy
   ◆ Review from session 1.

8:45   After-Workshop Get-Togethers
   ◆ Encourage after-workshop restaurant socializing.
   ◆ Any other plans for extra-workshop or small-group meetings must be cleared with coordinators.

8:50   Phone Calls
   ◆ Review that calls are vital to success and not optional.

8:55   Problems with Participants in the Groups
   ◆ List potential problem situations.
   ◆ "Problem people" should be reassigned immediately.

9:00   Co-Leader Meetings
   ◆ Allow time for co-leaders to schedule a meeting time during the week.

9:05   Brochures
   ◆ Pass out quantities of workshop brochure for leaders to distribute.

9:10   Prayer and Bible Reading Policy

◆ Review.

9:15 Other Matters to Cover

◆ Leaders should try to recruit new leaders.
◆ Turn in evaluations at end of workshop.
◆ Make sure everyone has coordinators' work and home phone numbers.
◆ Give instructions for when a leader can't come to a session.
    a) Let us know in advance.
    b) We will find the substitute.
◆ Veteran leaders should share their experiences.

9:20 Devotional

9:30 Closing Prayer

Session Two: Synopsis of Content

Several items dealt with in the initial leader training session will be included again in this second session. The reason for this is two-fold: Returning leaders, for whom this will be the first meeting, will need a "refresher course"; and there is always value in repetition, especially considering the short time available for training these very important small-group leaders.

Welcome. As people enter, a coordinator or the secretary should check off their names. Introduce co-leaders and encourage them to eat together. Give them their leader's laminated name tags.

Potluck dinner.

Introductions. Make sure that everyone has a chance to meet the various members of the leadership team and other workshop personnel—the coordinators, teacher(s), secretary, refreshments chairperson, potluck chairperson, greeters, and children's and teens' workshop coordinators.

Special speaker. You may want to invite in a speaker with expertise in an area such as group dynamics. Depending on the preparedness of your group leaders, you may choose to do this in a separate meeting where more time would be available. Note that if there is no special speaker, more time can be allotted for other items on the agenda. For instance, you may want to allow more time for veteran group leaders to share from past workshop experiences.

Distribution of folders. You should provide all leaders with folders containing information which will help them in their role as small-group leaders. These folders should contain at least the following information:

◆ Leader guidelines
◆ Publicity brochures
◆ Discussion questions
◆ A list of group leaders—listed by group (pairings) and by make-up of the group (nonparent, etc.)
◆ Names, addresses, and phone numbers of all group leaders, coordinators, and staff

Address/phone number corrections. Be sure to update all information in the folders and on any records maintained at the sponsoring church.

Discussion questions for each night. Review the discussion questions (included in the folders) for all six sessions. Use the suggested questions in chapter 7 of this book (beginning on page 82) or those you have put together from your own lectures. Go over the following discussion question guidelines:

◆ Tell leaders to consider each question as a starting point, a catalyst for discussion.
◆ Instruct leaders that there is no need to go through all the questions each night. Nothing is worse than rushing participants in order to get through all the questions.
◆ Indicate that questions can be a way to help move the group along if one person is dominating the conversation.

Discussion group guidelines. Hand out new copies of these guidelines (chapter 7 of this book, page 75) to stress their importance. Remind new leaders that they should be familiar with these by now; encourage returning leaders to review them.

Study books. Make sure everyone has a copy of the study book you are using. If you are using Jim Smoke's *Growing Through Divorce*, make sure they have the later edition, which includes a study guide.

Coordinators' goals for this workshop. Coordinators should take some time to communicate their enthusiasm for the upcoming workshop and their appreciation for the importance of what the small-group leaders will be contributing. They should stress that the small groups are truly the focal point of the workshop. Far more important than the content of the lectures is the personal interaction and the building of lasting relationships, both of which take place in the small groups.

Leaders' meetings. Stress once again the importance of these weekly meetings:

◆ Encourage leaders to arrive before 7:00 p.m. every night (except the sixth night). Ask leaders to be on time, as they always have a lot to cover in fifteen to twenty minutes.
◆ Let them know that babysitting is available at 6:45.
◆ Room/area assignments should be made for all small groups the first night.

Testimonies. Discuss the very strict procedure for giving testimonies during the workshop:

◆ Indicate that some of them will be asked to give testimonies.
◆ Testimonies are "by invitation only"; remind leaders that they are not asking for volunteers.

Small-group assignments. Session 2 should include information about assignment of all preregistered participants. Explain the different group categories. In most cases, leaders have been assigned to the category in which they best fit, but there are probably some exceptions. Since many more will be registering at the door, there is no way to guarantee that all participants will fit perfectly into the planned groupings.

Co-leader pairings are based on category (parent versus nonparent, etc.) and experience (a new leader paired with an experienced leader). Much thought goes into these pairings. If leaders feel they will have a problem working with their co-leaders, they should let you know immediately.

Hospitality. As much as their schedule allows, small-group leaders need to help make everyone feel welcome at the workshop. They should:

◆ Try to mingle.
◆ Not gather in groups with their fellow leaders.
◆ Introduce themselves to new registrants.
◆ Remember how difficult the first night was for them.

Dress code; alcohol/tobacco policy; dating policy. Review all information that was covered in the first session.

After-workshop get-togethers. Although these are not a requirement, urge the leaders to invite members of their small group for a time of fellowship, after the sessions, at a nearby restaurant. Any other plans for having their groups meet elsewhere must be cleared through coordinators first.

Phone calls. Making weekly phone calls to everyone in the small groups is a vital part of the commitment as group leaders. You can't overemphasize the importance of these phone calls; they are *not* an option. Ask leaders carefully to review the phone call guidelines (chapter 7). Our experience indicates that there really is a relation between the phone calls made by leaders and the attrition (or lack of it) in the groups. Over and over again we have heard of people opening up on the phone when they wouldn't open up in the group. Consider this a very important part of the divorce recovery ministry.

Problems with participants in the groups. Some potential problems to be prepared for are as follows:

◆ Ex-spouses in same group (or even in different groups in same room)
◆ Friends in the same group
◆ Someone the leader knows in his or her group

In such situations, group leaders should bring the person to the registration table as soon as possible for reassignment. A coordinator should plan to stay in the registration area during the first two sessions to be available to handle such problems.

Co-leader meetings. Encourage co-leaders to meet or at least talk by phone. Suggest that they could have dinner together right before the first session. Co-leaders will work together better if they have had some prior contact.

Publicity brochures. Brochures should be placed in the folders given to the leaders. More are available through the workshop ministry if they need them.

Prayer and Bible reading policy. My experience has shown that it is best not to have prayer or Bible reading in the small groups. Remember that there will very likely be several nonChristians in each group. They can easily be scared away if the emphasis of the group becomes too overtly spiritual, especially in the early stages. Our desire is to see all nonChristians come to faith in Christ, and many of our participants have. But first we must win the right to be heard. We win that right, in the context of a divorce recovery workshop, by demonstrating our concern and seeking to minister to their present needs.

Other matters to cover. Leaders should always be on the lookout for people in their group who could become leaders in future workshops. Remind workshop participants and leaders to complete and turn in their evaluation forms (see pages 91-94). These are very helpful in identifying future workshop leaders.

When leaders can't come to a session, they should let coordinators know as much in advance as possible. (Be sure to let leaders know how and when they can reach coordinators.) The coordinators will find the substitute.

As time permits, experienced leaders will be asked to share methods they have used and insights they have gained in past small-group settings.

Devotional.

Closing prayer.

CHAPTER SEVEN

GUIDELINES FOR LEADING A WORKSHOP DISCUSSION GROUP

The small discussion group is at the very heart of the divorce recovery workshop. What happens in this group, and in the relationships that blossom from it, is infinitely more important than any information a teacher can dispense in the weekly lectures.

The goal of the small group is to create an environment in which workshop participants feel comfortable and motivated to share their feelings, opinions, experiences, and needs. The group leader's task is to assist group members in responding to, integrating, and absorbing what they have experienced in the context of their lives, their divorce, and the divorce recovery workshop.

The leaders need to be "actively passive." They must recognize the weightiness of painful experience in people's lives while approaching them with the gentler attitude of acceptance.

Group facilitators are not expected to function as trained therapists. Participants are responsible for getting what they need from the group experience. Remember, as a small-group leader, *your job is to facilitate, not fix.* The purpose of the group is accomplished as each participant is able to deal with things that block his or her adjustment to and acceptance of the specific personal issues of their divorce.

Inherent in this process is the experience of the Christian community as loving, nonjudgmental, and strong, and as a source of comfort and peace.

In a very real sense, the workshop "happens" in the small groups. The quality of the total workshop experience is greatly determined by the effectiveness of these groups. The leader's role is crucial. The following pointers are fundamental in leading a successful and cohesive group dialogue.

A FEW GROUND RULES FOR SUCCESSFUL SMALL GROUPS

Here are some ground rules to share with your group before you begin discussion:

◆ You don't have to talk if you don't want to. We'll never go around the circle or room to get answers or comments on a question.
◆ Be careful not to talk too much. You don't need to reveal too much about yourself or talk too long.

◆ This is "our" group, not "my" group. We all share responsibility for its success.
◆ We should sit in a tight circle so we all can see each other.
◆ We'll use first names (from our name tags) when addressing each other.

Explain how you and your co-leader are going to lead the group and how you plan to work together. Co-leaders should sit across from each other in the circle, not side by side. If you are nervous or unsure of yourself in this new situation as a small-group leader, be honest and let your group know that.

There are to be no "observers" in the small groups. If observers slip through and say they are there just to see what is going on, either politely ask them to leave or contact a coordinator immediately.

Remember to listen. Don't dominate your group. Nothing will turn people off faster. This has been the chief criticism of many small groups. Use this opportunity to develop your active listening skills. You are not there to talk about your own experiences.

The group leader's role involves several responsibilities for you.

◆ Lead the group.
◆ Involve the participants.
◆ Draw out responses.
◆ Stimulate discussion.
◆ Keep things on track.
◆ Put people at ease.

As a small-group leader, don't let the expression of emotion bother you—but also don't encourage it. Discussion on a rational level is the most helpful in the long run. In addition be careful not to overspiritualize or use religious jargon. Stress to your group again and again how important it is to maintain confidentiality. When confidences are broken, it can destroy everything good that might otherwise have come from the workshop.

You should also be careful about how participants offer "advice" in your group. What may be helpful for one person may not necessarily be good for someone else. Also, remember your role is not that of advice giver, but of facilitator and enabler.

Watch out for those in your group who are obviously "on the make." Although you don't want to run other people's lives, consider suggesting that group members avoid dating each other during the workshop.

Look for opportunities to follow up or contact your people personally. Phone calls during the week and coffee after the meeting are ways of having a personal ministry.

Don't be overly concerned because of having to quit at 9:30 (which *will* be our firm policy) even though things are moving well in the group. Don't feel you have to deal with all the questions on the sheet in one session. Remember, too, that you don't have to have all the answers. Never be afraid to say "I don't know."

There are always a few people at the workshop who are unable to function normally in a group situation. They may either be too close to the divorce experience to deal with it honestly and realistically, or they may have serious psychological problems beyond the workshop's ability to heal. If you have such a person in your group, contact the teacher or a coordinator immediately following the first session. He or she can provide professional counseling referrals.

In the more common case of the overly talkative person, break in tactfully and ask other group members their opinion about what that person is saying. In this "emergency situation," you may need to solicit comments by calling on other group members by name. In some cases the leader may have to confront the excessive talker privately after the meeting.

On what, hopefully, will be very rare occasions, a group member who is disruptive may have to be asked to cease participation in the group. If you think that needs to happen, refer the case to the teacher or a coordinator. The guiding principle in such cases is that the group is more important than any single individual in it.

I recommend that you provide information about your church only if people request it. We provide materials regarding our singles ministry on the registration/materials table beginning with session 3. Of course you will need to follow whatever guidelines your own church or workshop leaders establish.

SMALL-GROUP COMMUNICATION

Typically, three levels of communication can occur in small-group meetings:

1. *Mouth-to-Mouth:* This is the first level of communication. It consists of merely talking and sometimes is carried out on a superficial level (introductions, etc.).
2. *Head-to-Head:* This is the "What do you think about . . ." level, the intellectual exchange of ideas.
3. *Heart-to-Heart:* This level means really sharing who you are, what you believe, what turns you on, or why you think this and why you react in a particular way. It's a deep, frank level of communication.

Usually, if a small group runs out of things to say in fifteen minutes or less, they haven't gotten out of the mouth-to-mouth stage. Once a group is in the heart-to-heart phase, no amount of time will be enough. Following the guidelines given above will help you lay the groundwork for honest, heart-to-heart communication in your group.

PHONE CALL GUIDELINES

A very important part of your responsibilities in being a divorce recovery workshop small-group leader is your commitment to making phone calls each week to each of the participants in your group.

Many times in the past, the weekly phone calls have been the means through which participants have opened up and even decided to return to the group. For others, it's enough just to know that someone cared enough to call. *There is a direct connection between weekly phone calls from group leaders and the cohesiveness of the group.*

Following are some guidelines and helpful hints in making phone calls to group participants:

Who Will Make the Calls?
Responsibility for calling can be divided between the leaders in various ways, at your own discretion. For example, male leaders can call all of the men, and female leaders can

call all of the women. Or leaders can simply divide up the names, switching the group of people each one will be calling every week. Most importantly, communicate with your co-leader each week to ensure that all the calls are made.

When Should You Make the Calls?
Don't wait until the night before the next meeting to make all of your calls! You will most likely not reach everyone if you do. It's a good idea to start making your calls three nights prior to each meeting. This way you'll have a better chance of reaching participants, and you won't burn yourself out or run out of time by trying to make all the calls in one night.

By starting early in the week, you can also try to avoid leaving a message on an answering machine. Instead, call back and attempt to talk to the participant directly. You are urged not to leave a message on a machine until your second or third attempt to reach the person.

If you do leave a message on an answering machine or with a person other than the participant, it is important that you keep in mind the participant's privacy regarding the fact that they are attending the workshop. Please do *not* say, "I am so-and-so from the divorce recovery workshop." Rather, say "I am so-and-so from St. Andrew's" or "St. Andrew's workshop."

What Do You Say?
Start out by simply saying you were glad to see the person at the workshop and hope to see him or her again next week. Ask how he or she liked the workshop. You might also ask about things like the person's work or children.

These conversations do not have to be long. The most important aspect of the calls is to let someone know that you care, that you have been through the same divorce process, and that you have survived and grown.

You might also want to say something about the topic of the next lecture and the corresponding chapter in the study book being used.

How Do You Handle Problem Calls?
The person who doesn't want to talk. The same rule holds true with phone conversations as in the small groups: No participant has to talk. If you reach someone on the phone who really doesn't want to talk, just let the person know you are glad he or she came to the workshop and you'll look forward to seeing that person again.

The person who doesn't want to stop talking. Obviously, you want to be a good listener. But you will inevitably end up needing to terminate some longer calls. The easiest thing to say to end a conversation is that you've enjoyed speaking with the person, you look forward to talking with him or her again, but you do have several other calls to make yet that evening.

It's important that you don't allow the fear of longer conversations to deter you from making calls. Before you make a call, rehearse your own polite way of ending an extended conversation.

The very distraught person. In this situation, just listen and offer your understanding. You are *not* expected to be a trained psychotherapist. Just be a friend. In an extreme case where you become concerned regarding someone's emotional and/or physical well-being, contact one of the workshop coordinators.

As the workshop progresses, if you have any additional questions about phone calls to participants, see one of the coordinators.

Calls Made Following First Session

Here are some things you should cover during the first phone call:

1. How did you feel about the first evening (both the small group and the larger workshop)?
2. Were you comfortable in your group? If not, why? (The main intent of this question is to make sure that the participant was placed in the proper group, e.g., parent versus nonparent, etc.)
3. Do you have any unanswered questions about the workshop?
4. Has anything particular happened this week that relates to what you learned the first evening?
5. I look forward to seeing you next week, and I'm sure the next session will be meaningful to you. It gets easier as we go along and become better acquainted.

Be sure to have details of church and community social events available when calling, in case you feel the person might need suggestions of activities to fill empty days.

GUIDELINES FOR GROUP LEADERS
WHO GIVE PUBLIC TESTIMONIES

Giving a testimony at a divorce recovery workshop is an awesome opportunity literally to become a wounded healer to many who are coping with pain, loss, anger, and confusion. The process of deciding who will be asked to give testimonies involves the prayerful thoughts and collective wisdom of several people.

The teacher and the coordinators are eager to assist as much or as little as the individual giving the testimony desires. Feel free to call regarding any help you might need during the week as you prepare. (By now you should have been given the office and home phone numbers of your workshop teacher and/or coordinators.)

If you are asked to participate in this important aspect of our divorce recovery ministry, you need to observe the following guidelines.

Five Minute Maximum

First, we ask that you strictly observe a five minute maximum for your testimony. This may mean that you have to write out and practice what you are going to say to be sure that it does not extend into the small-group time. The teacher is subjected to the same time constraints, so that the time allotted for the small groups does not suffer from his or her going overtime.

The coordinators will be standing in the rear of the room, keeping time. They will signal when you have a minute left, and again when your time is up. This will be a standard procedure for all testimonies.

A Positive Emphasis on Growth

The purpose of the testimony is not to tell your whole story. Certainly no one can do that in the brief time allowed. The thrust of the testimony, rather than being a rehashing of your pain, is to communicate a positive emphasis on how you are presently growing as a person. You want to encourage your listeners.

Relevance to Topic of Session
You have been selected to give a testimony on this particular night because it is felt that you have something to say regarding the topic of the evening. As much as possible, you should relate your testimony to the lecture topic. But don't feel overly constrained by this. The goal is to strive for a topical continuity, from the *lecture* to the *testimony* to the *small groups*. Other material can be inserted as it relates to your particular circumstance; yet the testimony should generally focus on the topic of the day.

A Balanced Spiritual/Practical Perspective
As you know, we try to delicately balance the practical and spiritual ingredients of the lectures, recognizing that there are many nonChristians present who may feel threatened by a high-powered spiritual approach. We never want to apologize for being Christians, nor water down how God has brought wholeness and healing to our lives. Without being schmaltzy or sloppily sentimental, we are trying to share how God has helped in our experiences.

We don't want to appear to be giving a hard sell for the Lord or the church. Yet, at the same time, there is nothing wrong with simply stating how God (and/or His church) has been instrumental in your healing.

A Word of Thanks
Thanks for all the work you are doing and your willingness carefully and prayerfully to offer a personal testimony in what has proven to be such a meaningful and vital part of our workshop. You are being undergirded with a whole lot of prayer support and love.

LAUGHTER IN THE SMALL GROUPS

It is important to help our attendees smile and laugh. Laughter is medicine for the wounded soul. I've had people come up to me and say, "I didn't think I could ever laugh again, and you have helped me to do so. Thank you." Laughter is part of a healthy divorce recovery ministry.

Discuss this aspect of your workshop with the leadership. How can laughter be encouraged in healthy ways? How can the small groups help encourage laughter?

A good group will have both laughter and tears. Just laughter or just tears is probably a sign that something is not in the right balance.

There are, however, some cautions. Neither laughter nor tears can be manipulated or forced. If you start making jokes at the wrong time or in the wrong context, it can trivialize a person's feelings and possibly even increase their pain. Encourage laughter, but allow it to be spontaneous, natural, and healthy.

PRAYER AND BIBLE READING IN WORKSHOP GROUPS

My experience has shown that it is best not to have prayer or Bible reading in the small groups of a divorce recovery workshop. Remember that there will very likely be several nonChristians in each group. Some of them could be intimidated or scared away from the workshop altogether if the emphasis of the group becomes too overtly religious, especially in the early stages. Our desire is to see all nonChristians come to faith in Christ, but first we must win the right to be heard. And we win that right, in the context of a divorce recovery workshop, by demonstrating our concern and seeking to minister to their present "felt needs."

You will, of course, want to abide by the guidelines established by your own workshop's leaders in this regard.

BEHAVIORAL GROUND RULES FOR SMALL-GROUP LEADERS

We have one main behavioral ground rule that we will ask you as a small-group leader to abide by: We ask that you not become involved in a dating relationship with any of the participants during the workshop. We make this request for two very important reasons: First, such a relationship could seriously compromise your effectiveness as a leader. Second, it is not healthy for most of our participants to be involved in a new relationship at this stage of their recovery process. We cannot keep participants from dating each other on their own, but we cannot allow our leaders to be personally involved in such a manner.

In addition, we ask that you as a group leader respect the rules of this church pertaining to smoking and alcoholic beverages on church property.

SMALL-GROUP DISCUSSION QUESTIONS

Following are some suggested discussion questions for use in your small group. These questions are based on the teaching for each evening, as well as the material in the study book *Growing Through Divorce*.

Here are some guidelines for using these prepared discussion questions:

- ◆ Do not feel limited to these questions.
- ◆ Consider questions to be starting points, catalysts for discussion.
- ◆ You do not need to go through all the questions each night. Nothing is worse than rushing participants in order to get through all the questions.
- ◆ The questions can be a way to help move the group along if one person is dominating the conversation.

Important Note for Workshop Teacher or Coordinators
Whether or not your workshop uses the sets of questions on the following pages will depend on whether or not you choose to follow the suggested lecture outlines presented in the next chapter. In either case, we highly recommend that you do provide your small-group leaders with suggested discussion questions.

SESSION ONE

IS THIS REALLY HAPPENING TO ME?

(Chapters 1 & 2—*Growing Through Divorce* by Jim Smoke)

Have everyone introduce themselves, share what they do, and tell something about who they are.

1. What was it that brought you here tonight? Do you have some particular idea of what you would like this workshop to do in your life?

2. Which of the three stages of divorce recovery are you in right now: shock, adjustment, or growth? Where are you struggling or hurting the most right now?

3. How did each of the following people react to your divorce? Ex-spouse. Friends. Children. Relatives.

4. What effect has your divorce had on the social areas of your life?

5. How are you handling the absence of a spouse in your home?

6. What effect is your divorce having in the spiritual areas of your life?

Conclusion

Leaders should make a closing statement summarizing what was said in the group that evening. You should also remind the group to read the suggested chapter(s) of the study book before the next session. (Since they will have just received the book that night, you'll want to encourage them to read the chapters for the first week as well as those for the second week.)

SESSION TWO

COPING WITH YOUR EX-SPOUSE

(Chapter 3— *Growing Through Divorce* by Jim Smoke)

1. Which of the seven basic causes of divorce best describe your divorce?

   a. The victim divorce
   b. The problem divorce
   c. The little boy/little girl divorce
   d. The "I was conned" divorce
   e. The shotgun divorce
   f. The menopause divorce
   g. The no-fault divorce

2. In one word, describe your current feelings toward your ex-spouse.

3. How would you *like* to feel about him or her?

4. Which of the five growth guidelines in coping with your ex-spouse are the easiest for you? Which is the most difficult? (See Smoke, pages 39-44.)

   a. Take detachment one day at a time.
   b. Try to make the break as clean as possible.
   c. Quit accepting responsibility for the ex-spouse.
   d. Don't let your children intimidate you into seeking reconciliation.
   e. Don't get trapped in your "child state."

5. For you, what is the toughest part of breaking up?

6. Share together regarding your personal goals for this next week. (Group leader may offer suggestions.)

Conclusion

What did you hear being shared in our group tonight? Next week's study book reading will be _____.

SESSION THREE

ASSUMING NEW RESPONSIBILITIES
(Chapters 4 & 6 — *Growing Through Divorce* by Jim Smoke)

1. How do you react to the statement, "Plan your life as if you will always be single"?

2. It was said tonight that we all need to assume responsibility for our part of the break-up. We can then identify areas where we need to grow. Have you identified any areas of needed growth for yourself?

3. Will you share with us the struggles you're having in assuming responsibility for your present situation?

4. In what area do you have the greatest struggle: thoughts, feelings, or actions? Explain.

5. Discuss what goals you would like to set for yourself in the following areas: money, job, career.

6. What are you thinking about doing in the future?

7. Develop a series of seven to ten goals for yourself for the next three to six months. (See Smoke, pages 79-81.)

Conclusion
Next week's study book reading will be _____.

SESSION FOUR FOR PARENTS

BEING A SINGLE PARENT FAMILY
(Chapters 5 & 7—*Growing Through Divorce* by Jim Smoke)

1. How do your children feel about Mom or Dad not living in the home?

2. What is the biggest problem you face in being a single parent?

3. How did you tell your children about your divorce? What was their reaction?

4. Have you been honest with your children about your divorce?

5. How do you represent your former partner to your children?

If not all the members of your group are parents, you will need to include some of these questions:

1. Describe the kind of relationship you have today with the family you were born into. How did your family feel about your divorce?

2. How did your divorce affect your concepts and feelings about your family?

3. If you have a supportive family around you, describe how you feel about it and how it helps you.

Conclusion
Next week's study book reading will be _____.

SESSION FOUR FOR NONPARENTS

COPING SKILLS FOR WORRIES, DARK THOUGHTS, AND DOWN DAYS
Lecture by Dr. John Fry

1. What are some stress-producing beliefs you have been able to recognize in your own life?

2. What are some of the distortions in thinking about your divorce that you have been able to identify? What might be a more realistic, less depressing way of perceiving that situation?

3. Describe the kind of relationship you have today with the family you were born into. How did your family feel about your divorce?

4. How did your divorce affect your concepts and feelings about your family?

5. If you have a supportive family around you, describe how you feel about that and how it helps you.

Supplemental Questions (Not Based Directly on Lecture)

1. When you tell people that you are single again, how do they usually respond? What feelings do you have if their response is a negative one?

2. What is the most difficult thing you face in being single again? What do you like *most* about being single?

3. Describe one or two things you are doing to try to get your singleness "in gear."

Conclusion
Next week's study book reading will be _____.

SESSION FIVE

FINDING AND EXPERIENCING FORGIVENESS
(Chapter 8 — *Growing Through Divorce* by Jim Smoke)

1. If you have experienced God's forgiveness in your divorce, describe how this came about and what brought you to it.

2. Where are you in the struggle to forgive yourself?

3. If you have asked your ex-spouse for forgiveness, what happened? If you have not, how do you feel about doing it?

4. How are you handling the "forgetting" in your divorce?

5. Describe an experience in your life where you wanted forgiveness and received or did not receive it.

6. How do you feel about the statement, "God does not like divorce, but He loves divorced people"?

Leaders need to be particularly sensitive as to where group members are in their personal journey of healing. For many, it is just too early to discuss the subject of forgiveness openly.

Conclusion
Next week's study book reading will be _____.

SESSION SIX

THINKING ABOUT NEW RELATIONSHIPS
(Chapters 9 & 10—*Growing Through Divorce* by Jim Smoke)

1. What are some of the fears you have when you think about building new friendships?

2. What have you learned about yourself at this stage of your divorce?

3. What is important to you in selecting the kind of person you would like to marry?

4. How do you feel about dating? Does dating frighten you?

THINKING ABOUT REMARRIAGE

(Chapter 10—*Growing Through Divorce* by Jim Smoke)

1. Finish this statement: "The thought of remarriage makes me feel _____." Explain your response.

2. Describe how you might feel about loyalties in a remarriage: your ex-spouse; children (yours and inherited); former in-laws; new in-laws; spouse's ex-mate.

3. How do you feel about inheriting someone else's children? About someone else inheriting yours?

4. What would be your greatest fear as a step-parent?

5. Explain how you have kept or lost relatives and friends through your divorce.

6. What three goals would you set for yourself in a remarriage?

MISCELLANEOUS GROUP LEADER RESOURCES

CHECKLIST FOR SMALL-GROUP LEADERS

❑ Have I prayed for each person in my group this week?

❑ Have I (or my partner) called all the people in the group this week?

❑ Have any special needs of people in my group been addressed?

❑ Am I adequately communicating with my co-leader?

❑ Am I adequately communicating with the coordinators?

❑ Have I read the relevant chapters in the study book?

❑ Have I previewed the lecture material (if available)?

❑ Have I thought about this week's discussion questions?

❑ Am I prepared to deal with theological questions?

❑ Are there any emerging relational problems within the group?

❑ Do I need to work on any relational skills myself?

❑ Am I dominating the discussions?

❑ Is anyone dating another person in the group?

DIVORCE RECOVERY WORKSHOP: LEADER'S EVALUATION

Name _____

We are interested in hearing your thoughts as a group leader on various aspects of the divorce recovery workshop. Could you please take a few moments to fill out this form following the last session of the workshop? That will help us make our next workshop even better! Your comments will remain confidential.

1. Would you like to be a leader again?

2. How do you feel about your co-leader?

    Preparation:

    Compatibility:

    Follow-through (phone calls, etc.):

    Additional comments:

3. Please list participants in your group who you think would make good leaders.

Name   Phone

_____

_____

_____

4. Please comment on the leadership training you received. Was it sufficient? Is there any additional information that you feel would have helped you? Please use the back of this form if you need more space to answer.

5. Do you have any suggestions for additional publicity?

6. Do you have any comments that might be helpful in regard to:

a. Registration

b. Refreshments

c. Space

d. Leaders' meetings

7. Please evaluate the main lectures.

8. Please comment on special speakers.

9. Please comment on testimonies.

10. Do you have any suggestions regarding coordinator roles/responsibilities?

11. Were there specific problems in your group? How did you handle them?

12. Do you have any additional comments?

TURN IN AFTER LAST MEETING. THANKS!

DIVORCE RECOVERY WORKSHOP: PARTICIPANT'S EVALUATION

Name (optional) _____

Date _____

Lecture	1	2	OK	4	5
1. Pace of speaker (1 - too slow, 5 - too fast)	—	—	—	—	—
2. Length of talk (1 - too short, 5 - too long)	—	—	—	—	—
3. Spiritual content (1 - too little, 5 - too much)	—	—	—	—	—
4. Other _____ (1 - too little, 5 - too much)	—	—	—	—	—

5. What topics needed more emphasis or time?

6. What topics needed less time?

Small Groups

7. What, if anything, did you dislike about your group?

8. What, if anything, was personally most helpful or valuable to your small group?

9. What would you like to see changed or improved about this workshop?

Other

10. What has been the most helpful or valuable part of this workshop to you personally?

11. What comments would you like to share that might be helpful for the leaders and planners of this workshop?

DIVORCE RECOVERY WORKSHOP: ROSTER OF SMALL-GROUP PARTICIPANTS

(Confidential—for Group Leader Use Only)

Group Leaders

_____

_____

Participants

Name _____   Name _____

Address _____   Address _____

_____   _____

Home phone _____   Home phone _____

Work phone _____   Work phone _____

Name _____   Name _____

Address _____   Address _____

_____   _____

Home phone _____   Home phone _____

Work phone _____   Work phone _____

Name _____   Name _____

Address _____   Address _____

_____   _____

Home phone _____   Home phone _____

Work phone _____   Work phone _____

Name _____   Name _____

Address _____   Address _____

_____   _____

Home phone _____   Home phone _____

Work phone _____   Work phone _____

Dealing Effectively with Group Members' Relational Styles

Not every group member's style of relating will be easy for you to deal with effectively. Listed below are some typical ways people relate and some suggestions for group leaders who need to cope with these styles.

Overly talkative: a show-off, eager beaver, or just plain gabby. Cut across with a summarizing statement and direct a question to someone else.

Highly argumentative: a combative personality, a professional heckler, or someone upset by emotional problems. Try to find merit in one of the person's points and get group agreement on it; then move on to something else. Try to apply the process of conciliation. As a last resort, talk to the person privately after the meeting and see if you can get his/her cooperation for future meetings.

Quick and overly helpful: one who has the right answers but keeps others out. Cut across tactfully by questioning others (for example, "Let's get several opinions"), but be sure you express your appreciation for the person's help.

Rambler: one who talks about everything except the subject, or who tends to get lost in his or her own thoughts. When the person stops for breath, extend thanks, rephrase one of the person's statements, and move on. Ask direct questions of others. Indicate in a friendly manner that the discussion has moved away from the topic.

Poor voice or poor language skills: one whose voice is not clear, who can't find the right words, whose ideas are good but inadequately expressed. Repeat the person's ideas in your own words but say "Let me repeat that," rather than "What you mean is . . . ." Protect the person from ridicule.

Obstinate: one who won't budge, who has prejudices, or who simply may not see the point. Try to get others to help the person see the point. If time is short, tell the person frankly that it is necessary to get on with the meeting.

Griper: someone with a pet peeve, a professional griper, or one who may have a legitimate complaint. Explain that the relevant issue is how to operate under the present system. Direct attention to the topic under discussion. Indicate the pressure of time.

Wrong subject: someone who's off base. Direct attention to the topic under discussion (for example, "Something I said may have thrown you off the subject, but the question we are considering now is . . .").

Definitely wrong: someone who is completely missing the point of the discussion. Say "That's one way of looking at it," and go on. Ask additional questions (such as, "Would we be able to reconcile that with . . .?"), but don't embarrass the person.

Personality clash: two or more members in confrontation. Emphasize points of agreement as much as possible. Cut across with a direct question on the topic. Bring a disinterested member into the discussion. If necessary, ask that personalities be left out of the discussion.

Attitude of superiority: one not disposed to help, whose attitude is, "I had to find out the hard way, so you do the same." Explain that the meeting is a cooperative effort. Flatter the person by emphasizing how much the others could benefit by his or her experience. But don't overdo the praise, or the rest of the group will resent it.

Common Excuses for Failure to Participate Within a Group

Here are some of the most common reasons people give for being unwilling to take part in a group discussion. We need to honor the rule that no one in a divorce recovery workshop discussion group should be coerced into participation. But the feelings revealed by the comments below may give you some insights as to how to encourage those who would really like to participate but seem hesitant to do so.

A lack of confidence in one's own ideas: "It doesn't make any difference whether I say anything or not, because I never have anything original to contribute."

A lack of emotional involvement in the matters being discussed: "I just don't feel excited about the subject."

A lack of skill in verbalizing ideas: "The others can state their ideas so much more clearly than I can, so I'd rather just listen."

An inability to think rapidly enough to keep up with the pace of the discussion: "By the time I have mulled over a point long enough to have something to say on it, the rest of the group has moved on to something else."

A deeper reflection of ideas: "Some people just seem to think out loud, but I prefer to think to myself a while before speaking."

An attitude of detached observation: "I just like to hear what other people have to say about things."

Habitual shyness: "I never talk much."

A lack of sleep or other physical disturbances: "I could hardly keep my eyes open."

Distraction of more pressing personal problems: "I didn't talk today because I was worrying about a midterm exam."

Submissiveness to more aggressive members: "A guy can never get a word in edgewise in this outfit, so I just keep quiet."

An interpersonal conflict: "I knew that if I ever got started I would have told that _____ off, so I decided not to say anything at all."

A nonpermissive atmosphere: "I don't feel free to speak when Ms. _____ is around."

An overly dominant leader: "He doesn't care what I think. He just wants an audience to make big speeches."

Fear of being rejected: "I'm afraid everyone will think that what I have to say is silly."

A solidified pattern of nonparticipation: "Everyone in the group has gotten used to my not talking much, so I feel uncomfortable, as though everyone were surprised when I do speak."

A feeling of superiority: "That was such a pointless discussion and no one really knew what they were talking about. What a waste of time."

A disbelief in the value of discussion: "Talk never changes anybody's mind, so why bother?"

Lack of knowledge or intelligence: "The discussion was way over my head."

Effective Listening Tips

For a small-group leader, knowing how to listen is far more important than knowing what to say. Remember: One of our most common complaints has been that group leaders talk too much! Here are some tips for becoming an "eloquent listener."

◆ Look directly at the person speaking.
◆ Takes notes when there is important information to receive and retain.
◆ Focus on the meaning behind the words you hear. The speaker's feelings and

emotions add meaning to the spoken words.

◆ Formulate questions in your mind as the speaker progresses. Wait until after the speaker has finished to ask questions.

◆ Be open to another's view and opinions, even if they differ from your own. Don't make judgments too soon.

◆ Avoid letting distractions interrupt your listening.

◆ Avoid reacting strongly to negative or inappropriate language. Listen to the whole message before responding.

◆ Work hard at paying attention, even if the topic is uninteresting to you. Create your own motivations for listening.

◆ Restate to the person speaking what you think you have heard. Rephrase her or his thoughts in your own words to check your understanding.

LAWYER/CLIENT ISSUE QUESTIONNAIRE[2]

During sessions 3 through 6, copies of this questionnaire should be available at the materials table for all workshop registrants.

Below are questions and issues we consider essential for gathering the information necessary to make a good choice in retaining a lawyer for a divorce settlement. Take this form with you to record his or her answers.

1. How much do you charge per hour?

2. How do you charge for items such as phone calls that may take only a fraction of an hour on a given day?

3. Are there any additional surcharges or bonus charges?

4. What is the smallest unit of time that you will charge for?

5. Do you charge for telephone calls?

6. What is your estimate of my total cost for the divorce, including items such as child and spousal support?

7. What are the costs in my divorce litigation?

8. How many family law cases have you litigated?

9. Will you give me a memo containing the operative facts of my case so that I may be sure that you have all of them?

10. What is your estimate of the length of time that this divorce will take?

   a. Shortest time:

   b. Longest time:

11. How many custody cases have you litigated?

12. Are you going to be responsible for the tax advice in my divorce?

13. If you will not be, who will be responsible for the tax advice in my divorce?

14. Will you communicate with my minister?

15. I want a meeting between yourself, the other lawyer, and my spouse. Will you arrange for that meeting?

16. Will you communicate with my psychologist?

17. What is your telephone call policy with regard to communication to and from me?

18. I would like a copy of each letter and each paper that you generate in this divorce as it is generated. Can that be arranged?

19. I would like in writing your appraisal of the major facts and issues of this case so that I may be made aware of them. Can this be arranged?

NOTES

CHAPTER EIGHT

LECTURE OUTLINES

The Appendix of this book (page 163) contains transcripts of the lectures most often used in divorce recovery workshops. This chapter provides brief overviews and outlines of those six lectures. These are presented to assist you, the teacher, in formulating your own workshop lectures.

The outlines are structured to show you what areas I believe should be addressed within each of the six general topics. You will, of course, want to fill in these outlines with your own thoughts and experiences in each area.

SESSION 1: IS THIS REALLY HAPPENING TO ME?

Overview

What are some of the myths, as well as the facts, of going through the painful process of a broken marriage? This session looks at the three stages of divorce recovery: shock, adjustment, and growth. The premise is that you can either "go" through it, or "grow" through it.

Outline

Introductory Remarks

I. Dispel misgivings.
   A. This workshop could be a very positive experience—a turning point in your life.
   B. (Introduce yourself. Explain why you are qualified to speak about divorce.)
   C. I know there are a lot of mixed feelings in this room right now.
   D. We are not here to exploit your vulnerability.
   E. We are here, basically, as wounded healers.
II. Make additional "warm-up" remarks.
   A. We can't possibly answer all your questions; but sometimes just answering questions doesn't really satisfy the need in your lives.
   B. Are you surprised to see so many people here?
      1. In tough times we often feel all alone; but obviously in this case, that's not true!

2. (Discuss divorce statistics, to show them that they are definitely not all alone.)

C. There are people from all walks of life here.
1. Some of you are only contemplating divorce.
2. Some are already divorced.
3. Whether you are hanging on, letting go, moving on, or settling down, we'll try to be aware of where you are coming from.
4. Everyone here is in a different place; yet you all have a common need.
5. You won't have to be in a small group with your ex-spouse.

III. State the five objectives for this workshop.
A. We are here to facilitate some new friendships in your lives.
1. It is not a "meet market."
2. It is a place to grow with other people.
3. (Invite attendees to take part in optional restaurant fellowship.)
B. We are here to practice "mutual need therapy."
1. Small-group leaders are not professional therapists; rather, they are just a few steps ahead of you in the healing process.
2. If you don't want to talk in your small group, it's okay to just listen.
C. We are here to share with fellow-strugglers, not to provide all the answers.
D. We are here to help you better understand your own divorce experience.
1. You will hear much misinformation from others about the dire consequences of your divorce.
2. Some of the things you learn here may be painful, but there is no growth without pain.
3. Many are here for the second or third time, and that is valid. We can always grow.
E. We are here to extend our hands to you as friends.

The Lesson

Jim Smoke writes about the three stages of the divorce experience:
I. Stage one is shock.
A. Shock makes us feel out of control.
B. Divorce is like death. We grieve for the end of the relationship. There are five stages in this grieving process:
1. We deny reality.
2. We become angry.
3. We bargain.
4. We become depressed.
5. We accept.
C. We handle shock in one of three ways:
1. We internalize (withdraw).
2. We externalize (go wild/run away).
3. We actualize (face the facts). Just by walking through the door tonight, you have begun to actualize!
D. Do you still hope for reconciliation in your marriage?
1. If you do, that's great. We can refer you to counselors. (This workshop must

be limited to those who have no hope of reconciliation.)
    2. If you hope for marital reconciliation, we suggest to you that there are four necessary ingredients:
       a) A willing man
       b) A willing woman
       c) A neutral professional
       d) God
    3. Smoke's four questions for those considering reconciliation are listed below:
       a) Do both parties really want the marriage?
       b) Will both parties accept professional help for as long as it is necessary?
       c) Has a third party become involved with either mate? (If so, there is relatively little hope.)
       d) Are both parties willing to learn through this experience?

II. Stage two is adjustment.
    A. Adjustment means moving forward and making important decisions for yourself.
    B. Adjustment means moving beyond self-pity.
    C. By walking through the door tonight, you exemplify that you are in the adjustment stage.
    D. Of course, you may slip back to the shock stage from time to time, but don't be discouraged.

III. Stage three is growth. You can either *go* through a divorce, or *grow* through it.
    A. When you grow through your experiences of divorce, you are able to think clearly.
       1. You are able to make a realistic analysis of the past, from which you can now learn (emotional growth).
       2. You are able to maintain an understanding of the present, where you are seeking healthy relationships and values (relational growth).
       3. You are able to determine a positive and optimistic plan for your future (practical growth).
    B. Smoke discusses eight things (pages 21-23) to help you adjust to the reality that this really is happening to you.
       1. Time is a healer; you need to walk through the process one day at a time.
       2. Take some "me" time.
       3. Allow time for reflection, meditation, reading, and personal growth.
       4. Get with some healthy people who are struggling and growing.
       5. Seek professional counseling.
       6. Accept the fact you are divorced or divorcing and are now single. Begin to see yourself that way.
       7. Put the past in the past and live in the present.
       8. Commit your new way to God.

SESSION 2: COPING WITH YOUR EX-SPOUSE

Overview
How does a person handle a relationship that in one sense has ceased to exist and yet in another sense goes on for life? Here are some positive principles for managing the frustration, anger, rejection, and hopelessness of such a relationship.

Outline
Introduction
The relationship with your ex-spouse is something you'll have to deal with, in one form or another, for the rest of your life. The question is simply, How do you manage it?

I. The relationship with the ex-spouse may take one of four basic shapes.
  A. It is a real, ongoing, continuing contact.
  B. It involves only your shared responsibilities for the children, and there is no other basis for the relationship.
  C. It is based entirely on the memory of the relationship that used to be—and there is no longer any actual contact.
  D. The ex-spouse is no longer living. But, even then, the relationship is not really over.

II. There are many different types of divorce. The way you relate to your ex-spouse is often directly related to the causes of the divorce (see *Growing Through Divorce*, page 36). Considering these various possible causes could also help you avoid a second bad marriage.
  A. The Victim Divorce: Suddenly a marriage is over and someone is left devastated.
  B. The Problem Divorce: The breakup of a marriage is caused by things like alcohol, gambling, money, sex, or unfaithfulness.
  C. The Little Boy/Little Girl Divorce: Two people can no longer live together because of emotional immaturity—which can strike at any age!
  D. The "I was conned" Divorce: A marriage is broken apart because one mate didn't get what he or she wanted from the other partner.
  E. The Shotgun Divorce: Friends pressure other friends into an unwise marriage, which soon comes unraveled.
  F. The Menopause Divorce: Both men and women may go through a mid-life crisis, during which they decided to trade their spouses in for newer models.
  G. The Rat Race Divorce: The pressures of life simply kill the marriage.
  H. The No-Fault Divorce: Spouses part as friends, and there's no big crisis.

III. Coping with the ex-spouse.
  A. The natural tendency is to be controlled by feelings such as hate. But that will only destroy you. Usually, with time, the initial strong feelings will "mellow out" to feelings of indifference to the ex-spouse and acceptance of your new situation.
  B. Sometimes feelings will vary:
    1. When an ex-spouse is absent, you may long for reunion.
    2. When an ex-spouse is present, negative feelings return.
    3. Such feelings are often caused by fear of starting a new life.
  C. Here are some guidelines for coping:
    1. Take things one day at a time; don't be discouraged by how slow the healing process can be.
    2. Try to make the break as clean as possible; avoid ongoing contact with your ex as much as you can.
    3. Quit accepting responsibility for your ex-spouse.
      a) Don't get trapped into thinking that he or she can't make it without you.

Few people learn to make it on their own until they have to.
b) You are actually the person *least* qualified to help your former partner.
4. Don't let your children intimidate you; don't try to revive a dead marriage *just* to please your children.
5. Finally, don't get trapped in your "temporary immaturity." The stress of divorce can cause you to revert to childish behavior (e.g., jealousy, temper tantrums, fighting over division of property).

SESSION 3: ASSUMING NEW RESPONSIBILITIES

Overview

How do you plan for yourself and for your future when the outlook may be very bleak and unpromising? This session examines how we can put some new structures and disciplines into life and take advantage of new opportunities for personal development. The premise of the presentation is: "You can't steer a parked car."

Outline

I. It is important for you to plan for the future during your divorce experience.
   A. Many people choose to "wallow in the mire" of the past. Many people have no direction or purpose in life.
   B. If you are to experience healing and recovery, sooner or later the past needs to be minimized.
   C. Our natural tendency in times of stress is to form dependent relationships.
   D. What we need is a willingness to take initiative, to assume new responsibilities, and to learn some new skills.
II. You can't go through life just "pulling strings" and letting others take care of you. Assuming responsibility takes courage and determination.
   A. You must assume responsibility for your part of the failure of your marriage. There are no 100 percent, black-and-white divorce situations. Assume your part of the blame, no matter how large or small that part may be.
   B. Assume responsibility for your present situation.
      1. Assume responsibility for practical things like household chores.
      2. Assume responsibility for your present happiness.
   C. Assume responsibility for your future. People often make contingency plans for their lives, hoping someone else will bail them out. Such plans can include the following:
      1. I won't go to work because I might remarry.
      2. I'll do this until something better comes along.
      3. I won't set goals because it might interfere with someone I meet.
      4. I won't join the church because I do not know how long I'm going to stay here.
      5. I won't put down roots. I'll just be rootless, trying to live life without any pain, because if I make plans I might miss out on something.
   D. Assume responsibility for yourself. This includes three elements:
      1. My thoughts: Are they negative or positive?
      2. My feelings: Am I in touch with them? Do I express them honestly?
      3. My actions: Don't blame them on the divorce situation.

Supplemental Material for Session 3
I. The story of the crippled man at the pool teaches us about our responsibility in the healing process.
   A. Jesus said, "Do you want to be healed?" We have to *want* to experience healing from divorce and get on with our lives.
   B. The man had to *begin* getting up on his own strength. He had to take the initiative, in order to be healed.
   C. Jesus said, "Pick up your bed and take it with you." This signifies taking responsibility for your life.
II. These ten commandments for divorced or divorcing people are good "laws" to live by.

Thou shalt not live in thy past.
Thou shalt be responsible for thy present and not blame thy past for it.
Thou shalt not feel sorry for thyself indefinitely.
Thou shalt assume thine end of the blame for thy marriage dissolution.
Thou shalt not try to reconcile thy past and reconstruct thy future by a quick new marriage.
Thou shalt not make thy children victims of thy past marriage.
Thou shalt not spend all thy time trying to convince thy children how terrible and evil their departed parent is.
Thou shalt learn all thou can about being a one-parent family and get on with it.
Thou shalt ask others for help when thou needest it.
Thou shalt ask God for the wisdom to bury yesterday, create today, and plan for tomorrow.

SESSION 4: BEING A SINGLE PARENT/BECOMING A WHOLE FAMILY

Overview
Divorce is not a process that turns a whole parent into a half parent. Here are some encouraging principles for being a healthy family in a one-parent home or in a situation where custody is shared. Some of the advantages as well as disadvantages of being a single parent are considered.

Outline
Introduction
The purpose and goals of this lecture are as follows:

♦ To develop a greater openness, communication, honesty, and sensitivity between parent and child.
♦ To assist the parents in sharing feelings and ideas with their children.
♦ To assure parents that their children are not being exploited in the workshop, that an attempt is being made to foster some healing in them.

I. Statistics support the need for this lecture.
   A. In 1970, 12 percent of North American children lived with only one parent. By 1981, this had increased to over 20 percent.

    B. (If possible, include some current statistics about who children are living with. Most libraries have that kind of information.)

II. Divorce affects children.

    A. The negative connotation in terms such as "broken home" creates a bad self-image.

    B. Divorce *is* traumatic for children.

    C. Children do recover and do not automatically become juvenile delinquents.

    D. It takes approximately two years for children (and parents) to achieve a new sense of security and adjustment.

    E. Children feel alone and isolated, and they believe that they are the only people ever to experience this particular problem. They feel angry, distrustful, betrayed, resentful, unforgiving, confused.

    F. Current research reflects the effects of divorce on children. (Use some of your own sources.)

    G. Those children who have difficulty or never recover from divorce tend to be those who never have the opportunity for dealing openly with the problem.

III. Single parents experience a unique set of problems.

    A. "My circuits are on overload." (This is exemplified by a lowered standard of living, insecurity, no one to share problems with, stress, and tension.)

    B. "Where were you when I needed you?" This includes a difficulty of achieving balance in assuming responsibility for the children.

    C. "I don't get any respect." One parent is seen as the entertainer parent, the other as the disciplinary parent.

    D. "Help, I'm a prisoner." Parents can become overly responsible out of fear of failing with children as they failed with their ex-spouse.

IV. You can learn to deal with your children in a healthy way.

    A. Don't try to be both parents to your children.

    B. Don't force your children into playing the role of the departed parent. That's simply putting too much pressure on an immature child.

    C. Be the *parent* that you are. Don't try to become a playmate to your children. They will consider it an intrusion, and you will be abdicating your parental responsibilities.

    D. Be honest with your children. Let them see you as you are. Also, don't try to be a role model all the time. Don't be afraid to cry together with them.

    E. Don't put down your ex-spouse in front of your children. Either consciously or unconsciously, we want our children to take our side. Resist the urge to make them do so.

    F. Don't make your children undercover agents to report on the other parent's activities. When they visit your ex, they need to feel the freedom to talk or not to talk, as they see fit.

    G. Children of divorce need both a mother and a father. Even though your ex failed with you, they can still be a great success as a parent. Allow them that— even if it points a finger at your own failure.

    H. Develop meaningful relationships with your children; don't become an entertainer parent.

V. Single parenthood has advantages.

    A. You gain an opportunity to discover your inner self and seek personal growth.

    B. You have the freedom to structure your household as you desire.

    C. You have the opportunity to develop a partnership with your children by giving them more responsibilities.

    D. You have a chance to develop new friends as an individual.

VI. Single parenthood also has disadvantages.

    A. You are sometimes lonely.

    B. Your life may lack structure and self-discipline. It's easier to do things like clean house for someone else than for yourself.

    C. Your time may be inadequate to fulfill responsibilities that were formerly shared with your spouse.

    D. You may experience guilt. Extended family can contribute to feelings of guilt by placing expectations on your overloaded life. If you have to work, don't feel guilty about it.

VII. We offer these principles to help the single parent survive being overextended.

    A. Change yourself, not those around you.

    B. Plan your time and how you use it.

    C. Lower your standards and share responsibilities.

    D. Learn to say no.

    E. Learn to be good to yourself.

    F. Share your feelings with your children.

    G. Develop alternate support systems.

    H. Nurture yourself and your family spiritually.

VIII. When it's all added up, we can only give our children two things: roots and wings.

SESSION 4 FOR NONPARENTS: COPING SKILLS FOR WORRIES, DARK THOUGHTS, AND DOWN DAYS (BY JOHN FRY)

Overview

Worry is circular in nature, while problem-solving is linear. Much of worry is caused by false beliefs which lead us to "catastrophize" about situations. Down days and depression are usually caused by our cognitive distortion. Recognizing our own cognitive distortion can help us change our thought patterns and overcome depression.

Outline

Introduction

Stress usually comes from external situations. You can reduce stress in one of two ways, the second of which is preferable.

    ◆ By dealing externally with each of those situations.

    ◆ By dealing with them internally, controlling the way you think about and respond to them. This is the cognitive approach.

   I. You must learn to acquire coping skills for worries.

    A. You need to learn to distinguish worry from problem solving.

1. Worry is *circular* in nature:
    a) I have to decide.
    b) There's no apparent solution.
    c) "This is awful! I have to decide."
2. Problem solving is *linear*:
    a) I have to decide.
    b) There's no apparent solution.
    c) I will explore possible solutions.

B. Dr. Albert Ellis has described certain false beliefs that can lead to following the worry pattern:[1]

1. *"I have to be perfect in everything I do."* Perfection is not achievable. What is possible is to strive for excellence in areas where you have a chance at it.
2. *"If there's even a faint possibility of danger or failure, I should dwell on it!"* Because there is a lot of pain in the divorce process, it is easy to start anticipating pain in all other areas of your life as well.
3. *"I have to have everyone like me. I have to have everyone's approval."* Even if you are the most popular person in your neighborhood, someone will be jealous of your popularity.
4. *"My feelings are caused by others and I have no way of controlling them."* You need to take full responsibility yourselves for what you do feel: "I am sad," rather than "You made me sad."
5. *"It's awful when things aren't exactly the way I want them to be!"* It would be much better to get down to business and try to solve the problem or make the best of a bad situation.
6. *"I'm a victim of my past and I always will be!"* Certainly your past does influence you. But you can change and grow.
7. *"Don't tell me to relax! It's only my tension that holds me together!"* Your best efforts usually occur when you're alert but not tense.
8. *"Life is supposed to be fair!"* Life isn't fair or unfair. It just is. It's a waste of time and emotional energy to complain rather than to cope.

II. You must learn coping skills for dark thoughts and down days. David Burns, in *Feeling Good: The New Mood Therapy,* lists ten basic types of cognitive distortions.[2] By acknowledging and then correcting your distortions you can "inoculate" yourselves from their power in the future:

A. *All-or-nothing thinking.* If you find yourself using the words "always" or "never," you are probably indulging in all-or-nothing thinking.
B. *Overgeneralization.* You do this when you take a single negative situation and tell yourself it is a pattern.
C. *Negative mental filter.* You pick out a negative detail and dwell on it, coloring your perception.
D. *Disqualifying the positive.* You find some reason to disregard the good things.
E. *Jumping to conclusions.* You practice mind reading, where you assume the negative, and fortune telling, where you predict disaster.
F. *Magnification or minimization.* Magnification usually involves catastrophizing or exaggerating your mistakes. Minimization involves reducing your view of strengths.

G. *Emotional reasoning.* You do this when you make your feelings your reality about something.

H. *"Should" statements.* You try to motivate yourself with guilt and put-downs.

I. *Labeling and mislabeling.* You lock yourselves out of possibilities when you too rigidly define yourselves; and you easily contribute to others' defensiveness when you label them.

J. *Personalization.* You mistakenly assume responsibility for a situation.

III. You must learn to cope with dark thoughts about your faith. There can be distortions in faith, too.

A. "I have to keep my act together for God to love me; and how can anyone going through a divorce have their act together? Therefore, God must be distant from me."

B. "I have to get my act together for God to use me. Since things are in kind of a mess right now in my life, He certainly wouldn't want my services."

IV. We offer these additional suggestions for coping.

A. Stay active.

B. Communicate with others.

C. Along with your "to do" list, keep a list of things you've accomplished.

SESSION 5: FINDING AND EXPERIENCING FORGIVENESS

Overview
Forgiveness is at the very core of healing from divorce. It has been defined as "surrendering my right to hurt back." This session looks at the principles of experiencing forgiveness from God, from yourselves, and ultimately, seeking the forgiveness of your ex-spouse.

Outline
I. Forgiveness is important in the divorce recovery process.

A. Forgiveness is absolutely crucial to recovery.

B. It is also a difficult thing to contemplate.

C. This may or may not be the right time for you to take this step. You'll have to discern that for yourself.

D. Listen to the principles of forgiveness, even if you are not yet ready to forgive. (Even if it's the right time to forgive, you may never feel quite ready.)

E. Forgiveness is crucial whether you are religious or totally secular in your thinking. (Personally, I can't separate forgiveness from the reality of God.)

II. Forgiveness has been the most controversial part of our divorce recovery workshops.

A. People have tended to react either very positively or very negatively to our discussions about forgiveness.

B. It would be a lot easier to go through a divorce recovery workshop and not talk about forgiveness. Most other workshops I'm aware of do not.

C. The notion of forgiveness draws the divorce experience "to a head." Most of you have come here filled with feelings of hate or hurt. You can drown yourselves in a sea of negative feelings toward others and yourself. Experiencing forgiveness gets the hate out of your life, permanently.

III. Forgiveness needs to be defined.

A. Ideally, forgiveness is a two-way street, a two-way experience. Forgiveness frees the forgiver and often the person who accepts the forgiveness.

B. Lewis Smedes says, "Forgiveness means to give up all claim upon the one who has hurt you, including letting go of all the emotional consequences of the hurt. This is the antithesis of our selfish human nature."[3]

C. Arch Hart says, "Forgiveness is surrendering the right to hurt back."[4]

IV. What happens to people when they don't forgive?

A. They are controlled by their anger, pain, or hatred.

B. They are directed by negative memories.

C. They do not act freely.

D. They keep a controlling grasp on situations and people.

E. They are pressured by lives of tension and stress.

F. They probably shorten their lives.

G. Their relationships with others are strained.

H. Their relationship with God is weakened.

I. They have very little sense of self-worth.

J. They feel unrelieved guilt.

V. Forgiveness is at least the following seven things:

A. Forgiveness is a decision; it is not a feeling. You must forgive even when you don't feel like it.

B. Forgiveness is showing mercy. This means forgiving even when the person in no way deserves your forgiveness.

C. Forgiveness is acceptance. When you truly forgive others, it means you are able to accept them just the way they are.

D. Forgiveness is risky. It means making yourselves vulnerable. It means some people will say, "You're a fool." It can hurt. But it is worth the risk, because it will bring about your healing.

E. Forgiveness is accepting apology. It involves being able to accept an apology from someone else.

F. Forgiveness is a way of living. It means developing in your lives a readiness to forgive. By pardoning others for little everyday hurts, you prepare yourselves to handle the bigger hurts.

G. Forgiveness is choosing to love. As in the story of the prodigal son, forgiveness comes out of your choosing to love someone unconditionally, no matter what they have done to you.

VI. God is willing to forgive you. "If we confess our sins, he is faithful and just and will forgive us our sins and purify us from all unrighteousness" (1 John 1:9).

A. Divorce is a sin. Sin simply means missing the mark.

1. Divorce is a tear in the fabric of God's divine intentions.

2. God did not want divorce to happen. It was not a part of His plan for us.

3. God says, "I hate divorce."

B. Why does God hate divorce?

1. First, it is a tearing asunder of something He meant to be united. It shatters a divine ideal.

2. Second, He hates it because of what it does to us. He takes no pleasure in our pain.

3. Remember: God hates divorce, but He *loves* divorced people!

C. You, as a divorced person, need to accept some responsibility for the failure of your marriage.

 1. Even if you claim no responsibility in your failure with your ex-spouse, you must with your God.

 2. Somewhere along the line, in order for you to become whole again, forgiveness has to take place.

VII. There are three crucial principles of forgiveness. Too often, the words "I forgive you" are too easy to say; you need to see what true forgiveness really involves.

A. *God forgives me.* God is willing to forgive you, and not just to forgive you, but to cleanse you from all unrighteousness.

B. *If God can forgive me, then I can forgive me.*

 1. For a lot of you, that's harder than accepting God's forgiveness.

 2. This doesn't relate as much to the one who was left (the dumpee); this is more for the person who left or chose to seek a divorce (the dumper).

 3. Here are six helpful keys to forgiving yourself (Smoke, pages 99-100):

  a) I accept my humanity as a human being.

  b) I have the freedom to fail.

  c) I can accept responsibility for my failure.

  d) I can forgive myself for my failure.

  e) I accept God's forgiveness.

  f) I can begin again.

C. *I forgive my ex-spouse.* Some of you are not quite ready for this final step.

 1. You can call, write, or visit in person (if you are brave enough!).

 2. Don't start by saying, "I forgive *you.*"

 3. Instead, say, "Will you forgive me for what I did?"

 4. It may lead to what will be a two-way experience of mutual forgiveness. It may not. There are no guarantees.

 5. Do it because it's the right thing to do, not because of how your ex may respond.

 6. Such forgiveness will give you a sense of cleansing from hatred, a sense of being ready to grow again.

 7. The church can provide you the support of a forgiven community. The ground at the foot of the cross of Jesus Christ is absolutely level.

 8. Extending forgiveness involves risk; but to avoid all risk in life is to die.

SESSION 6: THINKING ABOUT NEW RELATIONSHIPS

Overview

The great majority of divorced persons marry again, but the failure rate for subsequent marriages increases rather than decreases. This session looks at the principles for building relationships that last.

Outline

 I. We are not made to be alone. We are designed by God to be a part of human relationships.

A. We all tend to hope for satisfying relationships for ourselves as well as for others.

B. We all have the capacity to love again, even after the disaster of divorce. Why? Because we were designed that way—to have meaningful relationships with other human beings.

C. This capacity for relationships applies to ordinary friendship as much as to dating relationships and marriage.

II. Unfortunately, however, second marriages fail at a greater rate than first marriages. Therefore, you must exercise great caution in pursuing new relationships.

A. As a divorcee, you are emotionally vulnerable. You have many unmet needs.

B. You may be tempted to settle for the first good relationship that comes your way.

C. You may feel the pressure of time: "I'm not getting any younger; I'd better find someone quick."

D. The second time, many people remarry the same wrong kind of person as they did initially.

III. How do you develop new relationships that are healthy? There are three dimensions of mature relationships, three things for you to look at as you develop a new relationship.

A. *Speed.* Relationships take time. No matter how old you are, how mature or compatible you are, you still need to go through some of the crises of life together.

B. *Quality.* Do you like each other only when you put on a mask and are on your good behavior, or do you like each other's true selves?

C. *Depth.* Depth comes when you have gotten to know the other person well, through the *time* (speed) and the *quality* of your relationship—when you have learned to love each other in spite of all your shortcomings.

IV. "Five C's" will contribute to a successful relationship.

A. *Confidence.* Many of us lack confidence in ourselves and in our ability to have a good relationship. In practice, confidence means that you begin to trust yourselves and others. That takes time. Give yourself time.

1. Lack of confidence may relate to past mistakes in the area of sex.

2. We all have a sex drive; but our deeper need is for intimacy and love.

3. Intimacy and love come only when you learn to give instead of take.

4. Only when you learn to give will you have the confidence to enter into an intimate relationship with another person.

B. *Communication.* As you try to communicate, you need to learn to look beyond the superficial. Communication is like an iceberg that's 80 percent hidden below the surface; you need to learn to communicate with an understanding that goes beyond the obvious.

C. *Commitment.* Most of the commitments we make are conditional. But when you get into significant relationships, particularly ones that are going to last for life, the relationship is unconditional: "For as long as you both shall live."

D. *Criticism.* A healthy relationship is able to endure criticism. But you have to win the right to be critical, and it must be constructive and guided by love.

E. *Community.* No relationship is going to survive purely on its own energy. No one person can supply all your relational needs. (This workshop provides a place to begin to experience community; as the workshop ends, you can continue that experience in the context of a church.)

SESSION 7: THINKING ABOUT REMARRIAGE (OPTIONAL)

Overview

Divorced people often remarry quickly, and these second marriages usually fail. Caution is in order! There are many things to consider before entering into a second marriage. These are issues that must be resolved *before* the marriage, not after.

The Bible holds up a high ideal for marriage, and has some very serious things to say about divorce and remarriage. Many Christians have concluded that the divorced person should not remarry. But a clear overview of Scripture will show that both God's law and His grace must be taken into account.

Outline

Part One: Practical Considerations of Remarriage

I. Remarriage calls for sober evaluation.
   A. Fifty percent of first marriages fail; but 65 percent of second marriages and 75 percent of third marriages fail! We think that we learn from our mistakes, but usually we do not.
   B. The greatest danger facing recently divorced people is jumping into a quick new marriage.
      1. Even as adults we can go through times of great emotional immaturity.
      2. Right after a divorce we can be especially prone to immaturity and bad judgment.
      3. As you seek healing, you can all too easily connect that healing to someone else who you think is going to bring new happiness into your lives.

II. Many unique issues are involved in a second marriage.
   A. You must account for many differences.
      1. You have different personalities.
      2. You have different needs.
      3. You have different commitments.
      4. You have different lifestyles.
      5. A blended family involves different pressures.
      6. Family life carries with it different traditions.
      7. You each have different rhythms of operating.
      8. You have different ways of settling disagreements.
      9. You respond differently to physical relationships.
      10. You have different ways of coping with money.
   B. You should be aware of some "pre-remarriage considerations." Some things must be resolved *before* the new marriage. If you wait until after you're married to discuss these things, you've waited too long.
      1. How many children will be directly involved in the marriage? Who will have custody? Who will support them? Where will they live?
      2. How much of the new family's income will go to support the ex-spouse and children?

3. Where will you live . . . his house, your house, or a new house? (Going to a new house is recommended.)
4. How will the children address their new parents?
5. Where will the children who live with ex-spouses stay when they come for weekends, vacations, or overnights?
6. What about legal adoptions and name changes for the children? (Caution is urged, to protect the children's sense of identity.)
7. Who is going to discipline whom?
C. Three things never seem to be totally resolved in remarriages:
1. The ongoing relationship with the former spouse is, by nature, irresolvable.
2. The fair and even treatment of the children on both sides is difficult to control.
3. Stretching the family budget over two households creates a strain.
D. Remember: What you establish in your relationship prior to marriage will be a preview of what it is going to be like afterward. "What you see *is* what you get."
E. Even some loyalties that have been clearly thought out may change with new circumstances.
1. If your ex-spouse were to become critically ill in another state, would you drop everything to run to his or her bedside?
2. If your new mate exacts severe discipline on your children, will your loyalty be to him or her or to your children?
3. If your children seem to be getting in the way and trying to wreck your new marriage, where will your loyalties be placed?
F. These are all very difficult questions. Many couples are afraid to face them, so their new life together turns into a living hell. People get hurt all over again; only this time it is worse than the disaster of the previous marriage.

Part Two: A Biblical Perspective of Remarriage
I. The Bible specifies four things that should characterize a marriage relationship.
A. Marriage is monogamous. (Genesis 2:18-25, Matthew 19:5)
B. Marriage is permanent. (Genesis 2:24, 1 Corinthians 7:39, plus Scripture's overall harsh attitude toward divorce.)
C. Marriage is intimate—two personalities becoming one in spirit as well as one in flesh. (Genesis 2:24, Ephesians 5:28)
D. Marriage is mutual. (Genesis 2:18-23, Ephesians 5:22-33)
II. The Bible contains specific guidelines for divorce and remarriage.
A. Eight important passages, which are not part of the lecture, are made available at the materials table for private consideration and discussion.
1. Genesis 2:18-25
2. Deuteronomy 24:1-4
3. Malachi 2:13-16
4. Matthew 5:31-32
5. Matthew 19:3-12 (and its parallel, Mark 10:2-12)
6. Luke 16:16-18
7. Romans 7:1-3

8. 1 Corinthians 7:1-17

B. You should also keep in mind these five important principles of biblical interpretation.

1. You need a clear, biblical definition of terms like adultery and fornication.

2. You must study each Bible passage in its proper context.

3. You need to appreciate the tension between the letter of the law and the spirit of God's grace and forgiveness. God judges us and is hard on us because He cares about us. He wants what is best for us.

4. You have to take into account biblical silence as well as what is clearly stated for you to understand and to obey. The Bible is not an almanac with an answer to every one of life's questions.

5. When you study the Scriptures from the point of view of faith and see it as having some binding authority on your lives, God expects you to make some appropriate response.

C. Although He sometimes permits us to live and to operate at a sub-ideal level, God by His very nature cannot legislate imperfection.

D. The Bible nowhere gives specific permission for the remarriage of a divorced person. Indeed, Christians may conclude that, if they are divorced, they cannot remarry during the lifetime of their former partner.

E. On the other hand, divorce is nowhere listed in the Bible as an unforgivable sin.

F. God's law has not changed, but Christ's atoning death has redeemed all of us if we will accept that redemption.

1. This forgiveness is appropriated when we express genuine sorrow for our sins.

2. God's grace not only enables forgiveness, it also gives us the strength to endure pain and guilt.

3. And it gives us a new start in life. God does not forgive us and then hold our failures over our heads.

a) Consider His attitude toward the woman caught in adultery (John 8).

b) We also see this attitude in John 3:17. This has always been the way of God—forgiving people and letting them begin again.

III. How do we come to terms with our attitudes toward divorce and remarriage?

A. The dissolution of a marriage is always a moral and spiritual tragedy.

1. It is a serious transgression against the design of God in creation.

2. It is a tear in the fabric of a community and a deep injury to everyone directly involved.

B. The laws of God are perfect, but the people who live under them are not. And that is all of us, whether we are divorced or not.

1. The penalty for breaking the law is eternal separation from God.

2. But Jesus Christ has come to pay the penalty for you and for me.

3. The church must:

a) Sound a clear note of divine truth and judgment about sin.

b) Also be merciful and forgiving.

4. At the risk of spoiling our own image, we must love the sinner, and give that person a chance to begin anew.

C. All of you who are thinking about remarriage must struggle.

1. You must struggle with the full force of what the Bible says.
2. You must deal with the full gravity of all the practical questions we have considered.
3. Only then can you begin to set your lives on a new path according to God's plan.

PART THREE

MAKING THE WORKSHOP HAPPEN

CHAPTER NINE

FACILITIES

Here are some of the important things to keep in mind when arranging for your workshop location.

A CHURCH IS THE BEST LOCATION

A few people who would attend a divorce recovery workshop in a neutral setting such as a hotel might never darken the door of a church. But I still believe that the best place for a workshop is a church.

The divorce experience is unique. Just as a thirsty man on the desert is not too particular about where he finds water, the divorced person, in most cases, is not overly concerned about the exact building where he or she finds healing and hope. The wide variety of people who come into our church for this recovery workshop is amazing. The workshop attracts those who have never been in a church, or at least not since childhood; cult members; agnostics; and people from a wide spectrum of denominations and religious groups.

Some of them may want nothing to do with the church and may even be very vocal about this feeling. But the divorce experience—more than just about any other experience in life—puts people on a level playing field. They have each experienced rejection, loss, and a sense of failure, and they are searching for wholeness and healing in their lives. The location of the workshop seems to make little difference.

A church facility requires less hassle and expense. Because of the reason above, there seems to be no real advantage in going to the trouble and additional expense of renting a more neutral setting. Renting an outside facility will make it more difficult logistically for you and your staff. Providing childcare will be more difficult (since many churches have excellent childcare facilities on site). A nonchurch facility would probably necessitate your charging a higher registration fee, possibly prohibiting some from attending. So I find little to be gained by going to a neutral place. I can see possible benefits to sponsoring some other types of ministry events on neutral territory; but this does not seem to be the case in the area of divorce recovery.

It facilitates "building a bridge" to the church. This is the most important reason to hold the workshop in a church. Part of the goal in our workshops is to let this ongoing divorce recovery experience serve as a bridge into the life of the church. We want those who attend to begin feeling comfortable coming to our fellowship of believers. We want them to see that we genuinely care. We want them to see the church building as a place where they can experience healing and the love of God. The church-sponsored divorce recovery workshop that meets on neutral ground is going to have a harder time building this bridge.

It can provide a safe place to grow. My only caution in using the church as your meeting place is that you guard against being heavy-handed in your evangelistic zeal. As I have already stressed, if you attempt to make your workshop an evangelistic seminar in the disguise of a divorce recovery workshop, your church will lose credibility as a safe place to come for help. If you are more concerned about getting them to join your church or to listen to your preaching, your church will not remain a viable divorce recovery outreach in your community.

A Large Central Meeting Room

The fellowship hall in most churches works well for the main teaching session. Ideally, it should lend a warm, friendly atmosphere and should not look too "churchy." You definitely do not want to meet in a room with pews, which rules out meeting in most sanctuaries.

Small-Group Meeting Facilities

The perfect scenario is that each of your small groups have its own room, because of the privacy, quiet, and sense of focus needed. If some groups must remain in the main meeting room, use movable chairs and do everything you can to keep the groups as far apart as possible.

Make do the best you can based on the facilities and the size of your group, but keep in mind that in the small groups people are sharing some of the most painful parts of their life. They need maximum privacy and as much comfort as possible.

It is best to schedule your workshop on a night when you can use all the meeting rooms in your church.

Easy Access to a Kitchen

Although this is not essential, easy access to a kitchen is very helpful for serving refreshments during each meeting and for preparing the potluck dinner. Access to a kitchen makes it easier to provide soft drinks, coffee, finger foods, and serving utensils.

Nursery/ChildCare Facilities

Because many of those attending will be single parents of young children, it is essential to provide some kind of childcare during your sessions. This is one of the real advantages of using a church.

We have found that providing this service free of charge for all preschool children has been a tremendous benefit in allowing many of our participants to come. The cost of this service is paid by our church, but it can also be built into the registration fee.

Adequate Parking

Parking is another area where churches have an advantage. But is your parking lot well lighted? Is it a safe place to be alone at night? Is extra security needed to make first-timers feel safe? And can those newcomers find their way, from anywhere they may choose to park, to the door of the church nearest the workshop registration area?

Signs Giving Clear, Easy-to-Follow Directions

One of the most frustrating things for people unfamiliar with your church is not to know where to go. Some of the people who come—especially on the first two nights—are going to be looking for the slightest excuse not to go into the meeting. Not having clear signs and directions may be just enough excuse for them to turn around and go back home.

CHAPTER TEN

THE WORKSHOP BUDGET

Although I do not believe that a divorce recovery ministry should be designed to make money, I have found over the years that you will at least cover your costs and most likely see a surplus. In fact, as I discussed on page 24, a divorce recovery workshop can be a wise investment for your church. You are meeting a legitimate need in your church and community. Thus, you will gain much more, both spiritually and financially, than the workshop will cost. (At St. Andrew's we receive great joy from giving some of our workshop profits to other ministries that benefit our divorced and single-parent families.)

BUDGET OVERVIEW

Setting the budget should be primarily the responsibility of the coordinators, with assistance from the secretary. If you (or someone on your pastoral staff) is the teacher, then you or that person will want to be involved with these decisions as well. The basic items to consider in your workshop budget include the following:

- ◆ An honorarium for speaker (This will not be necessary if a pastor or member of the church staff is teaching the workshop.)
- ◆ A catered dinner for your leadership team
- ◆ A copy of the study book for each participant
- ◆ Refreshments for each workshop session
- ◆ Postage for follow-up letters to attendees and for promotional flyers and letters
- ◆ Printing cost for the promotional flyers/brochures
- ◆ Newspaper and radio advertising; other promotional items
- ◆ Appreciation gifts for any long-term or special leaders/facilitators
- ◆ Miscellaneous supplies (name tags, etc.)

SAMPLE FINANCIAL REPORT

Below is an actual financial report from our March-May 1989 workshop. It is quite typical of our workshop expenses. I have also included the percent of the total budget that each area represents. This may be helpful in planning your own budget.

RECEIPTS

Registration Fees

305 @ $20 (Full registration) $6,100.00
43 @ $15 (Fee without study book) 645.00
66 @ $5 (Alumni) 330.00
    Total $7,075.00 (96%)

No-Shows

6 @ $20 . . . . $120.00
1 @ $15 . . . . 15.00
4 @ $5 . . . . 20.00
    Total $155.00 (2%)

Extra Books and Miscellaneous

31 *Growing Through Divorce* books @ $5.00 . . . . $155.00
Other 9.00
    Total $164.00 (2%)

TOTAL RECEIPTS $7,394.00

EXPENSES AND DISBURSEMENTS

ADVERTISING
Newspapers
The Register $773.20
Daily Pilot 462.30
Irvine World News 220.80

Brochures
Quick Print (7,500 brochures) 731.40

Mailings
Letter to all alumni 75.00

TOTAL ADVERTISING $2,262.70 (35%)

Program
Growing Through Divorce books @ 7.95 each less 30% discount $1,368.78
Honorarium for speaker 400.00
Children's ministries 400.00
(Childcare plus craft materials for children's workshop sessions.)

TOTAL PROGRAM $2,168.78 (33%)

Food and Refreshments

From church (coffee and punch) $450.75
Cookies for refreshment time 295.61
Ingredients for new leaders' dessert 8.58
Coordinators' dinner meetings 72.61
Catered "thank-you" dinner for leadership team 436.73

TOTAL FOOD/REFRESHMENTS $1,264.28 (19%)

Materials and Services

Paper goods for leaders' potluck and sixth-night potluck $154.61
Quick Print (printing and laminating DRW bookmarks) 147.34
Quick Print (singles ministry calendars for handouts) 115.12
Typesetting 106.00
Flowers for the sixth-night potluck 101.76
Stationery supplies (folders) 34.18
Stationery supplies (name tags and markers) 171.55
Update posters 15.00

TOTAL MATERIALS/SERVICES $845.56 (13%)

TOTAL RECEIPTS $7,394.00

TOTAL EXPENSES 6,541.32

NET 852.68

BUDGET PLANNING SHEET

To help you think through your budget, here is a worksheet, which includes suggestions based on our experience from other workshops.

1. What will you charge for registration? _____
   (Your expenses will probably run between $12-$17 per person. Since you will want to keep the fee as affordable as possible, my suggestion is that you set a fee that will cover all your costs plus a 10 percent "profit margin." This extra 10 percent will help cover any unexpected expenses.)

2. How many people do you realistically estimate will come to your workshop? _____
   (This will depend on several variables: the size of your church, how much advertising you do, and how strongly your church is behind you.)

3. What is your estimated income from registration fees?

   _____ (fee) X _____ (people) = $_____ (total budget)

   (Multiply your registration fee by the number of people you expect to attend. This formula gives you a guideline for planning your expenses.)

4. What do you plan to spend on advertising for the workshop?

   35%_____ of total budget $_____ = Advertising $_____

   (If you seek to make this workshop a community outreach, advertising is one of the most important expense items. I would suggest spending approximately 35 percent of your total budget on carefully planned advertising. See chapter 11 for more information on how to advertise your workshop.)

5. What is your estimated program cost?

   32%_____ of total budget $_____ = Program $_____

   (An equally important budget item is your program, including speaker honoraria, books, child care, etc. I would suggest spending 30 to 35 percent of your total budget in this area. For smaller workshops paying travel expenses in addition to an honorarium for the teacher, this percentage could be much higher. In such a situation, a higher registration fee would be in order.)

6. What do you estimate as the cost of food and refreshments?

   17%_____ of total budget $_____ = Food/Refreshments $_____

   (Food and refreshments is one area where you may be able to reduce your total costs. For example, you may find a service group in your church willing to provide some of the food. By doing this, you may be able to reduce this portion of your budget to the 12 to 15 percent range. Keep in mind that food and refreshments add warmth to a setting and help your people relax and open up. So, for planning purposes I would suggest that you consider approximately 19 percent of your total budget going for this item.)

7. What does your workshop need to allow for cost of materials and supplies?

    12%_____ of total budget $_____ = Materials/Supplies $_____

    (Materials and supplies are always going to be necessary. Figure around 10 to 15 percent of your total budget going for this.)

8. To serve as a safety valve, reserve up to 10 percent of your total budget as "profit."

    4%_____ of total budget $_____ = Profit $_____

SAMPLE BUDGET FOR A SMALL WORKSHOP

Let's suppose you are hosting a divorce recovery workshop for the first time and would like to plan your expenditures using our budget planning sheet. You expect approximately forty people to attend. You, as the pastor, will be the main teacher. And since this is your first time, you have decided not to attempt a separate workshop for children and teens.

While you will be saving honorarium expenses, the cost of the study book will take up a proportionally higher amount of the program budget since your workshop is so small. You may want to increase the percentage for your program budget and decrease the percentage for your advertising budget to make up for this. And you should probably charge a slightly higher fee, just to make sure this expense is covered.

Here's an example of the results you might come up with.

SAMPLE BUDGET PLANNING SHEET

---

1. What will you charge for registration? $25.00

2. How many people do you realistically estimate will come to your workshop? 40

3. What is your estimated income from registration fees?

    $25 (fee) X 40 (people) = $ 1,000 (total budget)

4. What do you plan to spend on advertising for the workshop?

    35% 30 of total budget $1,000 = Advertising $ 300

5. What is your estimated program cost?

    32% 37 of total budget $1,000 = Program $ 370

6. What do you estimate as the cost of food and refreshments?

    17% 17 of total budget $1,000 = Food/Refreshments $ 170

7. What does your workshop need to allow for cost of materials and supplies?

    12% 12 of total budget $1,000 = Materials/Supplies $ 120

8. To serve as a safety valve, reserve up to 10 percent of your total budget as "profit."

    4% 4 of total budget $ 1,000 = Profit $ 40

EXPENSES AND DISBURSEMENTS

ADVERTISING
Newspapers
Yourtown Gazette $150.00
Shopper's Weekly 25.00

Brochures
Rapid Print (500 brochures) 100.00

Mailings
Letter to area churches (stationery, stamps) 25.00

TOTAL ADVERTISING $300.00 (30%)

Program

50 *Growing Through Divorce* books @ 7.95 each less 30% discount $280.00
Children's ministries 90.00
(Childcare plus supplies.)

TOTAL PROGRAM $370.00 (37%)

Food and Refreshments

From church (coffee and punch) $45.00
Cookies for refreshment time 25.00
"Thank-you" dinner for leaders (at nearby restaurant) 100.00

TOTAL FOOD/REFRESHMENTS $170.00 (17%)

Materials and Services

Paper goods for leaders' potluck and sixth-night potluck $20.00
Printing and laminating DRW bookmarks 40.00
Flowers for the sixth-night potluck 30.00
Stationery supplies (folders) 10.00
Stationery supplies (name tags and markers) 20.00 (12%)

TOTAL MATERIALS/SERVICES $120.00 (12%)

RECEIPTS

Registration Fees

44 @ $25 (Full registration) $1,100.00
   Total $1,100.00

Extra Books and Miscellaneous

3 *Growing Through Divorce* books @ $5.00 . . . . $15.00
   Total $15.00

TOTAL RECEIPTS $1,115.00

TOTAL EXPENSES 960.00

NET 155.00

Notice that, because attendance at your workshop was better than expected and you sold some extra copies of the study book, you actually made 14 percent profit—much more than expected. As you look back over your budget, you realize that one area where you had to cut corners was in childcare. You had to rely on mostly volunteer help and were not able to supply adequate craft material. You may want to apply this year's profits toward doing better in that area next year.

START-UP MONEY NEEDED

Registration income should cover all your costs in most situations. But you will need some advance "seed money" to get started. I would suggest that you take this from your own singles ministry budget or request funds from the general church budget.

The primary start-up expenses include:

◆ Study books such as *Growing Through Divorce*. To get a good quantity discount, and to assure that you have enough on hand, these will need to be ordered several weeks in advance.
◆ Newspaper advertising
◆ Printing the brochure/flyer
◆ Name tags

As registration receipts come in they should cover all your other expenses.

ONE IMPORTANT ITEM NOT TO FORGET IN YOUR BUDGET

Just as I believe it is important to have a thank-you dinner for your leaders, I also believe it is of great benefit to acknowledge publicly some of those leaders who have contributed in significant ways. For example, one of my core leaders has been responsible for refreshments since 1981. She has been a valuable, long-term member of our team. I recently presented her with a special gift in front of the entire workshop to express our appreciation.

It is not feasible or realistic to give gifts to all of the leaders. But for those who are especially deserving, find a way to acknowledge them publicly.

CHAPTER ELEVEN

ADVERTISING AND PUBLICITY

A divorce recovery workshop can be a valuable bridge-building ministry in a community. We conduct extensive advertising prior to each workshop so that people throughout our community get the word. In fact, the largest percent of our workshop budget goes to advertising.

I discussed earlier in this book the importance of making a long-term commitment to this ministry. The benefits of such a commitment are especially evident when it comes to advertising.

When you establish a healthy, ongoing ministry, you build credibility and exposure in your community. Around 70 percent of the people who come to our workshops come because they were personally invited. Your credibility will advertise for you as you continue to provide a consistent, dependable, credible ministry to divorced people in your community year after year.

Today, many people just call our church and say they heard about our divorce ministry and would like some information. Typically, the number of workshop alumni continuing to grow will have a ripple effect throughout your community.

LETTERS TO WORKSHOP ALUMNI

Therefore, our first and most important means of advertising each new workshop is a letter to all who have participated in past workshops (see sample letter, page 136). We send this out about six weeks prior the new workshop, along with a promotional brochure announcing the new workshop. We encourage alumni to pass the information on to someone they know who might benefit from the experience.

LETTERS TO AREA CHURCHES

We also send letters along with promotional brochures to all the churches in our community about three to four weeks prior to the workshop and invite them to announce our workshop to interested parties in their church. (See sample letter, page 137.)

SAMPLE LETTER TO FORMER WORKSHOP PARTICIPANTS

[LETTERHEAD]

January 18, 1991

To All Participants in the Fall 1990 Divorce Recovery Workshop

Dear Friend:

I trust that since the Divorce Recovery Workshop last fall you have been experiencing growth and fulfillment in your life. I am writing this letter in order to send you a brochure regarding our next workshop, which is to begin on Thursday, February 21, 1991.

I know you are aware of the depth of the problem of broken marriages in our nation and community and are continually in touch with people who are undergoing the struggle of a broken relationship and are in need of a loving and healing touch in their lives. The best promotion that we have had in the past for our Divorce Recovery Workshop has been the personal, word-of-mouth encouragement of those who have taken part in past workshops.

Therefore, the enclosed brochure is for you to share with someone you know whom you feel could benefit from our six-week experience, which begins soon. You can be a great help in encouraging someone to come, perhaps even in bringing them to the workshop and making sure that they follow through with their intention to register and attend. In past workshops we have had many people call our office and indicate their desire to attend, but then not show up for the workshop. Perhaps that encouragement you could provide would be just the extra push such a person might need actually to attend the workshop.

If you need additional copies of the brochure, please call our office [INSERT PHONE NUMBER], and we will be glad to send you as many as you need.

We deeply appreciate your joining with us in our common concern to share the good news of Christ's love. We ask that you also join us in extending the hand of human concern to those who need to be reached through the Divorce Recovery Workshop.

Sincerely,

[SIGNATURE]

SAMPLE LETTER TO AREA CHURCHES

[LETTERHEAD]

September 7, 1990

Dear [NAME OF CHURCH OR PASTOR],

Enclosed are two brochures describing the Divorce Recovery Workshop experience to be held here at [NAME OF YOUR CHURCH] on six consecutive Thursday evenings beginning September 27.

The workshop has been offered over seventeen times since the fall of 1981 with more than 8,000 persons participating. Last fall a significant number of churches shared this information, and many people came to the workshop through hearing about it from these churches.

We would like to extend a cordial invitation to your church to participate in this experience of wholeness and healing. Perhaps members of your congregation or others with whom you are in contact could benefit from the workshop.

Undoubtedly, divorce is one of the most painful and emotionally draining experiences a human being can go through. It is a hurt that cuts deeply and is usually accompanied by doubts that healing will ever come. This workshop will offer some practical guidelines, along with supportive relationships, for anyone struggling through the tragedy of a broken marriage.

If you desire any further information or additional brochures, please call our office [INSERT PHONE NUMBER], and we will be glad to accommodate you.

Sincerely,

[SIGNATURE]

THE PROMOTIONAL BROCHURE

On pages 139-141 is a sample of the advertising brochure we have used for our workshops at St. Andrew's. Use this as a starter and customize it for your own church. It should include a registration form (see page 59).

Besides sending out these brochures in letters, we distribute them in several other ways, as detailed on page 142.

Divorce Recovery Workshop ™

St. Andrew's
Presbyterian Church
(714) 631-2885

**A Seminar for
Divorced and
Separated Persons
of All Ages**

Workshop Leader: Dr. Bill Flanagan

Six Thursday Evenings
April 4-May 9,1991
7:30 p.m.–Dierenfield Hall
600 St. Andrews Road
(at 15th Street)
Newport Beach, California
(714) 631-2885

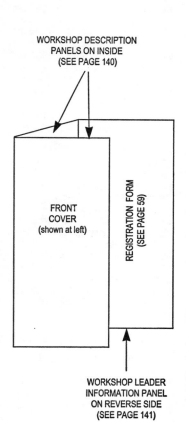

WORKSHOP DESCRIPTION
PANELS ON INSIDE
(SEE PAGE 140)

FRONT
COVER
(shown at left)

REGISTRATION FORM
(SEE PAGE 59)

WORKSHOP LEADER
INFORMATION PANEL
ON REVERSE SIDE
(SEE PAGE 141)

Growing Through Divorce

Last year over 30,000 people in Orange County experienced the dissolution of their marriage. The numbers reveal a problem and tragedy of epidemic proportion. The figures on second marriages are even more alarming. Close to 65% of these unions end in divorce.

Thousands of people in our community have had their lives deeply affected by the reality of the tragedy of divorce. There are deep and very specific needs that should be dealt with so that the fullness and joy of life can be restored. No matter how close or distant in time the divorce experience may be for you, there is something in this workshop that can touch your life and lift it to a new realization of your personhood and infinite value as a human being. Rev. Jim Smoke, whose book we will be using, has said, "You can go through a divorce or you can grow through a divorce." The mutual support and concern of others dealing with similar issues can be tremendously helpful in making one of life's most difficult adjustments. The sessions are designed to meet the needs of those who are adjusting to the finality of a broken marriage, rather than dealing with the possibility of a reconciliation.

Special Workshop for Children and Teenagers

The last three weeks of this seminar we will invite all of the children and teenage young people of the workshop registrants. On April 25, third- through sixth-graders will begin a three-week experience with our Children's Department using an exciting new curriculum developed to meet the needs of children from single-parent families. Junior and senior high young people will also have their own lecture and special small-group experience beginning April 25, led by our Youth Department staff and Marriage, Family and Child Counselor, Randy Smith. There is no charge for these special seminars and further details will be given early in the workshop.

Offered semi-annually since 1981, this workshop has attracted over 8,000 individuals from the geographical limits of Orange County and beyond. It is the largest seminar of its kind in Southern California.

The fall workshop will be offered six Thursday evenings beginning September 19, 1991.

Workshop Details

WHEN: Six Thursday evenings
April 4-May 9
7:30–9:30 p.m.

WHERE: **St. Andrew's Presbyterian Church.** The church is located at the corner of St. Andrews Road and 15th Street. We are directly across the street from Newport Harbor High School. Parking is available in the church parking lot, on the street, or in the school lot. The workshop will be help in **Dierenfield Hall** adjacent to the church sanctuary. There will be signs to guide you and hosts to greet you.

WHO: **Any divorced or separated person**

COST: $20.00. This will include Jim Smoke's book *Growing Through Divorce*, on which the workshop is based, and will cover other costs as well as refreshments each week. (Tapes of the workshop are available.)

REGISTRATION: We would like to know if you are planning to come. Please send in your registration, or call any weekday to register between 9 a.m. and 5 p.m., (714) 631-2885.

CHILDCARE: Childcare for infants through second grade is available free of charge, by reservation.

Supervised study for third- through sixth-graders is available by reservation the first three weeks, April 4, 11, and 18, prior to the Children's Department program the last three weeks of the workshop.

Topics to Be Considered

April 4
Is This Really Happening to Me?
The Three States of the Divorce Experience

April 11
Coping with Your Ex-Spouse
A Relational Reality That Continues to Exist

April 18
Assuming New Responsibilities
Planning for Yourself and Your Future

April 25
Being a Single Parent
Becoming a Whole Family

For non-parents
Coping Skills for Worries, Dark Thoughts, and Down Days—John Fry, Ph.D.

May 2
Finding and Experiencing Forgiveness
Discovering a New Family

May 9
Thinking About New Relationships
Relating, Dating, and Mating

Workshop Leader

Dr. Bill Flanagan

"Flan" is Minister with Single Adults at St. Andrew's Presbyterian Church in Newport Beach, California. He coordinates a ministry that reaches hundreds of single people each week. Starting in 1971, Flan has focused his attention on the issues that face never-married, separated, divorced, and widowed persons of all ages.

Since 1977 he has conducted Divorce Recovery Workshops across the country, reaching out a hand of hope and healing to over 8,000 persons. St. Andrew's Presbyterian Church began sponsoring his seminar in 1981. It is offered each spring and fall.

Bill has a B.A. degree from the University of Redlands, a masters in theology from Princeton Theological Seminary and his doctorate from Fuller Theological Seminary. The material relating to this workshop has been published by the National Association of Single Adult Leaders. Bill is chairman of the board of this coast-to-coast Network of Single Adult Leaders. He is also an adjunct faculty member at Fuller Seminary. Flan spends considerable time in personal counseling, writing, and speaking at conventions, seminars, and singles' conferences across America.

Our Church Bulletin

We do this about three or four weeks before the workshop begins. Again, this contributes greatly to our word-of-mouth advertising. Many of the people in our congregation are acquainted with recently divorced or separated people.

Key Places in the Community

We simply pile them around the church and people take them to distribute. The brochures get delivered to such places as divorce courts, human services offices, health clubs, the Y, laundromats, apartment complex clubhouses, company and supermarket bulletin boards, and law firms. Because so many people in our church have been helped by the workshop, we have an army of brochure distributors, who advertise for us in places we don't even know.

Newspaper

Newspaper advertising has been very effective and worth the money for us. We spend an average of $1,500 on newspaper ads (placed anywhere except the church page) for every workshop. Below is a sample of our newspaper ads. You have permission to adapt this ad to your own use. However, you are encouraged not to limit your creativity. Probably some talented person in your church—possibly even someone directly involved with your workshop—could come up with an ad design that is distinctively yours. There are many great ideas for logos and graphic design.

If you do feel drawn to using this logo in your divorce recovery ministry, then please contact us. There is no cost for you to use it; but since it is trademarked, we ask that you write us and request permission.

DON'T JUST GO THROUGH IT—GROW THROUGH IT!

SEMINAR

Over 8,000 persons have attended the previous workshops

A SEMINAR FOR DIVORCED AND SEPARATED PERSONS OF ALL AGES

Six Thursday Evenings
April 4–May 9
7:30–9:30 p.m.

ST. ANDREW'S PRESBYTERIAN CHURCH
Newport Beach—St. Andrews at 15th Street
(across from Newport Harbor High)—$20 Registration
For more information call 631-2885 Mon.–Fri., 9-5

Radio

We have experimented with radio but it has not been cost-effective for us. This will vary from place to place so you may want to experiment with radio in your community. However, be sure to take advantage of the free public service announcements offered by most local stations. Below is one of the scripts we have used for this free air time.

Divorced or separated people face many deep and specific needs. That's why St. Andrew's Presbyterian Church in Newport Beach is sponsoring a divorce recovery workshop April 4 through May 9, with Dr. Bill Flanagan. For six Thursday evenings, from 7:30 until 9:30, Dr. Flanagan will lead discussions on recovering from divorce. Thousands of people have been helped by this workshop in the past. You will be, too. Call (714) 631-2885 to make your reservation. The cost is $20.00, so call (714) 631-2885 today.

Announcements from the Senior Pastor

My senior pastor, Dr. John Huffman, has been very faithful about encouraging our people to take brochures and share them with family members, neighbors, friends, or coworkers. People have graciously and enthusiastically done this year after year.

A key principle is at work here: Without the enthusiastic endorsement and encouragement from the head of your church staff, your workshop is ripe for failure. Public support and encouragement from the senior pastor and other key staff are vital for a well-publicized, successful divorce recovery workshop.

Posters

The poster could simply be an enlargement of your brochure and would be mainly for displays in your church and other churches.

Joint Advertising with Your Children's/Youth Ministries

If your church is conducting a teen and/or children's divorce recovery program in conjunction with your adult workshop, find ways to advertise the events together. This not only allows each group to save money on their advertising but helps communicate that this is a ministry for the family unit.

ADVERTISING CHECKLIST

Check to make sure you have included all the items on this list every time you produce an advertising piece for your workshop:

- ❑ Where the workshop is being held. (A map is helpful—the more detailed the better. Don't give anyone an excuse not to come.)
- ❑ The starting time for all six sessions.
- ❑ The name(s) of the workshop teacher(s) (optional).
- ❑ The cost for the workshop.
- ❑ The deadline for registration, if any.
- ❑ Nursery/childcare information.
- ❑ A brief summary paragraph describing the workshop, with an invitation for any adults to attend who need healing and recovery—who want to grow through their divorce.
- ❑ Announcement of any concurrent programs for teens and children.

MEDIA RESPONSE SURVEY

The advertising that works best for you may be considerably different than what works for another ministry in another part of the country or even in another part of the same city. It is important always to evaluate what method of advertising is working best for you so that you are getting the maximum mileage from your expenditures.

We do this with a media response survey, which is circulated to all participants sometime during each seminar. On the following page is a copy of our survey.

SAMPLE MEDIA RESPONSE SURVEY

I heard about the workshop in the following way (check as many boxes as applicable):

NEWSPAPERS
❏ *The Register*
❏ *Daily Pilot*
❏ *Irvine World News*
❏ Can't remember which one

RADIO
❏ KBRT
❏ KYMX
❏ KEZY
❏ Can't remember which one

ST. ANDREW'S PRESBYTERIAN CHURCH PUBLICITY
❏ Sunday bulletin
❏ Church newsletter
❏ Singles classes
❏ Workshop flier
❏ Pulpit announcement
❏ Other

PERSONAL RECOMMENDATION OR CONTACT
❏ Friend, family
❏ Associate at work
❏ Neighbor
❏ Attorney
❏ Former workshop participant
❏ Other

MEDIATION COUNSELOR OF COUNTY COURT

MISCELLANEOUS
_____
_____
_____

Please include on this or another sheet any suggestions or comments that could help us improve in our efforts to publicize future workshops:

_____
_____
_____

CHAPTER TWELVE

GETTING ORGANIZED

We've all had nightmares about having a job to do, a speech to give, or a college exam to take, and waking up one day to the stark realization that the deadline had arrived and we were unprepared. Such a nightmare could become a reality if you do not adequately plan ahead for the many things that need to be accomplished—each at their proper time—in preparing for a divorce recovery workshop.

PLANNING TIME-LINE

Perhaps this Planning Time-Line can help you be better organized as you prepare for your workshop.

4-12 Months Ahead
Confirm the following:
- ❑ Workshop dates
- ❑ Workshop facilities (see detailed questions below)
- ❑ Workshop budget
- ❑ Your core leadership team
    - ❑ Teacher(s) (if other than yourself)
    - ❑ Two coordinators (one male and one female)
    - ❑ Secretary

2-4 Months Ahead
- ❑ Develop a promotional brochure or flier.
- ❑ Confirm mailing list and distribution network for advertising.
- ❑ Order estimated number of study books, such as *Growing Through Divorce*, that you will need. It's better to over-order than to have too few. You'll sell extra copies at the workshop, and you can always use leftover copies at your next workshop.

2-3 Months Ahead
- ❑ Distribute and mail the brochures/fliers.

1-3 Months Ahead
Confirm the following:
❑ Small-group discussion leaders
❑ Greeters
❑ Potluck/refreshments coordinators
❑ Newspaper/radio ads
❑ Name tags
❑ Literature (to be available on nights 3-6)
❑ Telephone resource person

MEETING FACILITIES

In chapter 9, we discussed the kind of physical facilities needed for the workshop. According to our time-line, you will have chosen your facility by four months before the workshop, at the latest. Here are some of the things you'll need to make sure the facility includes:

❑ Room large enough for main teaching sessions
❑ Adequate rooms for small groups
  ❑ Are those rooms comfortable?
  ❑ Do they provide adequate privacy?
  ❑ Do we have access to all those rooms for all sessions?
❑ Adequate facilities for childcare
❑ Chairs
  ❑ For main teaching room
  ❑ For small-group rooms
❑ Tables
  ❑ Registration/materials (number needed _____)
  ❑ Others needed (number _____)
❑ Chalk board/flip chart
❑ Podium
❑ Sound system
❑ Tape recorder
❑ Background music
❑ Audio-visual equipment[1]
❑ Separate phone line (if needed)

THE WORKSHOP SCHEDULE

The following is a brief outline of exactly what will take place each night of the workshop, along with reminders of preparations you will need to have made for each of those agenda items.

6:45 Childcare Begins

7:00(a) Greetings; Coffee and Refreshments
❑ All greeters on hand
  ❑ All areas covered (entrances, parking lot, etc.)

❑ Official greeters present ahead of time (especially first night)
❑ Coordinators and group leaders on hand as soon as their meeting ends
❑ Refreshments
    ❑ Refreshments purchased
    ❑ Serving tables and utensils in place

7:00(b) Leaders' Meeting
❑ All leaders present
❑ Allow time for:
    ❑ A brief devotion (two to three minutes)
    ❑ Announcements
    ❑ Small-group room assignments (first night only)
    ❑ Brief sharing (what's happening in groups or with follow-up phone calls)
    ❑ Group prayer
❑ Leaders dismissed by 7:20 to help greet participants

7:00(c) Registration (Nights 1 and 2 Only)
Plan for 30 to 40 percent of your participants to register at the door. During the first evening, participants are urged to invite other people to come the second week. But after the second week the workshop is closed to new registrants so that the small-group experience will have minimal disruption.

Registration will require the following items:

❑ Tables available and set up
❑ Adequate supply of registration forms
❑ Money box/petty cash for making change
❑ Registration and payment from those not preregistered
❑ Small-group assignments
    ❑ Lists of those pre-assigned
    ❑ Detailed procedure in place for assigning first-night registrants
❑ Adequate supply of name tags
    ❑ Plastic, permanent tags for all workshop staff
    ❑ Paper stick-ons for attendees (new tags each night)
❑ Signs
    ❑ In parking lot
    ❑ At main entrance
    ❑ At registration table
    ❑ Directing to main meeting area
    ❑ Directing to small-group locations
❑ Study books
    ❑ Free copies for each registrant (staff members should already have theirs)
    ❑ Extra copies for sale
    ❑ Extra copies for staff members who have given theirs away

7:00(d) Materials Table (Nights 3 through 6)
Have the following materials been selected and approved by the person(s) in charge of the workshop?

❑ Counseling referrals
❑ List of recommended resources (see Bibliography, page 251, for suggestions)
❑ Lawyer questionnaire
❑ Cassette tapes of workshop lectures
❑ Information on your church and other churches
❑ Extra copies of the study book

7:35 Welcome and Announcements

7:45 Main Teaching
❑ Teaching prepared
❑ Advance copies provided to group leaders
❑ Handouts ready

8:35 Brief Testimony
❑ Testimony-giver selected
❑ Knows of five-minute limit
❑ Testimony related to teaching theme
❑ Testimony-giver adequately helped and supported by prayer

8:40 Refreshments, on Way to Small Groups
❑ Necessary supplies on hand
❑ People guided to their groups

8:45 Small-Group Discussion
❑ Rooms available and adequately set up
❑ Group leaders present and prepared for session
   ❑ Substitute leader present if needed
   ❑ Any current problems resolved
   ❑ Leaders have read study book, advance copy of lecture, and discussion questions
❑ Required phone calls made by all leaders to all group members
❑ Leaders in agreement with all relevant guidelines (chapter 7)

9:30 Adjournment

9:45 Optional Gatherings in Nearby Restaurants
❑ Reservation made (An average of 20 to 25 percent of attendees will go to these restaurant gatherings.)

6:00 Leadership Thank-You Dinner (Fifth Night Only)
What arrangements have been made to prepare and serve the meal? (Group leaders should not have to pay for the meal.)

❑ Catering service, or
❑ Church service group

6:00 Potluck Dinner (Sixth Night Only)
❑ Details of potluck adequately publicized in main sessions and small groups
    ❑ Time and place
    ❑ Bring children
    ❑ Bring enough to feed six to eight people
    ❑ Carry-out food from restaurants is acceptable
❑ Attendance estimated _____ (based on number attending nights 3 and 4)
❑ Tables and chairs in place
❑ Centerpieces for each table
❑ Helpers recruited to:
    ❑ Set tables
    ❑ Someone appointed to direct people as they arrive with food
    ❑ Set-up at 4:00, so that all is ready when people begin arriving at 5:00
❑ Placemats and napkins purchased
❑ All other items on hand: flatware, serving spoons, salt and pepper shakers, baskets, sugar bowls, cream pitchers, packets of cream and sugar, covering for serving tables, coffee, tea, hot water, cups
❑ Adequate help for cleanup
❑ Begin on time—6:00
❑ Time allowed for "roving mike" sharing near end of meal
❑ End on time—7:30
❑ Cleanup completed, including removal of coffee and hot water pots

WORKSHOP RESPONSIBILITIES CHECKLIST

	Teacher	Coordinators	Small-Group Leaders	Secretary	Greeters	Refreshment Chairperson	Chairperson
Advertising				✔			
Attendance reports			✔				
Caterer for leader dinner		✔					
Counseling referrals	✔	✔					
Dates and schedule		✔					
Facilities—locate; prepare		✔		✔			
Greet newcomers at door					✔		
Group discussions			✔				
Group assignments		✔		✔			
Leader meetings		✔					
Lecture, content	✔	✔					
Lecture handouts	✔			✔			
Mailing list				✔			
Materials table, organize		✔		✔			
Materials table, select	✔						
"Mingle" with attendees	✔	✔	✔	✔	✔	✔	✔
Money box (petty cash)				✔			
Phone calls (weekly)			✔				
Potluck, sixth night							✔
Potluck, leader training		✔					
Problem people			✔				
Promotion				✔			
Recruit staff		✔					
Refreshments						✔	
Restaurant reservations		✔					
Schedule and dates		✔					
Signs				✔			
Study book, order				✔			
Study book, select	✔	✔					
Substitute leaders, recruit		✔					
Testimonies recruited		✔					
Train leaders		✔					
Troubleshoot		✔					

COORDINATION CHART FOR TRAINING AND WORKSHOPS

	Adults	Teens	Children
Week A Leader Training	✔		
Week B Leader Training	✔		
Week 1 Session 1	✔		
Week 2 Session 2 Leader Training	✔	✔	✔
Week 3 Session 3 Leader Training	✔	✔	✔
Week 4 Session 4 Session 1	✔	✔	✔
Week 5 Session 5 Session 2	✔	✔	✔
Week 6 Potluck Session 6 Session 3	✔ ✔	✔ ✔	✔ ✔

WEEKEND SCHEDULE: FRIDAY NIGHT/SATURDAY

Here's how the basic workshop schedule can be adapted for completion in a single weekend (Friday night/all day Saturday). Refer back to the checklist for the items you will be including in your shortened schedule. (Note that the single-parenting session is omitted in this format.)

Friday
6:00 Leader training session
      (If teacher is local resident, do training ahead of time.)
7:20 Leaders' prayer time
7:30 Leaders and staff greet and register attendees
8:00 Host gives public welcome
8:10 Lecture 1: Is This Really Happening to Me?
8:55 Testimony (optional)
9:00 Small-group discussion
9:30 Dismissal
9:45 Teacher debriefs small-group leaders

Saturday
 8:45 Late registration
 9:00 Welcome/announcements
 9:10 Lecture 2: Coping with Your Ex-Spouse
 9:55 Testimony (optional)
10:00 Small-group discussion
10:30 Refreshments
10:45 Lecture 3: Assuming New Responsibilities
11:30 Testimony (optional)
11:35 Small-group discussion
12:10 Lunch, free time, teacher/leader debriefing
 1:40 Lecture 4: Finding and Experiencing Forgiveness
 2:25 Testimony (optional)
 2:30 Small-group discussion
 3:00 Refreshments
 3:15 Lecture 5: Thinking About New Relationships
 4:00 Open question session
 4:30 Adjournment

WEEKEND RETREAT SCHEDULE (FRI. P.M./SAT./SUN. A.M.)

Here's how the basic workshop schedule can be adapted for completion in a weekend retreat format (Friday night/all day Saturday/Sunday morning). Refer back to the checklist for the items you will be including in your shortened schedule. (This format allows time for all six sessions.)

Friday

6:00	Leader training session
	(If teacher is local resident, do training ahead of time.)
7:20	Leaders' prayer time
7:30	Leaders and staff greet and register attendees
8:00	Host gives public welcome
8:10	Lecture 1: Is This Really Happening to Me?
8:55	Testimony (optional)
9:00	Small-group discussion
9:30	Dismissal/social activities; teacher debriefs small-group leaders

Saturday

8:45	Late registration
9:00	Welcome/announcements
9:10	Lecture 2: Coping with Your Ex-Spouse
9:55	Testimony (optional)
10:00	Small-group discussion
10:30	Refreshments
10:45	Lecture 3: Assuming New Responsibilities
11:30	Testimony (optional)
11:35	Small-group discussion
12:10	Lunch, free time, teacher/leader debriefing
1:40	Lecture 4: Finding and Experiencing Forgiveness
2:25	Testimony (optional)
2:30	Small-group discussion
3:00	Refreshments, free time
5:30	Dinner
7:00	Lecture 5: Thinking About New Relationships
7:45	Open question session

Sunday

8:00	Breakfast
9:00	Special music presentation
9:30	Lecture 6: Being a Single Parent
10:15	Testimony (optional)
10:20	Small-group discussion
11:00	Lunch/adjournment

CHAPTER THIRTEEN

AFTER THE HEALING BEGINS

The ministry of divorce recovery cannot take place in just six weeks. The workshop merely begins the healing process. And some wounds will never totally heal. The best indication that your workshop has been successful will be that a substantial number of those who attended will have chosen to get involved in Christian fellowship, or perhaps will have even made a first-time faith commitment to Jesus Christ. That is what the divorce recovery workshop is really about—building a bridge to Christ and His church.

Even as you plan for your initial divorce recovery workshop, you should be asking: Will the unchurched people who come to our church for the first time during the workshop be attracted to the larger ministry of the congregation? The size of your church and church staff will determine whether you can have an organized program for your workshop graduates. But no matter what its size, your church should be prepared to minister to workshop graduates on a personal, individual level.

The most important thing to do in preparation for a post-workshop ministry is to nurture within your church membership and staff an attitude of acceptance toward the divorced. As I asked at the outset of this book, will workshop graduates be viewed by the people of your church as second-class spiritual citizens? Or will they be welcomed with open arms as men and women who have the potential of being productive members?

I think of Sharon,[1] who came to our ministry as a single mother with teenagers going through a very difficult time of adjustment. Drugs gradually became a part of Sharon's family, and one of her children eventually committed suicide. But rather than treat Sharon as some sort of problem person, our whole church surrounded her with love and acceptance. Today Sharon holds an important leadership position, not only in our singles ministry but in the larger church.

This spirit of acceptance is especially important in dealing with the many workshop people who are unaccustomed to "the church scene" and not inclined to become involved in Christian activities. I recall Roger, who came to our workshop totally broken after the end of his marriage of thirty-five years. Roger couldn't remember ever being in church in his life. Yet as he got involved in our church, he found a place of acceptance and love where he was able to grow. Today he is leading one of our small-group fellowships.

Workshop graduates need to feel that they are both welcome as friends and valued as potential servers and leaders in the church. At St. Andrew's, I encourage qualified divorced people to move into leadership positions, and I even nominate them for such positions when appropriate. I see this as part of the healing process. I apply the same high standards as for any other leadership candidate; but in recommending these people I am making a statement about the reality of God's forgiving grace. I know that as these workshop graduates become church leaders they will provide positive models for future workshop participants.

When divorce recovery workshops are offered, pastors need to demonstrate this attitude of acceptance in their sermons. Will the sermon topics and illustrations assume that the audience is composed entirely of married people? Will the divorced people in the audience hear their situation addressed in positive ways that demonstrate God's love? I am most grateful to Dr. John Huffman, our senior pastor at St. Andrew's, for setting an example in this regard.

Acceptance should be expressed both programmatically and personally. It takes into account the needs of the divorced, especially those who are single parents, when church activities are planned; and it lets them know, individually, that they are welcome, that their presence is valued, and that they will be taken seriously as part of the church community.

According to the Gallup survey, many of the people who attend your workshop have been brought to a strong faith in Christ through their divorce experience; but often they have little hope of ever finding a church that will accept them.[2] Will they find such a church during your workshop?

SPECIFIC WAYS TO CONTINUE THE HEALING MINISTRY

Preparing the hearts and minds of your church members and staff is the most important step toward effectively ministering to the divorced. Once that step has been taken, some more specific suggestions will help you implement a healing ministry.

Encourage Personal Spiritual Discovery and Growth.
While all the group activities I will suggest in the following paragraphs can help people who are recovering from a divorce, they need to be encouraged first and foremost to launch out on their own journey of faith. You or someone on your staff needs to see that each workshop graduate receives as much individual attention as they need—whether that means bringing them to an initial faith commitment or discipling them in their walk with the Lord.

One method we have found helpful is encouraging people to keep a journal of their spiritual and emotional progress. This helps them see their time of recovery in a positive light, as a time when God can speak to them in especially meaningful ways. It can provide a helpful discipline for the person who may not otherwise be inclined to meditate on spiritual matters. It can minister both to the Christian and to the person who has yet to come to faith in Christ. Ronald Klug's book *How to Keep a Spiritual Journal* has helped many to get started in journal writing.

Invite Small Groups to Continue After the Workshop Ends.
We always let our small groups know that they are welcome to continue meeting as support groups after the workshop ends, on either a formal or an informal basis. We do this

in such a way that the leaders will not feel they have failed if their group chooses not to continue. We also do not want leaders to feel guilty if their group does continue to meet but they are unable to be involved. We have found that a substantial number of groups do continue meeting, most often informally, in restaurants or homes anywhere from once a week to just once every month or two. A few groups have even gone on meeting for several years because the contact and mutual encouragement became so meaningful. In some cases, people simply keep in touch on a personal, one-on-one level.

Involve Alumni in Small Groups Within the Larger Church Fellowship.
Having found the small-group interaction meaningful, our workshop people often graduate to new small-group fellowships within the larger ministry of our church. These groups may take various forms, but they all have at least four basic characteristics in common:

1. *Fellowship* — Just enjoying each other as brothers and sisters in Christ.
2. *Sharing* — One step deeper than fellowship. It means beginning to say, "You know, I'm really hurting; I'm struggling with this; I need your prayers."
3. *Study* — The study of Scripture or a related book. Productive study needs to include some content and needs to provide something more than just an opportunity for people to get together to talk.
4. *Prayer* — The ultimate sense of belonging. This experience happens as those in the group regularly pray for each other.

I strongly believe that such opportunities for intimate fellowship should be a part of every church, no matter how large or small. But for those who have gone through the experience of divorce, such small groups are especially vital. Workshop graduates often find in their new group setting an opportunity to get beyond the immediate problems surrounding their divorce. They learn to both give and receive in the larger context of Christian fellowship.

Organize Special Study Groups.
This kind of group is suited for people who are ready to take a more active role in exploring the world beyond divorce. Such a group involves a higher level of commitment, and leadership responsibilities are shared. Two helpful study books for such sessions are Jim Smoke's *Living Beyond Divorce*, and Harold Ivan Smith's *Single and Feeling Good* (see Bibliography). Also Jim Smoke's most recent book, *Growing in Remarriage*, is excellent.

Extend the Workshop to Address Special Areas of Concern.
Participants in our divorce recovery workshops have often expressed the desire that the workshop continue a few sessions beyond its scheduled completion date. While we have preferred to stick with the six-week schedule, we have at times offered a three- or four-week extension, where new groups are formed and continuing conversation and mutual support is formally provided. It may be that such an extension would work well for you. It can afford an opportunity to address many special concerns such as:

◆ Finances
◆ Car and home maintenance

◆ Legal questions
◆ Single parenting
◆ Remarriage
◆ Discouragement
◆ Loneliness
◆ Depression
◆ Anger
◆ Stress

You might want to consider bringing in guest speakers to present these various areas. Ask the group leaders to develop discussion questions for their small groups while they are listening to the speaker.

A special word needs to be said about offering a session on remarriage. My informal surveys have shown that 75 percent of our attendees are involved in a new dating relationship. Most of them will remarry, and statistics suggest that most of those new marriages will fail. But most of them are not ready to hear what I have to say about remarriage.

However, some—especially those who are already committed Christians—do want to deal seriously with these issues. So a post-workshop session on remarriage can be an important opportunity to minister. You may want to begin with my lecture in the Appendix (page 241) and reshape it to fit the biblical literacy of those you will be teaching.

Provide Pre-Remarriage Counseling.
Even if a new couple doesn't want to hear a lecture on remarriage, you should strongly encourage them to come in for counseling. If 65 percent of second marriages fail, most of your workshop graduates need to be talked out of taking that fateful step without giving themselves adequate time to discuss all the potential problems (especially if children are involved) and prayerfully to consider the wisdom of their choice.

Provide Counseling Referrals.
In some cases, of course, professional counseling will be a part of the continued healing process. The quality of referrals you provide can be crucial. You'll want to be well-informed concerning all the counseling resources available in your area. Unfortunately, some of these referrals will need to be for agencies that minister to battered women.

Provide Opportunities for Healthy Social Life.
This is especially important for nonbelievers or new Christians, who may be honestly unaware that divorced people can have any ongoing social life beyond the bar scene. Plan some fairly regular activities and make an extra effort to be sure that everyone is included. Many of these people will need regular encouragement to stay involved. Don't hesitate to invite even the habitual no-shows; at least they'll be reminded that someone cares.

Provide Activities and Services Geared for Single-Parent Families.
As your church becomes home to more and more single-parent families, you'll find a whole new area of needs to address. Look at these as exciting opportunities to get your entire church family involved as an extended family for these people. Your teens, single adults, and retirees especially can minister by providing free childcare to a financially strapped

parent, by tutoring a child who no longer has access to his math-wizard dad, or by running errands for an overly extended mom.

And keep in mind that, with an added number of single parents in your midst, child-care will take on an added urgency for all church functions. For instance, while others at your all-day leaders' retreat will have left the children at home with their spouses, this will not be possible for those who are single parents. Also, paying for a full day of childcare may be out of the question for them.

Provide Career Counseling and Job Interview Training.

This kind of help will be especially appreciated by the life-long homemaker who finds herself suddenly in the job market for the first time. But even men can experience disruption of their work situation because of the emotional stress of their divorce or because they have had to relocate. Don't let an impersonal government agency provide this service if someone in the church family can provide it just as well!

Provide Creative Ministry Opportunities.

Few things are more helpful in getting people beyond the initial trauma of divorce than simply putting them to work meeting the needs of others. The service opportunities you provide will be a blessing to your workshop graduates, and their work will be a blessing to your church.

George came to our workshop as a recovering alcoholic. He used to drink well over a gallon of hard liquor a week and smoked two to three packs of cigarettes a day. He came to St. Andrew's as a broken individual, went through the divorce recovery workshop, and became integrated into our single adult ministry, where he met his present wife, Sandy. Even though both George and Sandy are career people, they give a lot of time to serving the church. Sandy has served on various church committees, particularly those working to develop service ministries and mission outreach. George has become an elder and, in that capacity, is a powerful witness to God's grace, healing, and forgiveness.

Encourage Workshop Graduates to Become Involved
in Planning and Leading Future Workshops.

Don't overlook this obvious opportunity to put your grads to work. What better way to promote the healing process than for your workshop people to give themselves back to the ministry that helped them!

I am reminded often how much our divorce recovery ministry is built around these wounded healers, who show others the way by both their leadership and their examples. I think of Frank and Jean, who came to our divorce recovery workshop at different times but met while serving as discussion leaders. Not long ago they were married at St. Andrew's and are working to blend their families. To do this they are battling incredible obstacles, yet they are in church every Sunday with their children. They are modeling to other workshop people a commitment to growth and Christian service.

I have shared some of the ways our people at St. Andrew's have helped extend the divorce recovery workshop into a rich and rewarding ministry. I trust many of these ideas will be applicable in your church as well. And I encourage you to use your own creativity—and that of others in your church—to come up with additional ministry ideas.

No divorce recovery workshop, however well planned and presented, can bring total recovery from the trauma of divorce. The workshop should be viewed as a catalyst, an open door. But "after the healing begins," it will take your entire church family to minister adequately to workshop alumni. As you prepare for your first workshop, make it your first order of business to begin preparing the people of your church for their ministry to individual divorced men and women. Challenge them to join with you in reaching out with God's love, forgiveness, and grace to this very appreciative audience!

APPENDIX
WORKSHOP LECTURES

PREFACE TO WORKSHOP LECTURES

Following are the six lectures I generally use in my divorce recovery workshops. Since 1977 they have been used in approximately fifty workshops. They are to be viewed as a resource for your own study and preparation. The outlines of these lectures in chapter 8 will help you develop your own teaching material as you prepare for your workshop.

Workshop teachers will have their own opinions concerning what information needs to be communicated in these main teaching sessions. My own conviction is that *content* is much less crucial than using this time to create an atmosphere of acceptance and of excitement for what can be accomplished in the workshop. As I've stressed already, the small discussion groups are really the focal point of these workshops. My role as teacher is to set the tone for each evening and to give the small-group leaders a platform from which to launch meaningful interaction.

The lectures use Jim Smoke's book *Growing Through Divorce* as a resource text. Workshop participants have a copy of the book before them during the lectures, and I have frequently quoted excerpts from Smoke. More than once in each lecture I utilize the structural outline of his book.

All this has been done with the permission of Jim Smoke. In addition, he has provided me with his unpublished notes, which I have incorporated into my work. I am deeply grateful to Jim as a helpful mentor, professional colleague, and close friend.

Also included in this Appendix is "Thinking About Remarriage," an optional seventh lecture. Please refer to my comments preceding that lecture to assess whether or not you want to include that material in your workshop. And, finally, Dr. John S. Fry's lecture "Coping Skills for Worries, Dark Thoughts, and Down Days" is a perennial favorite as an alternate fourth night lecture for nonparents.

"IS THIS REALLY HAPPENING TO ME?"

It is important to me at the beginning of this workshop to try to make you feel as comfortable as possible as quickly as possible. You very well may have arrived with a whole lot of tension and apprehension, wondering what this workshop is all about. My hope is that you will look back on tonight and the sessions that follow as a very positive step in your life, a turning point, a new beginning. I want you to know, if you are here for the first time, that there are some folks around you who have attended previous workshops . . . and they will say that the divorce recovery workshop has been a significant time for them.

Let me spend just a moment introducing myself. My name is Bill Flanagan, and I am a Presbyterian minister. But I hope you won't hold that against me! I have been a pastor for twenty-six years. I have stood before divorce recovery workshops like this since the spring of 1977. This is my fiftieth divorce recovery workshop, and it has been a wonderful privilege for me to have been able to stand before almost 8,000 individuals who have taken up the challenge of learning and growing through this painful process of divorce.

I am not divorced. Last July, Christy and I celebrated our twenty-seventh wedding anniversary. Our marriage is not a perfect marriage. I don't know of any that are. But it is a marriage that has endured, a marriage that has thrived, a marriage that has been a very fulfilling experience in my life.

So perhaps you are asking, "What in the world qualifies you to speak to my particular situation?" That's a good question. I can only say that I am here by the grace of God, by invitation, and by a desire to help in some way to meet a need.

I consider it a privilege to be here. Divorce recovery workshops have been one of the most significant parts of my life as a minister. Although I've led these workshops many times, my enthusiasm for them has never slackened. I have been working with single people in the church since 1971; and through my relationships, counseling, and friendship with thousands of single adults through the years, I have been taught much and have been sensitized in many ways.

From many phone conversations over the last couple of weeks, I know there are many mixed feelings in this room right now. Some of you wish you had a seat belt to hold you in the chair. Some of you are glad you *don't* have a seat belt. Some of you have positioned yourselves close to a door so that, if the seminar doesn't fly, you can quietly slip out. I understand that feeling, too. I really want you to know that we are not here to "lay a heavy trip" on you. We are not here to exploit your vulnerability or cram something down your throat. We are not here to preach at you. We are not here to involve ourselves in the paralysis of analysis, or tell you where you went wrong or what went wrong with someone else. We are not here to analyze your situation.

We are here, basically, as wounded healers. We are here as people who feel we have some understanding, some sensitivity to your particular situation. And we hope that in the midst of the pain, the hurt, the fear, and the stark terror in some of you right now — that as this workshop gets going and you swallow hard a few times, you'll be able to say, "I'm glad to be here. There isn't a better place for me to be at this particular time in my life than right here."

We want you to know that we are going to take great caution to respect your dignity as a human being and not try to lay anything on you that you are not ready and willing to deal with.

We are all here tonight because of a need in our own lives. And we are here because we want to do something about that need, about that hurt, about that pain, about that anger, about that frustration.

We can't possibly answer all your questions. And I'm not so sure it would make you feel all that much better if we did. Sometimes just answering questions doesn't really satisfy the need in our lives.

I know that many of you were surprised, as you came into the room tonight, to see so many people here. Often, when you are surrounded by a tough thing in your life, you think you are the only one who feels that way, the only one going through that kind of experience. I hope you already see that many other people feel the way you do. It's true that the divorce rate is leveling off. But this year in Orange County there will be approximately 15,000 divorces. That's 30,000 people going through this experience. So the numbers here, in a real sense, represent only a tiny fraction of the folks in our geographical part of the world who are going through this very difficult experience.

There are people from all walks of life here, from all kinds of backgrounds. Some of you here are only thinking about divorce. Some of you are hanging on to a sliver of hope that things may yet work out. Some of you are divorcing—the divorce is in process and you are looking for ways to move on and settle down. Whether you are hanging on, letting go, moving on, or settling down, we're going to try to be aware of where you are coming from. You may have been left for someone else; or you may have left a relationship because of unsolvable problems. Everyone here is in a different place, yet you all have a common need.

There are some ex-spouses in this room tonight. (Whenever I say that, I see people looking around and thinking, "Is mine here?") Every workshop I have ever been a part of has had ex-spouses in it. Later on, we are going to be in small groups, and I promise you we will work things out so that you will not have to be in a small group with your ex-spouse.

I have five objectives for this workshop, five things I hope we will do in the six weeks that we are together. First, I want to facilitate some new friendships in your life—friendships begun in the very healthiest way possible. I always notice that on the first night people sit in little "ones." An hour before we began, a number of people were sitting around the room by themselves. We hope that by the time this gets rolling there will be no little "ones" anymore. We hope you will meet some people, and we hope this workshop will facilitate some very wholesome and healthy friendships.

The divorce recovery workshop is not a "meet market." We have come here to focus in on a very specific need in our lives. Yet it is really helpful, in the process of growing toward wholeness, to grow with other people. I guarantee that, if you will open yourself to this experience, you will find some real needs met in your life by some new friends. One of the things we do in the workshop is invite you to join us at Coco's for coffee after each evening session. It's an informal, optional part of what we do here. You might have to get home and pay the baby-sitter, or get up early and go to work tomorrow. The format of the workshop will conclude here each evening promptly at 9:30 p.m. We will not stay here until all hours of the morning. But if your schedule allows, you are very welcome to join the gang at Coco's.

Second, we are here to practice what I call mutual need therapy. Therapy is a loaded word. I almost hesitate to use it because when some of you hear the word your hair stands on end. You may have had a negative experience with various things going by the label of therapy. On the other hand, some of you have had very positive experiences with counselors. This workshop does not deal with therapy in the professional sense of the word. Later on you will meet some folks who will be facilitating small-group discussions. They are not professional therapists; they are just folks who may be a couple of steps ahead of you in the healing process after their own divorce. They, like you, are here to share in a mutual need therapy, to have some healing take place in their lives, to come to terms with some of the real issues, and to discover some wholeness.

Let me just say one more thing about these small discussion groups. For some of you it will be more comfortable to just sit and listen to somebody else talk. A small-group experience can suddenly seem closer than some people want a time like this to be. Naturally, some of you are afraid you'll be asked to reveal more than you want to reveal. That will never happen in our small groups. We have a very clear rule that you don't have to talk if you don't want to. You can just listen. Sometimes just listening is very therapeutic. Sometimes it is very therapeutic to share as well.

Third, we are here to share our struggles with fellow strugglers. I find tremendous encouragement in my own life when I have someone to talk to about the things that I am struggling with, particularly someone who doesn't have it all together and doesn't claim to have all the answers. I usually feel turned off—and you probably are too—by people who have all the answers to our struggles. We are not here to provide all the answers. We do not have all the answers. Already tonight I have been asked questions that I cannot answer.

We will make no attempt here to deal with specialized areas. We won't try to answer legal questions, for example. We're not equipped to do that; we are here to share struggles with fellow strugglers.

Fourth, we want to help you better understand the divorce experience. One of the advantages I have is that I can address you from a position of emotional neutrality. I can stand more or less outside your experience and hopefully look at it from a sensitive, analytical perspective. Sometimes when you are in the midst of an experience, it is impossible to see it clearly. I want to help you with that—to help you understand what is really going on in your life right now.

Tonight's lecture is entitled "Is This Really Happening to Me?" We'll be talking about some of the stages of the divorce experience. You will hear some incredible myths about divorce from those around you:

◆ You are going to die.
◆ Divorce is the end of your world.
◆ No one understands you.
◆ Your relatives all hate you.
◆ God hates you and will never forgive you.

- ◆ Your children will all become delinquents because of your divorce.
- ◆ You will starve to death.
- ◆ Your house and car will disintegrate.
- ◆ You will be fired from your job.
- ◆ Everyone is looking at you!

Some of these things can give you a lot of pain. But remember, there is no growth without pain.

How many of you have ever been in a divorce recovery workshop before tonight? There are many of you, and I appreciate your raising your hands. That does not mean, friends, that they didn't get it right the first time. It simply means they are now at a different place in their own experience and have concluded that, even though they'll cover the same subject matter as before, they are going to hear and perceive things in this workshop that they were not ready to deal with before. That is the process of growing through divorce, and we are delighted that people do come back. In fact, we find that, in any given workshop, somewhere between 15 to 20 percent are here for the second or third time.

Fifth, and finally, I am here to extend my hand to you as a friend. Although I wish it were possible, I cannot relate personally to all of you. But through our group leaders and through many other concerned people, we desire to extend a hand of friendship to you. There's a hand for you to grasp. There are boxes of Kleenex nearby, if you need them. There are folks here who understand and who care.

All of us who are involved in this workshop, and that includes almost eighty group leaders, want this to be a very special opportunity for you. We want to:

- ◆ Provide a genuine healing experience.
- ◆ Help you develop a sense of belonging and identity for this critical transition time in your life.
- ◆ Present an opportunity for you to do some emotional draining—to dump some garbage you need to get rid of.
- ◆ Offer an atmosphere for real caring, sharing, and growing.

Remember, a divorce is not an event; it is a process you have to go through one day at a time.

Let me make a few announcements. We urge you, particularly if you do not have one of these brochures, to pick up one. We also urge you, if you know someone else who could benefit from the workshop, to invite them to the next session.

This part of the workshop is open to anyone who wants to come. We have numbers of people who come from all over to see what is happening. We are delighted if you are here as an observer. You are welcome in this part of the workshop; but you are not welcome as an observer in the small groups. That is only for those who are registered for the workshop. If you would like to register, you may do that next week. But as of week 3 registration will be closed.

We will be using Jim Smoke's book *Growing Through Divorce*. You received a copy tonight. Be sure to bring it each week.

I want to read several paragraphs written by Paul Bohannan, which I've used now for some time in beginning divorce recovery workshops. Listen to what he has to say:

Divorcees are people who have not achieved a good marriage. They are also people who would not settle for a bad one. Generally, they are not as some people would make them out to be: immature, disobedient, sinful, unstable, permissive individuals unable to stick it out and unconcerned about their children. Nor are they usually failures who deserve whatever suffering they are going through.

The church has no reason to categorize them as different, as a class by themselves, or second-class spiritual citizens. They are not people who threaten other people's marriages or contribute to the destruction of the marriage institution, predators, as it were, who only want to break up families. We falsely see them as people who think lightly of marriage, who treat sacred cows with disdain, who have some character defect for which we consign them to inferior status. Neither are they to be stereotyped as weak or selfish or as though they have somehow let the community down.

Surely, they are not people who by their decision to separate have purposely distanced themselves from their friends and no longer want their support. Divorce is not an act of independence. Divorce does not necessarily result in emotionally crippled, hostile men and women or in emotionally crippled, maladjusted children whose parents care more about themselves than for them.

We make a mistake when we say that since marriage is considered life's most noble undertaking, divorce must be one of its most ignoble shames. This simply does not follow. We have been conditioned for too long to believe that divorced people are inferior to married people, socially, psychologically, morally, and spiritually.[1]

On those words I take a very strong stand. People who go through divorce are hurt. They are deeply wounded. It is one of life's most wrenching, horrible experiences.

Terry Hershey, in his book *Beginning Again: Life after a Relationship Ends*, tells an unforgettable story:

Many years ago the English Duke of Portland owned a magnificent vase, a truly brilliant work of art. The Portland Vase, as it was called, was its owner's prized possession.

As he admired it one day, a thought came to the Duke's mind: "Beauty such as this should be shared with the world. I want to loan the Portland Vase to the British Museum for everyone to enjoy."

The vase was soon prominently displayed at the museum, and the immediate public acclaim of the vase gave the Duke a great sense of satisfaction.

Shortly after the opening of the display, the Duke found it necessary to dismiss one of his most trusted employees. The servant was so deeply hurt by this that he sought some means of revenge, some way to bring pain to the Duke.

Then he thought of the vase. Overnight, he traveled to London and paid the few pennies admission to see the vase. Planning his moves very carefully, he waited until there were no other visitors in the display room and the eyes of the guard were turned away. Carefully he crept under the protective ropes, picked up the vase, and dashed it to the ground.

The servant was quickly captured by the guards, and shocked museum officials sealed off the display room leaving the broken pieces strewn across the floor.

When the Duke was told what had happened, he immediately ordered that none of the pieces be touched. Even the tiniest chips were to be left where they had dropped. Then in Stoke-on-Trent, the pottery capital of England, the Duke searched for someone who would attempt to put the vase back together again. One craftsman after another turned him down. Everywhere he went he was told that the job could not be done.

The Duke was close to abandoning his search when he went to one last shop and told his story one last time. To his surprise, this craftsman agreed to try the restoration.

"But why are you willing to try?" the Duke inquired. "Everyone else has turned me down. I can't understand."

"Your Lordship, my father made the Portland Vase. The pieces on the museum floor are all that is left of his finest work. I must try to rebuild my father's masterpiece."

And so, working at the museum day after weary day, the craftsman added a piece here and a sliver there. At times he despaired that the job would ever be done. Then, finally, he was finished.

The duke was overjoyed at the results. "It is a masterpiece," he exclaimed. "A second masterpiece, more beautiful now than it was before."

Once more the great vase was put on display. And once more the doors to the display room were thrown open so that the world could see the great vase.

It may be difficult for us to believe that the pieces of our lives can be put back together again, but, like the Duke's broken vase, your life and my life can be restored after a relationship ends.[2]

What happens when people go through the end of a close and long relationship? In the first chapter of Jim Smoke's book he talks about three stages of the divorce experience, three different levels that describe what you are going through.

THE FIRST STAGE OF THE DIVORCE EXPERIENCE IS SHOCK

Shock is the feeling you get if you have been in a serious accident—or even if you just *see* a serious accident. Sometimes you become kind of immobilized by it. When you are in shock, you are unable to function normally; you are unable to reason clearly. The first experience of divorce is almost always the experience of shock. Even though you saw it coming, maybe for a long time, you still experience shock. The result is a paralyzing, frightening feeling that is beyond your power to really deal with or control, and you find yourself behaving in uncontrollable ways. You are afraid to go places in public, even places like divorce recovery workshops, because your feelings are so close to the surface. You find yourself letting those feelings out, even on the spur of the moment when you least want to.

Shock is a hard thing to go through because we like to be in control. When you are in shock, you are not in control. Some of you come here tonight as what I call "dumpers." Probably the majority of you here are what I call "dumpees." The shock experience is particularly harsh for the dumpee. You feel walked away from and helpless because you have been rejected at a very deep and profound level.

So where do you begin the healing process? You must start from where you are. Someone has said that there are three different kinds of people in the world: those who watch things happen, those who make things happen, and those who don't know what's happening.

I love the way Charles Schulz put it in one of his Peanuts comic strips. I clipped this out of the *Los Angeles Times* several years ago. Lucy is in her psychiatric booth, which reads: "Help—10¢." (Her rates are still reasonable.) She's saying to Charlie Brown, as he stands there with his perpetually furrowed brow and bewildered look, that life in some ways is like a deck chair.

That only adds to Charlie's bewilderment.

Lucy patiently explains to Charlie that passengers on a cruise ship spend a great deal of time sitting in chairs on the ship's deck so they can enjoy the sunshine. Some people decide to face the rear of the ship so they can see where they've been. Other passengers think it is more interesting to sit facing the front of the ship so they can see where they're going. Then Lucy asks Charlie which way he is facing as he sits on the cruise ship of life.

Poor Charlie Brown says he doesn't know because he's never been able to unfold a chair to sit in it.

You may have your chair facing one way or the other; or, like Charlie Brown, you may not even know how to get the thing unfolded yet. Many of us talk about cooking on all four burners. Sometimes it's down to three burners, or even two. But sometimes we feel like even the pilot light has gone out!

Some professionals who have studied stress have likened the experience of divorce to the experience of death. As a pastor who works with people in both of those stress situations, I have seen incredible parallels . . . because a divorce really is a death. It is the death of a relationship; and you will go through the process of adjusting and recovering from that death in a way very similar to people who are going through the process of adjusting to the physical death of someone close to them.

Five Stages of Grief

In recent years it has become common in the healing professions to talk about the five stages of grief.[3] The stages are painful, but at the same time they are key ingredients to the healing of a broken heart:

1. *Denial*—"This can't really be happening to me!" You bury your head in the sand in an attempt to recapture that which is now irretrievable.
2. *Anger*—Hatred, rage, and the desire for revenge can be very real. But after time and effort, the tears can turn from bitterness to simple sadness.
3. *Bargaining*—You want to make a deal. You play "what if" or "if only" or just "why." Your mind seeks alternatives to terrible facts you cannot justify.
4. *Depression*—Everything seems to stop. You want to drop out. You feel zombied and frozen in your inability to do anything positive for yourself. Life flows in slow-motion. It is a scary time of self-pity.
5. *Acceptance*—Now, at long-last, some healing steps are taken. You begin to live again even though the reality of the death is still all around you. At last you recognize some positive possibilities and realize you have only been temporarily out of commission.

Just as with physical death, that first step is shock and denial. Even when you know that someone close to you is going to die, you are not ready when they actually die. And so it is in the death of a marriage.

Three Ways of Handling Shock

In addition to going through the stages of grieving, people handle the experience of shock in three different ways. The first thing people may do is *internalize*. This is perhaps the most common way of handling shock: to go inside yourself, to become depressed. Clinically, that is what happens in shock: There is a depression of the body's whole nervous system. People in shock will find that they just cannot do the things they normally do.

Those of you who internalize become reclusive. You wall yourselves off from the outside world. You try to sleep a lot. If you render yourselves unconscious, you reason, the reality and the pain will go away for a while. But when you wake up there it is again. You drink. You take drugs. You do anything to try to escape, to wall out the reality that is pressing in on you.

The second way people deal with shock is to *externalize*. Externalizing is just the opposite of internalizing. It means you take off at ninety miles an hour, going somewhere—anywhere! Rather than walling it off, you decide to run, to escape. You have to move. You have to change. You have to go somewhere else. Thinking that if you leave where you are, you can escape the problem. You can escape the feeling. But you find out that no matter how fast you run or how far you go in externalizing your shock, you can't get away from it.

This is where the bar scene comes from. People in bars are often externalizing. They may be externalizing a lot of different realities. It may not be shock or depression. It may be a lot of other things. I'm not going to get into an analysis of why people go to bars, but it's an interesting thing to observe.

I don't know of anyone who stays in the bar scene very long. Most people wear out after a while because it is just like running anywhere: You can only run so far so long so fast before you collapse in a heap. Running will only get you so far and eventually you will end up panting and exhausted, only to find out that whatever you were running from is still looking over your shoulder.

The third way people can handle shock is to *actualize*. Actualizing is the most realistic way to cope with shock; it is also the most difficult. It demands a very conscious effort. Actualizers are the kind of people who *do* get up in the morning, who *do* get out of bed. They may not always want to, but they are able to stagger into the bathroom. And when they get their eyes open, they're able to look at themselves in the mirror and be honest about what they are feeling. Actualizing is to be able to look at yourself and say, "I am divorced. I am separated. I am single. I don't like it. I don't feel good about it. I wish it were different. But that's the way it is."

That is actualizing. And there's a real sense in which you have done that just by walking through the door tonight. You were saying by coming here that you have a need. "I have a need in my life. I do not have a full handle on it, so here I am."

Some people may look at that as a monumental sign of weakness. I look at it as a healthy, hopeful sign—a sign that there is something very good in your future. When you take that painful step of confessing to yourself, and maybe to some other people, just who and where you are—there is hope in that, my friends.

The Four Elements of Realistic Hope

I want to say a word about hope. A good number of you are separated. We take pains on the brochure to say that this workshop is for divorced *and* separated persons. We call it a divorce recovery workshop, but some people call and say, "Well, I'm not divorced. Can I come?" If you read the smaller print inside, where we try to help you understand what this is all about, we say that this workshop is really designed for those who are adjusting to the *final reality of a broken marriage*.

Some of you are here tonight hoping beyond hope that your being here may give you some handles by which you can put this broken relationship back together again. I want to say a word about that because I want you to know that is where the beat of my heart is, too. If there is any possibility for a reconciliation, I am with you.

Four things must be present for a marriage to be reconciled. This will help some of you determine if your hope is realistic. The first two necessary ingredients are (1) a willing man, and (2) a willing woman. Underline it fourteen times: *willing*. Are you *both* willing to enter together into the process of healing—the process of dealing with, of grappling with the issues that are tearing and ripping the relationship apart? If one of the parties is not willing to enter into that process and you know that one of the parties is not willing, then you probably are not hoping realistically for a reconciliation. It takes two people to make a marriage work, but only one to tear it apart.

Now I believe two other ingredients also have to be present. The third, after the willing man and the willing woman, is a competent, caring, emotionally neutral professional. You're kidding yourselves if you think just your willingness to sit down with a "we can work it out" strategy will do it. I have watched too many couples try and fail at this. If you are sitting here tonight saying, "I hope we can just talk and get it back together," you need a third party—someone who has been around the track a few times. I have a pocketful of cards that I will be glad to share with any of you. These cards list different people who can provide some positive professional assistance.

Fourth—and this happens to be a bias of mine that you may not buy into—I believe that God is necessary for reconciliation to happen. He is the One, you see, who designed the relationship we are dealing with in the first place. He's the One who created it. You did not think up marriage and neither did I. It was designed from the very beginning of the creation of humankind. And I believe that if you really want to deal with a broken design, it is very helpful to go to the One who designed it.

So those four ingredients can help you to cope realistically. From this point in the workshop we will proceed on the assumption that you are here adjusting to the finality of a broken relationship. We are operating on that premise in this workshop. We just can't go both ways. If you have reason to hope realistically within those categories I just talked about, we want to encourage you and give you some resources by which you can start putting things back together.

The Questions of Reconciliation

On pages 16-17 of Jim's book he raises four helpful questions concerning the possibility of reconciliation:

Do both parties really want the marriage? If this is not the case, hope is slim for reconciliation.

Will both parties accept professional help for as long as it is necessary? I know many people who have come to a counseling session with their hopes high. We spend an hour together and talk about a situation that took years to develop. And because we did not get it all put back together in an hour, they leave in a frustrated huff, saying, "I knew it wouldn't work. I knew that counselor couldn't help us."

A tremendously unrealistic expectation is put on many counselors who may be quite competent and quite able to help. But the time frame is too tight.

Has a third party become involved with either mate? If that is true in your case, the hope for reconciliation is markedly reduced. The added factors make things extremely complicated. It is not impossible, but it is very difficult to reconcile a relationship when the trust level has been shattered by one or both of the parties becoming involved with someone else.

Are both parties willing to learn through this experience? We're going to spend a great deal more time on this as the workshop goes on. If you think reconciliation is possible, by all means pursue it. But it is also important to know when to let go. For some, there is a time to realize that it is healthier to quit the marriage and to begin moving toward a new identity and a new life. Only you can truly discern that proper time.

THE SECOND MAJOR STAGE
IN THE DIVORCE RECOVERY PROCESS IS ADJUSTMENT

By walking through the door tonight, you exemplify the beginning of this stage. You are doing something about your situation, which is definitely a move forward. Of course, you may slip back and forth and up and down like a roller coaster between shock and adjustment. You may feel one day like you are getting a handle on the situation, that things are getting better. Then some calamity or a phone call will come, and *crash*—back down into the pit you go!

You think, then, that you have to start all over again, but not really. These steps are not so clean-cut. Some days you feel pretty good. Some days you feel pretty rotten. Many times you don't know why you feel good or why you feel rotten. You may be in deep mourning, and there's a sense in which everyone here is in deep mourning. That goes back to the analogy of death we used a few minutes ago. Mourning is a significant reality. There is a time to laugh. There is a time to cry. There is a time to admit "I'm in the pits."

Smoke talks about positive and negative mourning in chapter 1. There's not one of you, when you think honestly, whose marriage was all bad. I hope you haven't burned all the photographs in the scrapbooks and destroyed all the vacation slides all of those things you may one day want to look at again, particularly with your children. You may want to blank out someone in the picture, but adjustment involves beginning to realize that all is not lost.

You'll want to cling to some memories; others you'll want to deal with would best be either healed or forgotten. But there were some good times, so there is a need for positive mourning.

Some of you have grown very proficient at negative mourning. You have learned how to throw a very successful pity party for yourself. We're not here to teach you a new stroke in the sea of self-pity. No one is here tonight to feel sorry for you. Very little is constructive in your feeling sorry for your situation. When you stop feeling sorry for yourself at least some the time, you have begun to adjust.

SMOKE'S THIRD STAGE OF DIVORCE RECOVERY IS GROWTH

In fact the major premise of his book is that you can either *go* through a divorce or *grow* through it. You can let this tragic experience teach you something about yourself.

Of course, that does not mean divorce is a good thing. You're going to meet some people in a few minutes who have grown and adjusted enough to use their own tragedy in a constructive way in the lives of other people. But that does not justify the tragedy. None of these people are going to get up here and say, "I'm glad I got a divorce so that I can be a divorce recovery workshop leader." None of them feel that, but they *can* know the joy of using their own tragedy for good in another person's life.

Do you realize the whole Christian faith rests on that concept? Resurrection always follows death. You can go through it or you can grow through it. It *is* possible for you to grow. As mature adults, we know that rigor mortis begins to set in when we feel that we have grown as far as we can grow, that we've learned all there is to learn, that we've experienced all in life there is to experience, that we have it all together.

I don't think anyone here tonight has that attitude. So, there is a growing edge here. There are possibilities. There is hope. There is a promise—if you are willing to claim it—for healing and wholeness.

You may be saying, "I don't think I can ever feel good about myself again." But I am here to make a tremendously strong, radical assertion. I hope you are willing to claim it. You are not a piece of junk thrown on the trash pile of human existence! You are not a rejected human being with no value. You are not finished.

I want a positive truth to ring in your ears as you leave here tonight. I said earlier that, as you begin to actualize, you come to the place where you can look at yourself in the mirror and say, "I am divorced; I am single; I am alone." You may not like it, and it may make you feel terrible. But actualizing means being able to look into the same mirror after you've said, "I am divorced," and say, *"I am a unique, beautiful, unrepeatable miracle of God."*

Try to say that on the way home. Out loud. That is the beginning of growth, to be able to say that about yourself. You are valuable. You are worth this workshop. You are worth it! One of the most incredible experiences of my life is to watch people in these workshops heal before my very eyes. I believe you are unique. You are beautiful. You are a miracle of God's creation—and there is promise, and there is a future.

The battle to grow through a divorce is waged on three fronts:

- ◆ The emotional
- ◆ The relational
- ◆ The practical

When you grow through your experiences of divorce you are able to make:

- ◆ A realistic analysis of the past, from which you can now learn.
- ◆ A practical understanding of the present, where you are seeking healthy relationships and values.
- ◆ A positive and optimistic plan for your future.

Growing people learn to deal with reality for what it is, as opposed to fantasy for what it is not.

I want to be realistic with you, because divorce will leave a scar. You will not emerge from this workshop six weeks from now all healed. Divorce will leave a scar that you will carry for the rest of your lives. There is a sense in which you will always be adjusting and growing through this tragic experience. Always! Face that. It will be part of your healing. You will never completely get over it.

But I would remind you what a scar is. We all have scars of one kind or another on our bodies. Scars are reminders of something that happened in the past. But scars are also signs that something has healed. Scars do not hurt. We all bear scars in life. But scars are wonderful reminders that healing has happened—even though we carry the reality of those scars in our bodies and in our lives for as long as we live.

Adjusting to Reality

On pages 21-23 of *Growing Through Divorce*, Jim discusses eight things to help you adjust to the reality of "Is This Really Happening to Me?"

Time is a healer; you need to walk through the process one day at a time. As Robert Schuller says, "Inch by inch, life is a cinch." It's true. You can't have it all in one hour's session, but you can begin to grasp hold of a process. You will find that if you commit yourself to this six-week workshop, it will be a tremendously helpful experience.

Come to grips with yourself. Don't deny your own existence. Begin to do some things to value yourself. Take some "me" time. We'll talk more later on about balancing personal time with family and children and work.

Allow time for personal growth. Set aside some time for reflection, meditation, and reading. Find sources which are helpful to you, and give yourselves time to contemplate them. Look for opportunities, like this workshop, that will help you grow.

Get with some healthy people who are struggling and growing. Tonight you have taken a giant step in that direction. There are more healthy, growing divorced people per square foot in this room right now than anywhere else I know! You are in a healthy place.

Of course, this isn't a place where everyone has it all together. The discussion leaders I'm going to introduce to you in a few minutes don't have it all together, but they are basically healthy people. Too many people going through a divorce get involved with the most unhealthy people they can find. Isn't it ironic what we will do sometimes to try to escape? We'll get with people who are going to hurt us and not help us. Tonight, however, you are with some healthy people in a healthy place.

Seek professional counseling. The counselors I can refer you to are spiritually and emotionally healthy people. There are many *un*healthy people in the counseling field. For many, counseling is a racket. Some of you have had bad experiences with counselors. Of course, in some cases you may not have given the therapist a fair chance to really help you. But consider giving counseling another chance, if that is what you need.

Accept the fact you are divorced or divorcing and are now single. Begin to see yourself that way. Begin to accept that what has happened is the way it is going to be. If you are constantly projecting yourself into a never-never land that is totally unrealistic, you are not going to heal. You're going to stay wounded and bleeding. If there is truly no possibility for a reconciliation, then you must begin to accept your situation— and you need to allow the people here tonight to help you begin doing that.

Put the past in the past and live in the present. We all know people who live in the past, and they are not growing people. Like Charlie Brown, we need to unfold our deck chairs!

Finally, we must confront the question of religion. Almost always we are asked, "Is this going to be religious?" We are not taking a poll of what denominations are represented here, or suggesting what church to attend or not to attend. I know if we went around the room tonight we would have a real smorgasbord of different people in different situations. We are not here to exploit you spiritually.

Many of you here have no church or faith. We are not here to have you sign a pledge card. We are not here to have you join the church. As I said, I am not here to preach. But you must understand that I am trained that way, and sometimes I may come through and sound a little bit like that. That is not my intention. What I am trying to do is communicate as honestly, as carefully, in as caring a way as I can, the authentic truths that I have been taught by others. My prayer is that this will be a very exciting and very healing time for you as you begin the process of growing through the difficult experience of divorce.

COPING WITH YOUR EX-SPOUSE: A RELATIONAL REALITY THAT CONTINUES TO EXIST

You will probably have people in the audience for this second lecture who were not there for the first session. This presentation takes that into account.

In this lecture I want to address the issue of ex-spouses. This is one of the tougher things we will talk about in our divorce recovery workshop. My remarks will correspond with chapter 3, "Getting the Ex-Spouse in Focus," in *Growing Through Divorce*. Jim begins his chapter with a poem:

> *To My Ex*
> You've made my life the way it is,
> Though it hasn't always been placid;
> And one of the things that you've given me
> Is excess stomach acid.

I said last week that we aren't here to feel sorry for anyone. We aren't here to help you throw a pity party for yourself. We are here for no other reason than to deal with reality. So we're going to jump right in, realizing that for some of you dealing with reality will mean hitting some tender spots.

Jim headlines his discussion with the words, "I loved you, I hate you, I'll get you." Or, as someone else has said: "Hurt people *hurt* people." That's the way some of you are feeling, and we will talk about some of those feelings tonight.

One of our group leaders called a person in her group this week and got hung up on because the person she called was not ready to hear constructive, positive words. I really can identify with that. Have you ever hung up on someone? I have. "Don't talk to me about anything positive. Don't talk to me about anything constructive. I don't want to hear it. I'd rather wallow in my own despair right now."

Some of you need to take very good notes tonight. Some of you will say, "Bingo! I need to deal with that now." Some of you will say, "Whoa—I'm not ready for that one yet."

Some of you could produce a mini-series about your ex that would compete with the most prime-time soap operas. But we do not want to write a soap opera here; rather, we want to zero in on some of the issues you are grappling with. The question now is this: How can we cope with or handle a relationship that in one sense has ceased to exist and yet in a very real sense still exists? How do we deal with that reality in a mature, adult way?

You can't totally put aside a relationship with someone to whom you were once married. That, my friends—and here comes a dose of reality, so hold onto your chair—is a relationship you will deal with for the rest of your life. There will be no forever-putting-it-behind-you. That relationship is there and always will be. So, the question is not how do you cover it up, how do you deny it, how do you close your eyes and make it go away; the question is, how do you manage it?

Dealing with your former husband or wife involves much more than just property settlements, child and spousal financial support, custody of children, and visitation rights and schedules. How do you cope with that person to whom you once said "I love you" and to whom you may now be saying "I hate you," or a whole variety of other things? Not all of you are saying that, but some of you are. Some of you are just saying, "I still love you, but I'm so hurt I don't know what else to do." And some of you are saying, as Smoke says at the beginning of this chapter, "I'll get you if it's the last thing I do."

The relationship with the ex-spouse can take one of four basic shapes:

1. It may be a real, ongoing contact filled with revenge, anger, and hostility—or, in some cases, emotional neutrality. Perhaps it is a relationship that is somewhere in between and has flare-ups now and then.
2. Your relationship with your ex-spouse may simply involve sharing in the mutual responsibility of relating to and caring for your children—with no other basis for the relationship.
3. It may be a relationship based entirely on the *memory* of what used to be. You may have no actual ongoing contact. Consider yourself fortunate if you are in a situation where there are no children or where one parent has total custody of the children.
4. It may be that the ex-spouse is no longer living. But even then the relationship is not totally over. There is something about people we have loved and lost that still clings to us and influences us and touches our lives and our feelings and all we are for as long as we live.

Each of you fits somewhere in that panorama of possible ex-spouse relationships. Assuming that the majority of you are in the category where there is still a relationship, where there is still contact, how do you adjust to that? How do you have an equitable relationship with someone who has taken part in destroying something in you? How do you attain mobility, wholeness, freedom, and growth through a divorce? That is the premise of Jim's book. You either *go* through it or *grow* through it.

The growth option requires making a deliberate choice. You say, "I choose to grow. I choose not to let this destroy me. I am a beautiful, unique, unrepeatable miracle of God. I am not junk. I am not a piece of garbage thrown on the trash heap of life. I am a useful, productive human being. I am not perfect, and I don't like being divorced and all that goes with it."

Singleness is not a very exciting prospect to someone who is just going through this. Yet many people in this room would say that being single is not the worst thing that can happen to you. It is not the end of everything. There is life after marriage—a good life, a life full of wholeness.

But in order to establish that wholeness, you have to try to work out an equitable, satisfactory human relationship with your ex-spouse. That kind of reasonable agreement is not easy in many cases. Timing is crucial. Finesse, diplomacy, tact, wisdom, compassion, and sensitivity are words that describe how smart and careful you must be in initiating this kind of relationship.

"I loved you, I hate you, I'll get you." That may describe you. Many of you are in that revenge mode and shared that sentiment in the groups last week. That is some of the baggage you brought here—hopefully to dump. Our custodian will go through here tonight at ten o'clock and shovel it all up and put it into the dumpster out back. You dump it and leave it here! But, unfortunately, many of you *aren't* leaving it here. You are still carrying that old, smelly baggage around with you every day.

There's a lot of energy in hate; you can live on it. For a while, it will sustain you. I know some couples who have gone through some tough stuff in their lives—people who have gone through a divorce who find that their hatred, as an energy, will carry them a long way. But do you know where you end up? You become a warped, bitter, hollow, empty, hardened human being. You know people like that. You know people who have burned out their insides, burned out any instinct for love and compassion with their hate. We are going to talk about that more throughout the workshop because we all need to get rid of that hate. It's something you have to do, because sooner or later hate consumes you. Hatred will not allow you to be the kind of person you want to be. "I'm not really like this," you will say; "I'm not really like this."

Okay. Then don't *be* like that!

All of us have some semblance of control over ourselves. Sometimes we lose that control, but most of us have some semblance of being able to decide what we're going to do. So maybe it will be good for you to say to those in your group, "I'm going to dump some of my bitterness tonight," and then dump it! Or simply agree that you're going to go home and scream for an hour. Do whatever it takes. Let it out! Get rid of it!

All that hatred isn't ultimately going to help you bring about any kind of healing or equitable relationship with your ex-spouse. You need somehow to deal with the hatred and then get on with the rest of your life.

I'm not talking about marital reconciliation here. Nor am I saying that a perfect relationship with your ex-spouse is possible in every one of your situations. Some of you are saying, "I can't do that because he or she won't let me." I understand that. Many different kinds of situations are represented here.

Some of you are sitting there thinking, "If he knew my situation, he wouldn't even suggest such a thing." I love the eye contact in these lectures. Many of you are saying, "Yes, yes, yes, that's right, that's right," while others are saying, "W-e-l-l, I—don't—know."

As the saying goes, "different strokes for different folks." In fact, I will almost guarantee you that, somewhere in these six weeks, I will hit your target dead center and you'll think, "Yes, that's me. Thank you very much. I needed that." There will also be times when you'll say, "That's just not where I am at all."

Be patient. I won't be speaking to all of you all the time. But some of you have to come to realize that healing is going to take some time. Eventually, you may have to say, "I can't work it out with him or her. There's no way I can do that; there's a four-foot-thick brick wall that I simply cannot penetrate." At that point you need to concentrate on yourself and begin to do some good things for yourself. That's when you need to get rid of the garbage and begin to work with positive direction in your own life.

Some people, when something horrible happens to them, will say, "Why is this happening to me? I don't understand this. How could God do this to me? How could fate have allowed this horrible thing to happen?" I can't begin to tell you how many folks I've heard say that during a crisis time—not just during a divorce, but in a death of someone close, or in any kind of tragedy.

But if I had the answer to *why* for you, would it make you feel any better? Let's face it, folks: We're never going to understand some things that happen in our lives. They just don't add up. They just don't make any sense. We're not here to answer all the why's or to deal with all the questions you bring. We're here to extend a helping hand of hope to your life. Sometimes that's a whole lot better than answering the questions and dealing with all the nitty gritty issues.

Turn in the book to page 36. Here Jim describes some of the kinds of divorces you may be experiencing. Understanding the cause of your divorce will help you cope with your ex-spouse, and it may help you avoid making the same mistake in a second marriage. Some of you may be saying, "This will never happen to me again." Do you know the statistics say that for most of you — this is going to hurt — it *will* happen again? Statistics tell us that about 50 percent of first marriages fail. Do you know how many second marriages fail? Almost 65 percent. You would expect just the opposite; you would think it might be 25 percent. But it isn't. We seem to make the same mistakes over and over again. When we have failed once, we are prone to fail again. We are prone to label ourselves as failures. The minute something goes wrong in that second relationship, we say it is happening all over again, and we bail out and give up. That is a very simplistic, superficial answer to the very profound question, why?

We're having this workshop because a majority of you are going to get married again within the next four or five years. Even many of you who are saying, "No way. Not me!" will try marriage again. I am determined that, by having been to this workshop, you will not be one of the 65 percent who fail at a second marriage. I want you all to be different. This is one group that is not going to fit into the statistical abstracts.

DIFFERENT KINDS OF DIVORCE

Let's look at the kinds of divorces Jim describes in his book.

The Victim Divorce

This relates to the "dumpee." A marriage is suddenly over and someone gets squashed like a bug; someone is left devastated. For some it happens rather unexpectedly; others see it coming for a long time. In the victim divorce, one partner doesn't want divorce to happen, but it happens anyway.

The Problem Divorce

This is the breakup of a marriage that is caused by a specific problem on the part of either you or your ex-mate. Whether the problem was alcohol, gambling, money, sex, or unfaithfulness, some kind of issue became so overwhelming that the marriage could not survive.

The Little Boy/Little Girl Divorce

This kind of divorce involves emotional immaturity. I'm not talking about chronological age, because we don't have very many teenage marriages anymore. That went out of style a number of years ago. Now the average age for marriage is over twenty-five. But something about the little boy/little girl lingers in all of us.

We all have the capacity for great emotional maturity and we all have the capacity to behave like wailing two-year-olds. Very often a marriage is conceived in immaturity and never rises above it. Or sometimes the immaturity develops later on. I know people in their fifties and sixties who are involved in little boy/little girl divorces.

The "I Was Conned" Divorce

Smoke says this means that one mate didn't get what he or she expected from the other partner. Dr. Jekyll turned into Mr. Hyde, and you woke up one morning and discovered the person you were married to was not the person who courted you. You say, "I was robbed. I was conned." Generally, these statements indicate that you didn't spend enough time in the courtship and the engagement. You met during your mature years, thinking you knew what you wanted. But even mature adults make some dumb mistakes.

That's hard to admit. Just because you are twenty-five or thirty-something, you somehow think you know exactly what you want. You think you can make up your minds in a very short time about life's deepest and most ultimate relationship, but you can't. I know you can always point out cases where the couple knew each other a week before they got married and they have been married forty years. Some people do beat the odds, but maybe you did not.

When couples come to me for premarital counseling, one of the first questions I ask is, "How long have you known each other?" If they say three or four months or less, the red flags go up.

The Shotgun Divorce

You have all heard of shotgun marriages. You have probably never heard of shotgun divorces. This is a first cousin to the "I was conned" divorce. Sometimes it's not the other partner that cons us; sometimes it's the people around us. "You are the perfect couple." "You look terrific together." "What beautiful children you'll have." "You just seem so much in love." "You are so right for each other."

Often the people who say such things don't know what in the world they're talking about. They have no objective, informal, intimate knowledge of the situation. They have no educated information on which to make such an evaluation. But you think, "Oh, everybody thinks this is a good thing, so I guess it's okay. I hope it will work out. We have some good things going for us. We can overcome this particular problem. It will go away in time. I'll change him or her in time."

But sooner or later the shotgun goes off and the relationship collapses. There are very few storybook romances. Stories in storybooks usually are not true; they are fantasies. And some of you are living a fantasy, dreaming a fantasy, and looking for a fantasy to happen to you.

The Menopause Divorce

Smoke is very helpful in broadening this term. Menopause is not just a female experience: We are finding out more and more about the complexity and reality of male menopause. I am becoming increasingly interested in this, since I celebrated my fiftieth birthday last year. Now I wonder when and how it will strike me. I can't see as well as I used to; I can't hear as well either; and my bald spot is rapidly spreading. There is that sense in which we all live in a world that says, "Youth is where it's at; you have to be trim and firm and you have to look good."

All of a sudden, anything that is old has to be traded in for a new model. Many males I know have traded in their corduroys for designer jeans or have even traded their sedans for sportier models. Unfortunately, we have allowed changes in life, changes in environment, and changes in situations to change a relationship that is supposed to be for life, that is supposed to be "for better or for worse, in sickness and in health, for as long as you both shall live."

The Rat Race Divorce

This is the fast lane divorce. The rapid pace of living simply kills the marriage. "But I was doing this for *you*. I was working seventy hours a week for you and the kids!" We succumb to the rat race, and some of us don't even know who the rats are. We're in this squirrel cage running as fast we can go trying to get somewhere. I don't know anyone who got to the top of the heap, wherever that is, and said, "I'm on the top of the heap and I feel great!"

The No-Fault Divorce

Probably most of you here aren't from this kind of situation—a marriage that ends with a kind of amiable parting, not a crash but a whimper. You part as friends and there is no big crisis. I know of some relationships that have ended that way, with the partners just going their separate ways. That doesn't happen too often, but it does happen.

It's often called the no-fault divorce. But that is misleading. We have no-fault insurance, but I don't believe we can have no-fault divorces.

DIFFERENT KINDS OF FEELINGS

I want to talk about feelings for a few minutes. Smoke talks about dealing with an ex-spouse in terms of feelings. Dealing with that successfully happens when your feelings of hostility, hatred, and revenge begin to mellow. The process of working through your feelings may take several years. There's no instant cure. Feelings are healed only with time. Growth will modify your feelings in new areas.

But you have to begin by being honest about your feelings. You have to acknowledge and try to understand their existence. "This is how I feel. My feelings may not be appropriate. You may not like my feelings. You may not be able to accept my feelings or understand them, but feelings are just feelings." Jim says, "Feelings are neither good nor bad. They just are."

That is a valid statement. Morally speaking, feelings are neither good nor bad. However, feelings *can* be either constructive or destructive. Growing through a divorce is coming to a place of neutralizing some of those destructive feelings.

When we talk about feelings, we come to a place where the difference between males and females is very important. Women and men express and understand their feelings differently. One of the big problems in marriage today is that we do not understand the differences between men and women. We do not understand how profoundly different we are. A lot of marriages really hit rough water because of that lack of understanding. We are aware of our basic biological equipment and know a few very obvious things, and yet what lies below the surface is largely a mystery to us.

I want to say something now especially to the men: Usually, women will look around a workshop like this and ask, "Where are all the men? If there were 30,000 divorces in Orange

County this year, exactly 15,000 of those people should be men and 15,000 women. But it doesn't look like that here!"

I speak here as a man and say that our world has done a number on us males in terms of our feelings. Somewhere down the line, someone told us when we were little fellows that big boys don't cry. We have been taught, as males, to swallow those feelings, to deny them, to cover them up, to bury them, and to control them at all times because real men should be like Clint Eastwood or Sylvester Stallone.

Men tend to be very guarded about their feelings. It's very important to us to be masculine, and one masculine quality is self-sufficiency. "I don't need a workshop like this. I can handle it myself." Some men going through divorces will look at a man coming to a workshop like this and say, "What's the matter? Couldn't you take care of it yourself, like me?"

I want to affirm every male here. It is my deep conviction that a man who comes to a workshop like this is running a very high risk; it is tougher for him to come than it is for most women. A male coming to a divorce recovery workshop is expressing a very clear sign of tremendous ego strength, not weakness. It exemplifies coming to terms with your feelings at a very realistic level and saying, "I hurt! Big boys do cry. Big boys hurt desperately and big boys are not self-sufficient. Big boys can't make it on their own. Big boys need other big boys, and they need big girls. They need a community of whole, healthy, realistic, authentic people to help them."

So I would say to you males, it is good to have you here. One of the things I have noticed in workshops, and I notice it here in this one, is that the percentage—the ratio of men to women—is slowly changing. The first few we held we didn't have enough men to go around to all the groups. We didn't even come close to getting enough male leaders. We do now, and I'm really encouraged by that. I'm encouraged by every man who is here. And I challenge you to be a part of the movement in our world that shuts down this macho mystique and calls it what it is—baloney!

PRINCIPLES FOR DEALING WITH YOUR EX-SPOUSE

On page 39 Jim gives five important principles for dealing with an ex-spouse. Here's a shopping list you can begin working on right now. Hopefully, these ideas will assist you in moving toward a more equitable, mature, human relationship with your ex-spouse.

Take Things One Day at a Time.
Don't be discouraged by your growth or lack of it. We find ourselves in that microwave world where everything is supposed to happen fast, and some things in life just don't happen fast enough for us. We want instant healing, and that kind of healing is often not to be had. It takes a redwood tree a long time to grow to maturity. Some of you need to be patient with yourselves.

Maybe you need to put some kind of little saying on your refrigerator door. We mentioned Robert Schuller's last week: "Inch by inch, life's a cinch." If that is too clever or trite for you, then try this one: "You only need strength for today." Have you ever thought about that? Have you ever tried to store up next week's strength? You can't do that, can you? It's interesting how, biologically, we are built to live day by day. We have to eat every day. We have to sleep every day. Our bodily functions work primarily on a daily basis.

We have to learn that we simply cannot store up strength. You only have strength for today. Don't bite off more than you can chew. Don't set goals that are too long-range. Growth happens, in most cases, very slowly. Perhaps there's a door or place on the wall where you have charted your children's growth. You'll notice that there are some spurts of growth, these are different in everyone, and they vary at particular times in your lives.

Try to Make the Break as Clean as Possible.
Some people don't know when to end a marriage. They grope on through an impossible relationship and somehow keep it going long after it is dead. They are, in the familiar analogy, beating a dead horse. Sometimes it's hard to recognize when something is dead, particularly when we don't want it that way. But some of us apparently enjoy beating dead horses. Some of us get strange and perverse pleasure out of this futile effort.

Make the break as clean as possible. I remember Bill and Carol, a couple I knew years ago in another city. When they got a divorce, everybody was mourning for them because everybody loved them. They were two wonderful people. Their marriage didn't work out. They did everything they could to save it and finally it collapsed after a lot of counseling and effort on their part. One of the problems after the divorce was that Bill felt so sorry for Carol that he still took care of her. One of the things he did was to take care of her car. He had done that all their married life. I don't think Carol knew where the gas cap was. This went on for a couple of years.

Finally Bill met someone else and Carol did, too. The man she met didn't know anything about cars either. One day Bill said, "Carol, you're on your own," and Carol was devastated. She had no clue what to do with herself or that car, and she came to me asking, "What can I do?" I put her in touch with a good mechanic who could help her.

Please understand, you are responsible for you! Make that break clean. You have to realize there are no ties left, other than the continuing responsibility you may have for your children. When a marriage is over, you have to take responsibility for yourself.

Quit Accepting Responsibility for Your Ex-spouse.
That's the truth Bill finally realized. He had made a mistake. He should have cut the ties much sooner than he did. Few people really learn to take care of themselves until they are forced to do so. You are responsible for you. You are not responsible for your ex-spouse. In actuality, you are the person *least* qualified to help your former partner. The sooner you can drill that into your head and begin to live accordingly, the quicker you will begin to heal. And the more equitable and appropriate that relationship with your ex-spouse is going to be. You are responsible for you.

Don't Let Your Children Intimidate You.
Don't let your children get in the way of what you decide to do. Don't try to rekindle a dead marriage *just* for their sake. If you have listened; if you have prayed; if you have struggled; if you are, in your best judgment, doing the right thing, then do it. Don't let an eight- or nine-year-old, or sometimes an adolescent who may be operating purely out of emotion and immaturity, derail the healthy direction that you need to take.

Kids often feel responsible for the divorce. Frequently, when parents sense that, they allow children to control, intimidate, or direct them. Yet children, who then have become the decision-makers, have no experience, expertise, or valid rational judgment. Be careful how you accept advice from your children. Yes, sometimes they can be right on target. Yet I find it amazing that many adults are accepting guidance from very young children. Remember, your children cannot really help you. They can love, support, and encourage; but seldom can they offer valid counsel in very complex situations. You do need to be very close to them. However, right now the greatest source of help for you is in this room as you listen and share with others like yourselves.

Don't Get Trapped in Your Temporary Immaturity.

The stress of divorce can cause you temporarily to revert to childish behavior patterns. You may find yourself becoming consumed by jealousy, throwing a temper tantrum, or fighting about trivial things relating to division of property. You can do many things that will ultimately cause you great embarrassment.

This can especially be a problem if your ex-spouse has either remarried or is in a relationship with another person. Sometimes that other spouse or friend, along with your children, can entangle your ability to think clearly. I have a very specific piece of advice about that. The best way to deal with an ex-spouse's partner, marital or otherwise, is *not* to deal with an ex-spouse's partner, marital or otherwise. Deal only with your ex. Don't allow the other person to become an intermediary or get in the way of the positive relationship you need to be developing with your former husband or wife.

One of my fantasies in these workshops has been to have a session where I speak to all your ex-spouses, instead of everyone who is here tonight. Imagine having to put on a workshop with all those evil, wicked, sinister people! It would be terrible—having to stand here in front of all those dregs of society. . . .

I'm glad you can laugh at that. Because we're not perfect either, are we? At the other end of all the feelings of injustice and unfairness you bring to this workshop are other people with their own particular points of view, with their own reasons and rationales—however unfair or untrue those reasons and rationales may be.

Whichever group I would talk to—those of you here tonight or my "fantasy group" of your ex-spouses—I would still be talking to the some truly "walking wounded"—people who are trying to get their lives together; people who are not perfect, who are full of blemishes and problems and issues in their lives; people who need healing.

However, *you* are the ones who are here. I hope that you are grabbing some handles that are moving your life in a new and positive direction.

I close with some final poetic words from an anonymous author:

I ask why, but the fog is too thick to see clearly . . .
I become anxious and panicky, then I'm numb, without feelings . . .
I need more insight, but I want to be insensitive and totally unaware . . .
I eat like a horse, but I have no appetite . . .
I can't sleep, yet I escape with sleep . . .
I react to nothing, then I overact to everything . . .
I sit at home daydreaming, yet wish I were busy doing something . . .
I hate being lonely and alone, yet being with others points out my need . . .
I look for answers and stability, yet I'm tired of too much thinking and feeling . . .
God, I know you understand, but I need to tell you about it to make sure . . .

I will strive
>to create a new direction for my life, even though that takes time;
>to make my own decisions and determine my needs as I understand them.

I give myself permission
>to change in the way I think best and not box myself in with the expectations of others;
>to learn to be my own person and not forever live in the past.

I will not
>discount my feelings,
>ask friends to choose sides,
>use the children as spies,
>make commitments I can't keep.

I will
>grieve over a marriage that has died,
>allow my pain to motivate my growth,
>rediscover myself and what is unique about me,
>attempt to make this divorce a creative rather than a destructive force in my life.

It will take time . . .
>for I live in a world of ambivalence.

ASSUMING NEW RESPONSIBILITIES: PLANNING FOR YOURSELF AND YOUR FUTURE

In this presentation I will be talking about how you plan for the rest of your life. People who live in the past, people who helplessly wallow in the mire of what has already happened to them, are people without a plan. They are people without direction and without purpose in their lives. If you are to experience healing and recovery as you go and grow through the experience of divorce, sooner or later the past needs to be minimized.

To minimize the past you first have to deal with it. You have to take a long look at it. All of us, to varying degrees, struggle with what it means to be a responsible person. In talking about responsibility I want to be very careful not to assume that, because you are down or because you are hurting, you are irresponsible. Struggling with responsibility is an ongoing human need, particularly in times of change and crisis. We all need to take a fresh look at responsibility, at our lives, at our future, at where we are going and how it is we intend to get there.

When we are in a time of hardship and stress, we tend to form dependent relationships. We begin to count on someone else. It's easy to become dependent. I once heard that there are two kinds of marriage. First is the marriage where two people lean on each other not only for strength and support, but also for a source of individual uniqueness and life energy. And slowly but surely, those two persons shrivel up and die as individuals. As a result, the relationship dies along with the personhood of each individual. Some marriages are dependent relationships. Either they are mutual dependencies, or one person in the relationship becomes totally dependent on the other person.

A second kind of marriage could be called the ideal marriage. I'm not sure exactly what that is. I don't think anyone has actually discovered it. On my shelf I have a big, thick book entitled *Ideal Marriage* that was written in the 1950s. That title would not fit into today's world. However, we still tend to want the ideal.

This ideal form of marriage is not a dependent kind of relationship, but rather an interdependent commitment where there is an ebb and flow. There is a mutual need for each other, and there is the capability of drawing strength from each other. That is what we are talking about.

We all have hoped to share our lives with someone who gives us something vital and significant and loving. But at the same time, people who are growing also recognize that they have something to give; they have something to offer. Very often a person going through the crisis of a divorce does not see himself or herself as having very much to offer. What you look for is a relationship that offers something to *you*, and you get trapped in a dependent encounter instead of a healthy relationship.

In assuming new responsibilities, you are going to have to learn some new skills. You are going to have to venture out into some unexplored territory. Many of you will have to get back into the job market. For some of you that involves learning new ways to manage your time—a real stress point for many of us!

Some people think that singles have all this free time on their hands; they don't have

189

much to do; they are free and loose. If anything needs to be done, you can always ask a single person to do it because they don't have anything better to do. This myth suggests that everyone who isn't married is just casually moving on through life without any pressure at all.

One of the things we all have in common, one thing that is exactly the same for each and every one of us, is that all of us have exactly the same amount of time available to us each day. We all have twenty-four hours. The trick is how we learn to manage that time. I find this an interesting struggle for me. I am working on that discipline because life for me is a very dynamic thing and I am constantly having to establish priorities. I carry around this little appointment book in order to live a life that is disciplined and structured.

Someone has said, "If you're wasting your time, you're wasting your life. And if you're wasting your life, you don't feel good about yourself." You don't feel any sense of going somewhere or accomplishing something. People who are responsible put structure and discipline into their lives. But when you are down, when you are in a time of stress, that is hard to do.

My friend Alice was ninety-eight when she died. We had an "affair" going for the last eight years of her life. Alice and I had a beautiful relationship. I visited her at least twice a month. Alice lived in a little rundown house on the west side of Colorado Springs. She couldn't see how dirty the place was. She didn't really care. She had a comfortable bed with an electric blanket turned up to nine no matter what time of year it was. Alice had a large print Bible that was so worn the pages were falling out. She kept counting the times she read it. Every time she finished, she put another check mark in the front.

Alice had not physically left her house in seventeen years. She had been bedridden for a long time. She didn't have many friends, just the folks who shared the little duplex with her, who took care of her and prepared her meals.

We took Alice to the rest home, and the first thing she noticed was the smell. That antiseptic odor was a lot different from her warm, cozy little wooden bungalow. Suddenly she had to share a room with someone else, which was a brand-new experience for her, at least since the death of her husband almost twenty-five years before. Now she had to restructure and reorient everything in her life. We took some of her favorite things from her little house and hung them on the wall around the bed so she would have some familiar surroundings.

The nurse instructed Alice, as we got her situated, that a string was attached to a switch on the wall above the bed. All Alice had to do when she needed something was pull on the string. When she pulled the string it flipped a switch and a light went on in the hallway outside. That would summon a nurse.

It was a nice rest home, but Alice didn't like it very much. She lived another three months. Then one morning, as she was in a coma, I had a feeling as I stood over her bed talking to her that this was Alice's last morning. I gripped her hand, gave her a kiss, said a prayer, and whispered goodbye. Ninety minutes later she died.

I think there was something in Alice that gave up when her life was reduced to pulling that string. But some of you here tonight would *love* to be in that situation! You would love to have someone put a string in your hand that you could pull and someone would come immediately and ask, "Yes, can I get you something?" We are often looking for strings. We are looking for someone to take care of us because we're in the pits. We want a string to pull because we are hurt, because we have a need, because we feel helpless.

I refuse to let any of you try to convince me that you need that string. I refuse to believe that the only way you are going to survive is for someone to hurry to your side and ask what it is they can do to help you out of the mess you are in. We are not here to put a string in your hand. Instead, we are here to extend a hand to you that says, "You know, you are a unique, beautiful, unrepeatable miracle of God." Something within you, if you will be open to it, can allow a new chapter of responsible, authentic, wholesome living to begin.

Some of you have commented about how helpful Jim's book is. It *is* a helpful book with many good things in it. But, so what? If whatever is helpful in this book doesn't take root, what good is it? This book is not a string. You can carry it around twenty-four hours a day, and you can put it under your pillow, along with any other book you can think of, the Bible included, and it won't help you one bit *unless* you begin to apply some of its contents to your situation.

It isn't good enough to say, "Yes, I agree with you, Jim. You're right." The next step is to take that which you find to be true, helpful, and practical and to appropriate it. Become responsible for *you*. Nobody else will do that. As much as I would like a string to be put in my hands at times, I find that generally when I most want it there's usually no one there to put it in my hands. I have to be responsible for me, and you have to be responsible for you.

Some of us think that marriage itself is a string we can pull, so that the person we marry can, on command, make us happy. You may recall the way Jim said it on page 48:

> People often marry other people with the assumption that the person they are marrying will make them happy. What an awesome responsibility is placed upon that person's shoulders. What if they fail? Who gets the blame? Where can other happiness be found? A marriage built upon that premise often leads to a divorce and unless the lesson is learned, the hunt is on for another person to provide happiness.

For some of us that statement hits painfully close to home.

GROWING MORE RESPONSIBLE

Jim goes on to make four important points about assuming responsibility.

I Assume Responsibility for My Part of the Failure of My Marriage.

This is the third lecture, so I'm getting a little bolder! Did you hear what Jim said? "I assume responsibility for *my* part in the failure of my marriage." Obviously, Jim doesn't understand your situation . . . because you don't *have* a part in the failure of your marriage! He or she did it to you, right?

You will never grow into a responsible person if you are going to play the blame game and come out as the totally innocent victim of your circumstances. I'm still looking for the black-and-white marital situation. I haven't found it yet. Perhaps you can enlighten me with your story, but you will find I probably won't be too receptive to black-and-white arguments. It might be 99.44 percent his or her fault. Maybe. But I have never found the 100-percent-the-other-person's-fault-situation.

You must assume responsibility for your part of the failure of your marriage—whatever that part is, however miniscule it may be, or however vast and overwhelming it may seem.

If at this point you still don't want to assume responsibility for your marriage, then let me ask you this question: What are some areas about yourself where you need to change right now? What are some of your new responsibilities? What are some things you need to look at and begin to work on in your own life experience? One of the ways you can begin to do that is to look for people who will begin to treat you authentically.

For some reason, I am drawn every morning to read "Dear Abby" in the paper. People are desperate to find a friend who will speak authentically. Do you have a "Dear Abby"? Do you have someone who can be emotionally neutral enough to deal with you honestly? Do you have someone who will not just say what you want to hear all the time? Occasionally, we all need to be like the man in the commercial who says "Thanks, I needed that" after he has been slapped in the face. It's hard to find friends who will take the risk of turning you off, turning you away, or making you mad at them.

I remember a young man named John, whom I met early in my ministry. He was one of the sharpest, most outstanding kids in our high school group and is now a Presbyterian minister in New York. But back in those days, he had body odor that was terrible, and nobody would tell him. After several months, I finally worked up the courage and some-how (I can't remember the words I used) managed to tell John that his body odor was offensive. His response was something like, "Thanks, I needed that. Thanks for caring about me enough to tell me." I wondered why in the world it took me so long to deal with him openly and honestly, but telling him about his problem was a hard thing for me to do.

We all need a friend who will do the same with us. We need to allow people to be authentic enough with us to be able to say what we need to hear; and then we need to have the grace and the guts to be able to thank them for it.

I Assume Responsibility for My Present Situation.

As we said a moment ago, many of you are in desperation and in pain; you are looking around for someone else to make you happy. For a lot of people that's what getting remarried is all about. It's finding someone who will make you happy. If you are falling into that subtle trap, you are heading for disaster.

In one workshop some time ago I was pointing out the dangers of waiting for "a knight on a white charger." A woman came up to me afterward and phrased the situation wisely: "She who waits for knight on white charger ends up shoveling manure." That's pretty close to the truth. Too many of us are willing to place all our hopes for future happiness on someone else.

Of course we do often find happiness through things other people do for us, or simply through enjoying their company. But if you are planning your whole lives on that eventuality, you are not being responsible for yourselves, and you are not going to discover true happiness. You are responsible for your happiness and your fulfillment. It is within another person's power to help make you happy — but not to be your lifelong caretaker.

I Assume Responsibility for My Future.

Some of you may say, "Future? What future? I don't have a future!" Unless you plan to stop breathing within the next thirty seconds, you *do* have a future. And you had better do something to plan for it.

When you are questioning and struggling with your future, you tend to start setting some very short-term goals, and you are prone to stop committing yourself to important long-term responsibilities. In his book, Smoke lists some ways that you may be opting for the short term rather than the long term, without even realizing it:

♦ I won't go to work because I might remarry.
♦ I'll do this until something better comes along.
♦ I won't set goals because it might interfere with someone I meet.
♦ I won't join the church because I don't know how long I'm going to stay here.
♦ I won't put down roots. I'll just be rootless, trying to live life without any pain, because if I make plans I might miss out on something.

Something better might come along, so you don't make any commitments. You just hang loose.

But hanging loose is the nature of a floating jellyfish, not the nature of a mature adult! The only thing a jellyfish can take in is whatever drifts by. That's not a very exciting prospect for existence. It's like being a clam that just opens its shell and is totally dependent for its life on whatever the current brings. The fact is that some of you are living like clams when you are meant to live like eagles, flying and risking and soaring in the high lofty places.

Who, after having seen a clam and an eagle, would still want to be a clam? Yet I know some people who do. Clams have hard shells. Clams live a *safe* life—not a very responsible or exciting one, but a safe one.

People discover themselves when they are on the move. Henrietta Mears, one of the great women of this century, once said, "You can't steer a parked car." Did you ever try to steer a parked car? You can only steer a car that is moving.

In the New Testament, every person Jesus called to follow Him was called in the middle of their work, not while they were out to lunch somewhere, immobilized and trying to escape life. He interrupted them in the middle of their life's task. He spoke to them in the middle of their going somewhere, in the middle of the life process. Some folks are just sitting twiddling their thumbs and hoping for some giant tablet of stone with heavenly instructions written on it to drop out of the sky.

But that's not the real life works. You have to be moving. You steer when you are moving somewhere. You may be going the wrong direction. You may have to make a mid-course correction. You may have to do an about-face. That's why we need those authentic friends to share with us. Perhaps you need to have somebody in the car. In fact, you may even need a driving instructor or somebody to help you learn how to steer properly and learn how to stay on the road.

You also have to start out in the slow lane. I'm working with my daughter now as she learns to drive. We haven't gotten out on the freeway yet. She's not ready for the freeway. She's still in the slow lane where she belongs at the present time. The freeway will come later.

I Have to Assume Responsibility for Myself.
You have to establish some goals for yourself. Shoot at nothing and that's exactly what you'll hit: nothing! Assuming responsibility for yourself is not an easy process. Divorce will either force you to assume responsibility by saying "I can," or it will send you looking for someone else to do it for you.

Do you remember the story of "The Little Engine That Could"? It's a story about positive thinking. That little engine, you remember, had to pull the toys for a town full of children at Christmas when all the other freight engines couldn't do it. "I think I can, I think I can, I think I can," it said as it pulled for all it was worth. After the little engine got over the top of the mountain and started down the other side, do you recall what it said? "I thought I could, I thought I could, I thought I could!"

Sometimes we need to surprise ourselves with what we can do. Think positively. The minute you say "I can't" you won't. You'll quit and you'll stop trying. It takes effort to go through a divorce. If you don't think you will get through it, you probably *won't* get through it. Don't look for that lifetime custodian, that caretaker, or that janitor for your life's future. It can be a tragic, sorry, and unfulfilling way to live. You need to look for some new directions, some new relationships, some constructive new input.

Who is it that keeps you honest? Which person is it who will not give you a snow job? Who in your life will deal with you authentically at the point of your hurt? Who will help you and listen to you as you struggle with these questions: Why is this happening to me? What went wrong? What can I do now? Can I make it on my own? How long will I hurt? Will I ever be happy again?

Alcoholics Anonymous has a beautiful prayer. I want to claim it now for a much broader purpose. Every one of us needs to pray it every day. Listen to this if you have never heard it before:

> God grant me the serenity to accept the things I cannot change, the courage to change the things I can, and the wisdom to know the difference.

Take that prayer home and put it on your refrigerator! Better yet, put it in your head and let it sink down into your heart.

Lloyd Ogilvie paraphrases the same thought this way:

> God, grant me the strength to hold on; the courage to let go; and the wisdom to make the right decision with dignity.

I said last week that the majority of you are going to marry again. If you are beginning some good, positive reconstruction, remarriage can be a happy, fulfilling experience for you. But there are those here tonight who will tell you that the second time around—or the third—is even more devastating. It doesn't get easier. It just gets harder.

But it doesn't have to happen that way.

I want you to consider the idea of planning the rest of your life as if you will never marry again. To some of you that comes as a breath of welcome relief; to others it is a dark, terrible cloud. You can't imagine living alone for the rest of your life.

And most of you won't. But it isn't a bad idea at this transition period to begin to plan the rest of your life as if you will never marry again. It could be a very positive step. Dear friends, anyone can get married! It's no big accomplishment to get married! The accomplishment is making it work, making it last, and making it right. Anyone can get married. And the tragedy, as I look across the singles community, is that so many folks are desperately hoping and trying to get married, as if that is some key or guarantee to happiness.

And who, better than you, ought to know that simply is not true?

"But I am not made to live alone," you say—which is a very biblical statement. That's what it says in Genesis. Humankind was not made to be alone. But that doesn't necessarily mean our total fulfillment comes through the marriage relationship. It's true that we were made for relationships. That's what those words from Genesis are teaching. We are not made to be in isolation. We are made to be with each other. We are made to live in community. We are made for relationships and fellowship. The real issue is how, as a single person, can you find those healthy relationships, those positive, meaningful contacts that can teach you something valuable as you learn about yourself?

Most of us are not willing to wait. We want what we want, and we want it now. When we hurt now we want to be healed now, because we live in an instant, microwave world where we expect immediate results. We simply can't conquer our impatience and slow ourselves down.

Let me tell you a story. It's my favorite story in the Bible. It's in the fifth chapter of John's Gospel. The story takes place in Jerusalem. Jesus was coming into the city through the Sheep Gate, which, by the way, is still there. In fact, they still sell sheep around this gate.

After you go through the Sheep Gate, you come to a pool. This pool, called Bethzatha in the days of Jesus, had a superstition about it. People who were sick came to the pool by the hundreds. They believed that, whenever an angel came and disturbed the water, the first one in the pool would be healed.

The story focuses on a man who had been paralyzed for thirty-eight years and had been lying by this pool, waiting to be healed, for much of that time. One day Jesus came with His disciples through the Sheep Gate. He saw all these people who were hoping that someone or something would come along to heal them. I can just see Jesus looking and wondering who had been there the longest. Finally, Jesus walked up to this man and stood over him.

At this point, pretend you are the man. You have been paralyzed for thirty-eight years, hoping for some healing in your body. A stranger walks up and looks down at you. What would you want to hear Him say to you? What do you think Jesus said? "Heal"?

No. Instead, Jesus looks down to the man and says, *"Do you want to be healed?"*

Just think about that. You have been lying by the pool for thirty-eight years, hoping for a miracle. A stranger walks up and says, "Do you want to be healed?" How are you going to react? What an insensitive, cruel, mocking thing to say to someone in that condition!

So how does this man respond to Jesus? He is open and honest. He says, "When the water ripples, I don't have anyone to help me . . . and someone else gets in first."

That was his answer. Then what does Jesus say to him? "Get up!"

Remember now, you are the man who has been paralyzed for thirty-eight years. If the first statement of Jesus was insensitive, this one really takes the cake. "What do you mean, get up? Can't you see I'm paralyzed? Can't you see I'm crippled? I've been lying here for thirty-eight years! I haven't been able to move my legs, and you come along and say get up!" Incredible!

Jesus didn't even hold out His hand. He didn't even volunteer to help the man. He just said, "Get up!"

So what do you think the man did? He got up! That's what he did. He got up, and he picked up his bed, and he walked.

Let me make three observations and applications regarding this story:

You must want to be whole. Do you want to be whole? Do you really? Is that actually why you are here? That is a legitimate question. It was an important question to the man by the pool, and it is an important question now. Somehow, this man had survived thirty-eight years by that pool. Somebody had been helping him. Somebody had been feeding him. Somehow his basic needs for living had been met. Perhaps an honest response on the part of this man would have been, "No, I do not want to be healed. I would just as soon be paralyzed. I would just as soon live life the way I'm living it now. Thank you very much, but I think I'll stay here and make excuses about other people who get in the pool ahead of me. I think I will stay paralyzed."

Perhaps you are like the man and are saying, "There isn't anyone to help me." But no one *here* can say that! Take a look around you. You cannot say there is no one to help you get through the experience of growing through your divorce. You cannot get away with that unless you get up right now and walk out the door and say, "I was never there. I didn't hear. There wasn't anybody there who really cared, who really wanted to help me."

The question Jesus asked was a very legitimate one. In it, He was teaching the truth that with wholeness comes responsibility; with wholeness comes risk. You have got to leave this pool! You have got to leave this dependent situation! You have got to walk out into that cold, cruel world and begin to depend on yourself! Do you really want to be whole? Do you really want to start a new chapter in your life?

Power must be appropriated. This man exercised an incredible power. There are actually two miracles in this story. One is the miracle of the power God was willing to give. The second miracle is the appropriation of that power. The man could have said, "I can't get up. I'm paralyzed."

But he did get up. He cooperated with the power God gave him. He appropriated it. He used it. He undertook a task he hadn't successfully performed in thirty-eight years.

In a few minutes you are all going to get out of your chairs and walk. You aren't going to think anything about it because you do it all the time. It's an automatic process. Do you realize how complicated it is to get up and walk? Do you realize the incredible sense of balance required of your muscles and bones in order to do that? It's a beautifully complex process. This man had to think about it because he hadn't done it in a long time. But he did it, and it is important that Jesus did not help him up.

Do it yourself. You get up. You can do it. God is saying to you, "I will give you power to do it if you will appropriate that strength and go about doing it yourself."

You must carry your own load. It is interesting that Jesus did not just say, "Get up." It is important that He also said, "Pick up your bed and take it with you. That bed has carried you for thirty-eight years. Now you carry it! You take with you the identification of your dependency. You carry it with you. Announce to the world that you used to be dependent but you're not anymore. You are whole. You are healed, and you are free, and you are now responsible for your life." He said that to the man at the pool, and He is saying it to you.

Bible study can be an exciting and dangerous enterprise when we really get into it and begin to look at what a passage truly says. Jim puts it in such an effective way. He writes, "Brother, sister, you can fly but that cocoon has got to go." You can fly. You can go somewhere. You can be that beautiful, unique, unrepeatable miracle of God. Stop playing the blame game. Stop blaming whoever it is that got you where you are. Begin now to pick up the bed. Pick up the thing that has announced your crippled state and begin to move forward into a brand-new chapter in your life. You can do that.

TEN COMMANDMENTS FOR DIVORCEES

On page 77 of his book Jim suggests ten commandments for divorcing people. (They are also reprinted in the back of the book on page 167.) I close with them.

Thou shalt not live in thy past.
Thou shalt be responsible for thy present and not blame thy past for it.
Thou shalt not feel sorry for thyself indefinitely.
Thou shalt assume thine end of the blame for thy marriage dissolution.
Thou shalt not try to reconcile thy past and reconstruct thy future by a quick
    new marriage.
Thou shalt not make thy children victims of thy past marriage.
Thou shalt not spend all thy time trying to convince thy children how terrible
    and evil their departed parent is.
Thou shalt learn all thou can about being a one-parent family and get on with it.
Thou shalt ask others for help when thou needest it.
Thou shalt ask God for the wisdom to bury yesterday, create today, and plan for
    tomorrow.

You can do it. You can do it by virtue of your own positive thinking. You can do it by virtue of authentic relationships with others who really care. You can do it because there is a God who loves you and who wants to give you a power beyond your wildest imaginings to start a new chapter in your life.

BEING A SINGLE PARENT: BECOMING A WHOLE FAMILY

In this session we want to look at a very important issue for those of us who are parents. We are all keenly aware of our parental roles. I understand many of the passages that we all go through as parents. I hope our time together will encourage you, no matter what age your children are or what they are going through, to develop a greater openness, communication, honesty, and sensitivity between you and them.

I want you, as a parent, to be better able to share both feelings and ideas with your children. That is my goal in this presentation, to create a sense of openness—between parents and kids and between kids and parents.

Some of you are very concerned when you bring your kids to an experience like this: You wonder what in the world we are going to pull out of them! Quite naturally, you care about how that is going to reflect on you. But I hope your concern about that will be minimal, because the folks who are working with the children do not know you. Nonetheless, even though these workers do not know you, we are trying to foster some healing in your kids and some openness with you.

In 1970, 12 percent of the children in America lived with one parent. By 1981, according to the Census Bureau, this had increased to over 20 percent. That is one in every five kids. (At this point, if possible, include some current statistics about who children are living with. Most libraries have that kind of information.)

A headline in the *New York Daily News* read "It Takes Youngsters Years to Recover from a Divorce." Two themes emerged in that article (a sort of bad news, good news perspective). First, divorce is a major traumatic event for kids. That's the bad news, and it is no surprise. But second, the article suggests that these youngsters *do* recover, and they do not automatically grow up to be juvenile delinquents.

I don't know how you feel about the term *broken home*. I hope it angers you somewhat and turns you off, because it ought to. I hope you don't feel your home is *broken*. Your home may exhibit the results of a broken relationship; but that does not mean your home itself has to be broken or that you are a broken parent. One does not necessarily follow the other.

But studies do indicate, and my own experience verifies, that it takes about two years after a divorce for parents and children to achieve a new sense of security in their lives. Of course, that is a generalization, and I don't say it to discourage you if you are recently divorced. I'm not trying to alarm you. But you do have a big adjustment to make, and it is not going to take place overnight. It is going to take some time. You will be better off and less frustrated if you begin to accept that right now. The adjustment takes time. When we go through traumatic events in our lives, we simply do not recover from them quickly.

It's even more difficult for children and for their parents when a second marriage fails. It becomes more traumatic, rather than less traumatic, every subsequent time. Having gone through divorce before does not make it less painful.

Children whose parents are divorcing, or who have divorced, usually feel quite isolated and alone. Even though nearly half of first marriages now end in divorce, most youths going through that divorce—even though they may know the statistics—will see themselves as the only ones who are experiencing that particular problem. In other words, they do not see the children in the breakup of other families as readily as you might think. Kids will, to some degree, talk about this in school and with their friends, but by and large they keep it to themselves. They see themselves as quite isolated, as the only ones going through this process. Our hope is that, at this very moment, your young people are sitting down with others who are going through the same thing, are being encouraged by those around them, and perhaps are even thinking to themselves, "I didn't know so many other kids had this problem too." Hopefully, our kids' workshops going on right now will create an openness for them to begin to talk and share.

Several years ago, an issue of *Psychology Today* contained a survey about kids from California. These young people were surveyed five years after their parents divorced. They were mostly adolescents; some were younger children. Of those surveyed, 34 percent seemed to be happy, thriving, recovered young people; 29 percent said they were doing okay; and 37 percent said they were still depressed over the divorce. So roughly speaking, a third of them were not doing well. I believe that those who were not doing well were the ones who, for one reason or another, were not dealing openly with what was happening to them. I would like to think that your children being here is a very hopeful sign that they are growing and recovering.

I said that recovery takes about two years. It's interesting that the younger you are, the longer two years becomes. If you are ten, two years is 20 percent of your life. If you are forty, two years is not quite that long. You talk to an adolescent about two years and it seems like "forever"! Sometimes we adults fail to identify with the frame of reference of the young person to whom we are talking.

Many folks come to a workshop like this looking for solid, practical answers to the issues, the dilemmas, the complications, and the hurts of the divorce experience. I hope that at some point I scratch you exactly where you are itching and that you experience that in your small groups as well. But more importantly, I am trying to give you some principles, some sweeping ideas, rather than a lot of little suggestions or bits of advice. I have a hard time with canned answers; you probably do too. I have no patience with simplistic solutions offered for very difficult and complex problems.

As I stand in front of you to speak to you about the issue of parenting, I feel less adequate than during any other session. Parenting brings more variables, more situations, more distinctly unique questions and struggles than any other subject we discuss. Listen to some of the questions and statements children raise when they struggle with the reality of their parents' divorce:

- ◆ What is going to happen to me now?
- ◆ What did I do to cause this divorce?
- ◆ How can I get my parents back together?
- ◆ I have lost respect for my parents.
- ◆ I will search for role models elsewhere.
- ◆ I will never get married.
- ◆ I'm mad at God.

We have found here at our church that our divorce recovery workshops are changing the total life of our congregation at every level. For one thing, it is changing the traditional emphasis of the church on the nuclear family—Mom, Dad, and the kids. That has been the traditional makeup of the church. This particular congregation of God's people is changing because now our potluck dinners are not just populated by Mom, Dad, and the kids. We have a unique blend of virtually every kind of family situation you can think of. Frankly, I think that is very healthy for everyone concerned.

Do you remember the image of the family where the father works and the mother stays at home and does not work and the family unit consists of two children and a dog? In today's world that kind of family comprises only six percent of the family structures in America! The institutional church has been very slow to wake up to that fact and to program itself and to strategize to meet this reality.

It is still frustratingly slow. I find myself traveling around the country raising the consciousness of pastors and church leaders. When I have shared those statistics with groups of pastors, they often don't believe it. They are shocked. But I noticed that none of *your* mouths dropped open!

I also want to lay to rest the stereotype that children from divorced homes are problem kids. This falsehood comes from the same source that says divorced women are preying upon married men, or single adults are all oversexed, and so on.

One of the things I confront all the time is young people from very nice homes, with parents who are still together and are providing all their needs, who have good moral and religious upbringing in the home, but who still somehow get off track. I also know many adults who have gone through horrible divorce situations where there has been abuse and many other problems, but who still produced wonderful kids.

Of course it doesn't always work out that way. But divorce is not necessarily the thing that is going to bring some insidious problem into your young person's life. Your child is not doomed to limp through life with a horrible handicap because of what you are going through. That is why I like to get away from the *broken home* terminology and why I strongly challenge this false stereotype. There may be brokenness in your home, but there is brokenness in every home. I don't care what the situation is. We live in a world of brokenness; and all of us, regardless of our backgrounds, have to deal with brokenness in our lives.

Let's consider the uniqueness of being the custodial parent—the parent with primary custody. In his book, Jim begins the chapter on "Single Parenting" with a little quotation that says, "Divorce is the process that turns whole parents into half parents." The rest of the chapter challenges that assertion and indicates how untrue it is. Unfortunately, however, that is the feeling many parents have when going through a divorce. They feel that, because they have lost a partner in parenting, they become half parents. You are not half a parent any more than you are half a person. You are a whole person.

But parents who are single do bear some heavy burdens. If you were to make a list of the things that drive you up the wall, that put a lot of strain and stress on your life, you would express frustrations like these.

- ◆ My support check doesn't arrive on time (or doesn't arrive at all).
- ◆ I'm tired all the time.
- ◆ I don't have any time for myself.
- ◆ I can't do the things I want to do.

PROBLEMS OF SINGLE PARENTS

I want to assess some of the frustrations listed above as we look at some of the issues that come out of a home caught in the stress of divorce. Jim mentions in his book, beginning on page 58, some single-parent problems.

My Circuits Are on Overload.

I often use that term myself. I often feel I am doing and carrying about all I can do and carry. When a circuit is on overload, it flips off. When people are on overload, they can flip out. Most of our houses don't have fuses any more, so we don't blow fuses. Now we have circuit breakers. If you have been out to that box on the side of your house when you put too many appliances on one of your circuits, you know that a switch flips to protect your whole electrical system from burning up. We have systems put there by the Creator that, in effect, do the same thing in us.

Many of you, because of your divorce, have undergone a lowering of your standard of living. Some of you have had to move from a beautiful four-bedroom home in suburbia to a two-bedroom apartment near a discount store. That can be a blow. Some of you who are still living in that beautiful house know that when settlement time comes, you'll no longer be able to live there. Something that represented security, that represented a goal in your life, you will soon lose. That's very difficult to face.

I remind you that the material things in life which seem so important to us are not what ultimately keeps us alive and growing. Many of you will probably benefit from having to cut back on some of those things because it will cause you to focus on more important realities. I know that speaks to some of you more than to others.

Where once there was someone with whom to share problems, now there is no one but you. Some of you have unloaded and unloaded on good friends, and they have finally begun to turn their backs and become unavailable. They have become tired of your unloading and dumping, and you feel very isolated and very alone.

This kind of tension and stress can be constructive. But first, let me differentiate between tension and stress. I work quite well under tension. Tension can be a very productive, constructive, positive thing for me.

Stress, however, is something else. There is a fine line where tension becomes stress. When we cross that line, something that can be positive and motivating instead becomes unnerving and negative.

Stress can immobilize you. It can plunge you into a downward spiral. It becomes hard to sleep. It becomes hard to concentrate. Very often you have a hard time getting up in the morning. Some of you fall prey to taking pills just to get a good night's rest. Then you need to take a pill the next night and the next and the next. Eventually you discover you need to take a pill in the morning to get going.

It might be helpful to get out a piece of paper and write down some of the things that are overloading your life. What is creating the stress? Perhaps you should sit down and talk about this with your kids. What are the specifics, the particular issues? As you make that list, you can also begin a corresponding column on the other side of the sheet. In this second column begin to brainstorm how you can work out that tension and pressure. How can you deal with it constructively?

You may have to prioritize your responses. You may have a particular need you cannot deal with this week; it may have to be scheduled for next week. But *these* particular goals you need to tackle this week. Those other five issues will have to wait until you have more time and energy. You need to plan, prioritize, and discipline. This goes along with what we were talking about last week when we discussed assuming new responsibilities. You have to look the tiger in the eye and begin to organize constructively and face your situation so that you can begin to deal with some of these problems even when your circuits are on overload.

Where Were You When I Needed You?
This has to do with the other parent, the person with whom you are now hopefully beginning to relate in a constructive, mature way. Usually, a primary custodial parent feels a lot of resentment. As I talk with single parents, I find that about half of them feel they have too much of the responsibility for the children too much of the time. You may have an arrangement that divides custody fifty-fifty; that, too, presents problems, particularly for the children. One parent usually finds his or her circuits on overload constantly and is very resentful, angry, and generally exhausted.

Though not on overload, the other parent is experiencing an emptiness and a loneliness. Frequently, that parent misses the experience and routine of being a parent on a more regular basis. I don't have a simple answer to that issue. It's a tough thing to work out. Hopefully, time will enable you to arrange things in a mature, satisfactory way for all concerned, children included. It is worth all the effort if you can eventually achieve an equitable balance.

I Don't Get Any Respect.
Very often, the out-of-house parent becomes the entertainment parent, while the primary custodial parent becomes the disciplinary parent. Usually the father is the entertainer, although that is now changing dramatically as more and more fathers are receiving primary custody. The entertainer is usually more lenient, and the child becomes confused, and very adroit at playing one against the other. Ultimately, it brings no satisfaction to anyone.

Jim talks about the Disneyland Daddy, where the father becomes the entertainer, taking kids to pizza parlors, movies, and amusement parks. A child ultimately will not find wholeness in just going places and doing fun things. They long for a true parental relationship, and they even desire the discipline of the relationship. Ice cream cones, pizza, and movies only go so far. Outside attractions lose their allure after a while. Then the parents have to look long and hard at their relationship and what they are accomplishing with their children.

Help, I'm a Prisoner.
Our children can imprison us. Some parents seem to become overly responsible. Because of the pain they are going through and because they want to insulate and protect their children, they become super-moms or super-dads. They say to themselves, "I may have failed in my marriage, but I'm not going to fail as a parent. I'm going to die in the attempt before I fail with my children."

But that kind of parent can drive a kid crazy! After one of our retreat weekends at St. Andrew's, I had several single parents come up and say what a great weekend it was, getting away from their kids. I said to one, "You know, I bet it was a great weekend for them, too." Both parents and children need their space. Sometimes you can smother each other and not recognize how badly you need to give each other some breathing room. I hope that if your children are not here in the workshop, you are talking to them about it. I hope that the experience you are having here is something you are letting them know about. I hope you are letting them know that you are undergoing some positive reflection, some reappraisal, some change, some healing, some wholeness. I hope that you can talk about it with your young person.

I want to share with you some things young people in these workshops have told me. Several years ago I went out into the hallway while the adults were in their small groups. (This was before we had a workshop for teenagers.) I got into a conversation with three teenage girls, fourteen or fifteen years old, waiting for their parents who were in the workshop. They didn't know me, and I didn't know them. I asked them if they would tell me some things they were feeling about their parents' divorce. Let me tell you what they said.

> What is happening to my family? What is happening to me? I'm angry at both my mom and dad. I'm afraid of marriage. I'll never get married myself. I don't like boys because I'm afraid that what happened to my parents will happen to me.

> How can I help my parents get through this? They won't let me help them. They won't let me say anything to them about how I think they can make some adjustments in their lives. How can I forgive my parents? I have feelings of hate for what they did to each other. How can I love them and hate them at the same time? That's how I feel, though. I'm mixed up in my love and hate. How can I be loyal to my parents? I feel like a Ping-Pong ball, being bounced back and forth.

> I can't trust them because they lied to me.

> I'll never get married because of what a man did to my mother.

> It's hard to hold things inside. I don't know who to talk to who will really understand. Do you understand how I feel? If I let my feelings out, most of my friends will not understand what I'm talking about.

These young people were crying out for some authentic help in their lives. I know that sharing some of the things I have just read to you will cut to the heart of where some of your children are and will wound you deeply. Yet these are the real issues. In the final workshop session last fall, I participated in a panel discussion with fifty teenagers whose parents were downstairs in small groups. We asked them to write questions on cards to which the panel could respond. No names were used. Here are the questions exactly as they were written:

◆ How do you get closer to the parent you don't live with?
◆ How can I see my mom more often than my dad will let me?
◆ Can a mom and dad ever not fight because of money?

- How can I make some new friends? I just moved into a new place.
- I'm sort of looking forward to my dad moving out. I *never* thought this before! Explain this, if you can.
- How can I deal with the hatred I often suddenly feel toward my step-mom?
- Why do parents hit you after they get divorced for about a year or two? Then they take you somewhere and ask you not to tell or they will lock you up in your room.
- How do you tell the parent you are living with that you don't like how many or who that person is seeing? How do you handle a mom who cries a lot?
- I don't see my dad much. I know that he feels left out but I don't have the time, nor can I think of anything to do with him. He doesn't have any money and we are tired of the movies. Now, when I suggest watching television together, he tries to get out of it. What can I do with him? I think he's afraid of me being bored with him (which I often am).
- Now that my father is gone, my mother has dumped a ton of responsibilities on me. Basically, I'm the man of the house, but I can't handle the whole load.
- How do I deal with a father who makes me feel guilty when I ask things from him?
- My dad is going to get married to the woman he cheated with—one of the many. Her divorce is almost final. I could just accept it and get along with her, but my mom indirectly puts a guilt trip on me. I don't know whether to just make life easier and become friends with "her," or keep the loyalty to my mom.
- Is it okay to cry in a divorce?
- I have a lot of anger towards my dad and step-mom. My dad was having an affair with her, and I hate her because she hurt my mom and me and doesn't seem to care. Also, they tell me that my feelings about this are dumb and their life is none of my business. What can I do to get rid of this anger?
- My parents use me for information about the other parent, but they won't listen to my protests to their questions.
- How do you deal with a parent who has an alcohol problem?
- How do you deal with a parent who wants you to do everything their way?
- What should I do about my mom's boyfriend who is as cold as ice to me?
- How can I talk to my dad? He has a temper, so I can't say anything. What can I do?
- How do you deal with your dad who has a girlfriend and you don't like her?
- What would you recommend for us to do in our own marriages so we won't have to get a divorce like our parents?
- Why do my parents still argue even after they have been divorced?
- Why do parents hate each other after divorce? Why can't they stay friends? Children often feel better when their parents are friends and talk.
- When I go to visit my dad on weekends, how can I get him to do something besides sit in his chair and read the paper or watch television?
- Is it okay for parents to have affairs?
- I like this workshop. When does the next one begin?

I know these questions are hard for many of you to hear. But you need to hear them and work through their implications when they are relevant to your particular situation.

My hope and prayer is that this kind of frankness will begin to unlock and open doors to the kind of communication and mutual understanding both parents and children long for.

SOME SUGGESTIONS FOR SINGLE PARENTS

Many parents talk about how they really trust their kids, but too few parents recognize how children can *lose* their trust in them. You need to get down to their level and not make excuses, throw pity parties, and play games. Children can see right through you like cheap cellophane. It is so much better to be authentic and honest with them.

On pages 60-66 Jim makes eight suggestions (slightly altered here) as to what parents can do. I want to move through them briefly and make some additional comments:

Don't Try to Be Both Parents to Your Children.

If you are a woman, you can be a mother, but you will have a difficult time being a dad. Similarly, you dads will have a hard time being a mother. If you are in a normal divorce situation, your children still have a dad. They still have a mom. Hopefully, both parents are still equipped to fill their roles despite the fact that the marital relationship no longer exists. Do not try to be both parents.

Don't Force Your Children into Playing the Role of the Departed Parent.

I've heard a mother say to her eight-year-old son, "Now you are the daddy in the house." Can you believe that? Perhaps you have even been guilty of saying that without fully realizing what you were implying. How can a little boy become the man of the house when he is totally incapable of understanding what that means or of being able to assume any of the responsibilities that kind of role necessitates?

Don't force your children into playing parental roles. They don't need that kind of pressure.

Find a Supportive Community.

As fellow divorcees, you can help each other find an extended family. You can link together and form some new relationships. I love it when I hear single folks talk about what is happening here in the midst of our singles ministry. They are saying, "I've found a family. This is my family." That doesn't mean they have ripped themselves away from blood relationships. It means they have found an extension of what it means to be part of a family.

You need to develop that, and it is going to take some time. You don't get "instant family" wherever you go, even if you remarry and suddenly inherit a new family through that marriage. Whether you are in a first marriage or a second or third marriage, you inherit the relationships of your spouse. But that is not instant family. It takes time to develop those relationships into family. It takes patience. It takes hard work. It takes sensitivity, and it is not easy. You need to be creative and open.

Be Honest with Your Children.

Let them see you as you are. Don't try to be a role model all the time. You do need to be role models. But at the same time you need to be authentic.

Sometimes we as parents try to shield our children from the pain we are going through.

Being able to cry and emote together and sharing the pain of the experience may be positive for both you and your children. Pain itself can be bonding. The mutual expression of need can create a unity of support and encouragement.

You must carefully gauge how to share your pain and express your needs. It all depends on the ages of your children and their emotional stability. As a mature adult, you need to discern what you can and should do in terms of being honest with your children.

Don't Put Down Your Ex-spouse in Front of Your Children.

It isn't very constructive to expose children to all the faults of your ex-mate. Some of you have so much venom, animosity, and anger that you want to let it spill out. Either consciously or unconsciously, you want your children to take your side. You want them to see the correctness of your position and the injustice of what he or she did to you. You can take great satisfaction in your children saying, "You are right, Mom. He is a stupid, evil, irresponsible worm." "You are right, Dad. She really is selfish and cruel."

Don't Make Your Children Undercover Agents
to Report on the Other Parent's Activities.

You probably have a morbid curiosity about what his or her apartment or the closet or bedroom looks like. You would love to know what the oven or refrigerator would look like if you opened it. You can use the children as undercover or not-so-undercover agents to let you know what is going on with the girlfriend or boyfriend or the new spouse. That puts children in a terrible position when they return from a time with the other parent. They feel like you are tying them to a chair, shining a light in their face, and giving them the third degree.

Perhaps the best thing you could say is, "Did you have a good time?"

"Yes."

"Good." And if the child wants to talk more, fine. But you place no expectation on that child to share anything. They need to feel the freedom to talk or not to talk as they see fit. Probably their wisdom at many points will outstrip yours. If they don't say anything, there is probably a good reason they shouldn't. Let it go at that.

Children of Divorce Need Both a Mother and a Father.

That almost goes without saying. These ex-mates may be guilty of tremendous failure in their relationships with you, but they can still be a great success as a parent. Allow them that. Discern that carefully by breaking down your wall of animosity. That their relationship with you wasn't successful does not mean they can't have a very successful relationship with your children.

But that often points a finger at your own failure. And you don't like to admit that. You hate to confess that your ex could have a successful relationship with anyone else when he or she couldn't develop it with you. So you instinctively want to lash out and to cut down. But your children need both a mother and a father.

Don't Become Disneyland Daddy or Magic Mountain Mommy.

Earlier I mentioned the entertainer parent. We discussed a child's need for meaningful relationships, not just exciting things to do. I have heard kids say, "My parents tried to buy me off. They didn't have time for me, so they dealt with their guilt by giving me money or presents." Developing strong, continuing relationships takes time, energy, and a lot of creativity. There are no short cuts.

POSITIVES AND NEGATIVES IN SINGLE PARENTING

I would like to spend the closing portion of this lecture discussing some general issues in single parenting. First, let me share four positive aspects of being a single parent.

Positives

Personal growth. In a marital relationship, we often give up who we are in order to make the relationship succeed. A single person has the opportunity to discover the inner self.

Freedom. As the only adult in the household, you are absolutely free to structure it any way you choose. If you have a craving for cantaloupe and ice cream for dinner instead of meat and potatoes, go right ahead.

Partnership with your children. It's crucial for survival. And by sharing, children are able to grow with the responsibilities that are given to them.

New friends. Your world opens up to a whole new group of friends once you're no longer part of a couple.

Negatives

But of course there are some negatives that go along with the positives in being a single parent. Some of them are:

Loneliness. Although it is rapidly changing, our society is structured in pairs. Many single parents feel there are no other adults to talk to when they need someone.

Lack of structure. Often we tend to do things for other adults, and if there's not another adult to appreciate a redecorated room or a clean house, it may be easier just to take a nap. People who like structure in their lives find that in being a single parent it is difficult to maintain discipline and order.

Time poor. There's simply not enough time to work, to care for the kids, to shoulder the household responsibilities, and to get the rest, recreation, and time for ourselves that we need.

Guilt. So often, working moms and dads feel guilty in general; single mothers feel even more so. Women tend to absorb the guilt that society delivers about divorce and neglected children. If you have to work, don't feel guilty about it.

Family. Relatives, parents, and those close to you can contribute to the feelings of guilt and add time and responsibility demands to your already overloaded life.

What can you as a single parent do when you are overextended and just trying to survive? Here are some thoughts and principles that hopefully will help:

- ◆ *Don't start by trying to change others around you.* Instead, look to the areas you need to change in yourself.
- ◆ *Think about your time and how you use it.* Often you take on things you don't need to, like cleaning everything until it's spotless. You need to give yourself permission not to do certain things, to set priorities, and to do those things that are most important to you.

- *Lower your standards and share responsibilities.* It might be a good idea to ask one of the kids to clean the living room. Then don't do it over again just because it isn't up to your standards. Make suggestions. Help them improve. You'll find your kids will blossom and grow.
- *Learn to say no.* Why feel guilty if you can't contribute home-baked cookies to the PTA? Do what you can and be satisfied with that. It's a good idea to give yourself a cushion of time for emergencies. If you're booked up 100 percent of your time, you're looking for trouble.
- *Learn to be good to yourself.* In order to be able to give, you need to nourish your own needs. The child that is in you, the part that wants to have fun, is important. If you don't take time for yourself, you'll grow resentful.
- *Share your feelings with your children.* Tell them you've had a rotten day and need an hour to yourself. Become a *person* to your children.
- *Develop alternate support systems.* Neighbors, friends, and co-workers often will help if you'll let them.
- *Nurture yourself and your family spiritually.* If you've been away from God and the church, take advantage of your changed situation. Put some spiritual discipline and structure into your life. Spend daily time in the Scripture, in prayer, and in meditation. If you don't say grace before meals with your family, begin to. Understand how important Christian education is, both for yourself and your children.

Someone once said, "The way out is the way through." When it's all added up, we can only give our children two things: roots and wings.

It takes good parents to understand that, whether they are single or not. There are few super parents in this life. The best parents are the ones who are honest and flexible and who depend daily on the grace of God.

I close with these poetic thoughts, given by one of our workshop participants a few years ago:

My Halfway House
Is in between where I've been and where I'm going.
It's almost a home—
　　especially when someone special comes to halfway between conditions in life,
　　visits and needs a friend,
　　to listen—
a refuge, where sharing is safe.

I feel safe here,
　　although, at times, I do feel lonely.

I've learned many things about myself—living alone,

I'm the same, yet I'm different.

No one can ever replace or be substituted for that part of me that is gone.

My void is being filled in a new way.

I'm becoming—
  more totally me.

    Halfway between where I've been
    and where I'm going.

COPING SKILLS FOR WORRIES, DARK THOUGHTS, AND DOWN DAYS, BY JOHN S. FRY

The following lecture has been an important dimension of our divorce recovery workshop at St. Andrew's. On the fourth night, I speak to parents of dependent children while Dr. John Fry delivers this lecture to nonparents and parents of grown children. This second group is usually about one-third of our participants.

Dr. Fry, who is divorced and single, is a clinical psychologist in private practice and is active in our ministry at St. Andrew's. I am deeply grateful for his willingness to give freely and sacrificially of his time and abilities. In the process he has become a valued colleague and personal friend.

Hundreds of times, in stress management seminars I have given, I have asked audiences the question, "What causes your stress?" Typical answers include "the workload," "driving the freeways," "satisfying my boss," "coping with difficult people," and "angry customers."

If I were to ask you, the attendees at a divorce recovery workshop, that same question, you would probably add answers such as "talking with my ex-spouse," "dealing with the court system," "working on my property settlement," and "paying the bills."

I would like you to notice that there is one thing common to all those responses: They are *external* stresses. They are about situations in your environment or experience that present difficulty or challenge. Therefore, the assumption is that you can reduce your stress by improving your skills at coping with particular situations.

Taking courses on time management and customer relations or going through this workshop on divorce recovery would all be helpful in reducing your stress because your abilities to cope with that particular stressful situation would be improved. However, I would like to expand your awareness of what you can do for yourself, beyond just improving your coping skills.

Another major stress-reduction method deals with *internal* processes instead of external challenges. It is called the *cognitive* approach to stress management. Do you tell yourself, "Oh, no. This is terrible"? If so, you make the situation worse for yourself by "catastrophizing" about it. Or do you instead tell yourself, "Well, this is a real problem in my life. It's a waste of time to fret about it. I had better figure out what to do"?

The nice thing about the cognitive approach to stress management is that you can have control over it because it is an internal process. It is dependent upon your thinking clearly. It is a learnable skill that almost anyone can acquire.

On the other hand, you probably don't have much control over what comes at you, even if you are proficient at coping with external situations. For instance, your spouse may choose to leave you, and you may not have any choice about that. In some situations no amount of effort to communicate and change will keep that person in the relationship. But you still can work on how you are thinking about the situation, even if your efforts to repair the situation by getting some marriage counseling are not successful.

The rest of this discussion will focus on what I consider to be some of the more helpful ideas and suggestions drawn from a cognitive approach to stress management. I can think of no time in my life when I needed these skills more than when I was faced with coping with a separation and divorce in my own life. What follows is what I have found to be the most helpful for myself as well as for my counseling clients.

COPING SKILLS FOR WORRIES

Worry is a bad mental habit. The definition I like for it is "problem solving gone pointless." It is *circular* in nature. See if this isn't how worry works for you.

You start out with the thought, "I have to decide." Your second thought is, "But there's no immediately apparent solution." Then your third thought is, "Oh, no! This is terrible!" Then, "I've got to come up with something!" (Your first thought again). "But what?!" (Second thought again.) "This is awful!" (Third thought again.) Round and round it can continue for minutes, even hours, with very little grounding in reality, rotating between a demand and a sense of inadequacy, and catastrophizing about it.

Problem solving, on the other hand, is *linear* in nature. You start out with the first two thoughts—"I have to decide" and "There's no immediately apparent solution."

But instead of closing the circle with a catastrophizing thought, you then go on to explore possible ways either to solve the problem or to get more information. You may make plans to talk with a friend, pastor, or psychologist. You may pick up a good self-help book on the issue. Or you may sit down with a pad of paper and brainstorm some ideas. You don't waste your energy dwelling on all the worst things that could happen.

So, one approach to combating worry is to notice the difference between worry and problem solving. Worry is circular and problem solving is linear. Whenever you find yourself going round and round in a mental circle, tell yourself to stop it and start looking for solutions or for more information that might lead to solutions.

Several decades ago Dr. Albert Ellis made the astute observation that we can hold certain beliefs which can lead to a great deal of needless stress in our lives.[1] Here are some examples of commonly held beliefs that can greatly increase our experience of stress. As I discuss each of them, try them on for size. If the belief fits, see if you can challenge yourself in that area to avoid needless stress.

I Have to Be Perfect in Everything I Do.

Perfection is not achievable. No matter how well we do something, there is always room for improvement. Since perfection is impossible to achieve, the undesirable prize we do achieve includes worry and anxiety while we are trying, and discouragement and depression when we give up.

Even "I have to be *excellent* in everything I do" isn't achievable, because few if any of us have the ability to be excellent in all areas. What *is* possible is to strive for excellence in the areas where we have a chance at it. It is certainly more helpful while going through a divorce to think in terms of making the best of a difficult situation than to torture yourself with unrealistic standards of perfection in a very imperfect situation.

If There's Even a Faint Possibility of Danger or Failure, I Should Dwell on It!

While it is important to examine the alternatives in a situation, it is a stressful mistake to have the attitude that extreme vigilance is necessary to avoid calamity. Because there is a lot of pain in the divorce process, it is easy to start anticipating pain in all other areas of your life as well. You then run the risk of not noticing the things that are going *right* in your life.

I Have to Have Everyone Like Me. I Have to Have Everyone's Approval.

Just by the very fact that you are going through a divorce, we know there is almost certainly one other person who won't give you this one! Even if you are the most popular person in your neighborhood, someone will probably be jealous of your popularity.

If you are trying to have everyone's approval, you can't take a meaningful stand on any issue. While it is a good thing to be a likable person, you give up some of your integrity and substance of character when you try to have *everyone* like you. And for every compromise you make to gain someone's favor, someone else will dislike you because of that very compromise.

My Feelings Are Caused By Others and I Have No Way of Controlling Them.

"She made me angry!" "He made me sad." "She upset me." "He hurt my feelings!" It's not what people do that gives us our feelings; it's our *interpretation* of what they do.

For example, I'm walking down the street. I turn around a corner and bump into someone. I say to myself, "That crazy fool! Why doesn't he watch where he's going?" I create anger based on my interpretation of the situation.

The next day I turn around the same corner and bump into someone. Only this time I say to myself, "There you go again, Fry! You clumsy fool!" I create lowered self-esteem and maybe even some mild depression by talking to myself that way.

The third day I again bump into someone. I say to myself, "The world is a risky place. You can get hurt!" This time I create anxiety out of the same situation.

The fourth day I turn the same corner and again bump into someone. (You'd think I would learn about that corner!) This time I shrug it off—"Those things happen"—and go on my way and soon forget the incident.

Life tends to work much better for us if we take responsibility for our feelings rather than blaming others for them. If we give others the responsibility for our feelings, we give up something important to people who may not have our best interests at heart. This is often how we relate to our ex in a typical divorce situation.

I'm not saying we should be phony or deny our feelings. But we need to take full responsibility ourselves for what we do feel: "I am sad," rather than "You made me sad."

It's Awful When Things Aren't Exactly the Way I Want Them to Be!

No, it's not necessarily awful. Rather, you have a difficult situation to deal with and "awful-izing" about it is a waste of your time and energy. It would be much better to get down to business and try to solve the problem or make the best of a bad situation. What good does it do to throw a pity party for yourself about your divorce or your property settlement when you could use your energies to cope with the situation?

I'm a Victim of My Past and I Always Will Be!

"My parents made me the way I am." "I can't change. That's just the way I am." Certainly our past does influence us. But we can change and grow. Some of that growth may occur through insight about our past. (It's okay to look back—just don't stare!) But insight alone is rarely enough. The next step is developing a plan for change, such as attending this workshop and/or getting some professional help.

Don't Tell Me to Relax! Only My Tension Holds Me Together!

Some people may know how to relax but don't use their skill because they superstitiously believe that they have to be tense in order to be good. The pattern probably started for them when they were in about second grade, studied hard and anxiously for a test, and got an "A" on it. They then made the assumption that their anxiety, rather than the fact that they studied hard for it, is why they did well.

Our best efforts usually occur when we're alert but not tense. Just because your life is difficult right now doesn't mean you are obligated to be nervous all the time!

Life Is Supposed to Be Fair!

Where does it say that? As part of their purpose, our laws and government try to make things more fair. But it certainly isn't in the order of things for situations to work out fairly all the time. Nor is such fairness a Christian concept. Jesus said that God "causes his sun to rise on the evil and the good, and sends rain on the righteous and the unrighteous" (Matthew 5:45).

Life isn't fair or unfair. It just is. And we need to cope with what presents itself to us. It's a waste of time and emotional energy to complain rather than cope.

COPING SKILLS FOR DARK THOUGHTS AND DOWN DAYS

For a long time medication had a better record than any single psychotherapy approach at helping those who were depressed. In the last decade or two, however, at least one therapy approach has also produced some very good results in extensive scientific research, as well as in practical use by thousands of psychotherapists.

During his many years of research, Aaron Beck noticed something that was always true of those who were depressed: they tended to have distorted views of reality.[2] Beck and his colleagues also found that if people could learn how to combat these tendencies to distort, they could learn to pull themselves out of their blues. Eventually they came up with something they called cognitive therapy. Cognitive therapy tends to be helpful whether the problem is serious depression or just feeling a bit low.

David Burns, a colleague of Beck's, lists ten basic types of these cognitive distortions in his excellent self-help book on depression.[3] As I define and give examples of each type of distortion, I would like you to write down any examples of such distortions that you recognize in yourself. By acknowledging and then correcting your own distortions, you can in a sense inoculate yourself from their power in the future. (I'll offer suggested corrections for each of the examples I give.)

All-or-Nothing Thinking

This is the tendency to think in black-and-white terms and to be perfectionistic. If you find yourself using the words "always" or "never," you are probably indulging in all-or-nothing thinking.

> Distortion: "If I'm not perfect (and how can anyone going through a divorce be perfect?), I must be a failure."

Correct thinking: No one is ever perfect.

Distortion: "If he's not perfect, he's not for me!"

Correct thinking: You'll never find anyone that way!

Distortion: "Now that I'm on my own, it will always be difficult."

Correct thinking: It really *is* possible to be complete and whole as a single person.

Distortion: "I can never again be happy without him/her."

Correct thinking: If you are stuck on someone in this way, try thinking of the situation like this. Let's assume that you had never met this person before. This person walks up to you right now and begins treating you the way he or she has been treating you lately. Would you even give that person the time of day? The way this person treats you is who they are *now*! That person may bear little resemblance to the person you knew in the past—the person who no longer exists for you.

Much of the difficulty in letting go of a relationship that is over comes from holding on to an idealized or black-and-white image of that person. This often takes the form of selectively remembering only the best times in the relationship and ignoring the difficulties of the recent past.

Overgeneralization
You do this when you take a single negative situation and tell yourself that it is a pattern. Examples include:

Distortion: "My wife left me. Therefore I'm unattractive to women."

Correct thinking: There are over two-and-a-half billion members of the opposite sex in the world. Just because you couldn't work it out with one of them, doesn't mean you can't do so with another.

Distortion: "Since I'm now single, I'll always be single."

Correct thinking: Most people who divorce do remarry.

Negative Mental Filter
You pick out a negative detail and dwell on it, coloring your perception.

Distortion: "Everyone else is happy and part of a loving couple."

Correct thinking: Not really. Think back to the last few months of your marriage, for instance. Recall that terrible loneliness you may have felt during that time. Just because a couple is still together in no way implies their happiness.

Distortion: "I've wasted the best years of my life in that relationship!"

Correct thinking: It has *not* been a waste. If you think about it, you probably learned quite a bit during that time even if things didn't turn out well.

Distortion: "Because I'm going through a divorce, my whole life is lousy!"

Correct thinking: Don't make your whole life lousy because of one aspect of life. You may still have good friends, a good job, and your health. Don't deny the good stuff!

Disqualifying the Positive
You find some reason to disregard the good things. Examples include:

Distortion: "They're being kind with their compliments. They don't really mean it."
Correct thinking: How do you know that? Soak it up!
Distortion: "They invited me over because they pity me."
Correct thinking: Again, how do you know that? They probably care about you and like your company.

Jumping to Conclusions

Mind reading, where you assume the negative, and fortune telling, where you predict disaster, are the two most common forms of this type of distortion.

Distortion: "She didn't say hello to me. Therefore, she must be angry with me."
Correct thinking: No, she's probably preoccupied with that traffic ticket she got while driving here.
Distortion: "People blame me for the break-up."
Correct thinking: Don't assume you know what people are thinking.
Distortion: "This is a terrible situation, and it's never going to end! I will always feel this badly."
Correct thinking: This is a very common version of fortune telling for those who are depressed. It seems that it will never end; but if you work constructively on your difficulties, the pain almost always diminishes as time goes on.
Distortion: "No one understands me."
Correct thinking: Since half of all marriages end in divorce, there are a huge number of people who do understand the pain you're experiencing. If some individuals don't understand you, it may be because you haven't tried to help them understand. Tell them! Others can't read your mind.
Distortion: "This property settlement will be a disaster for me."
Correct thinking: I remember how helpful it was for me to say to myself, "I am not my possessions!"

Magnification or Minimization

Magnification usually involves catastrophizing or exaggerating your mistakes. Minimization involves reducing your view of strengths.

Distortion: "Since finances are tight right now, I'm not going to survive financially."
Correct thinking: All it really means is that times are difficult now. It's not necessarily going to get worse.
Distortion: "How will I survive without a man to fix things?" or "How will I survive without a woman to cook for me? I'll starve!"
Correct thinking: Actually, you will be surprised at how quickly you can gain some competence in unfamiliar areas.

Emotional Reasoning

We do this when we make our feelings our reality about something.

Distortion: "I don't feel like dealing with the legal issues today, so I won't do it."
Correct thinking: Much procrastination comes from emotional reasoning. We tell

ourselves that, since we feel badly about something, we should put it off as long as possible. A different perspective says, "Since I feel badly about doing those legal forms, I'll get them out of the way so I won't have to be feeling badly about having to do them."

Distortion: "This flu makes me feel rotten. I feel rotten about you!"

Correct thinking: Beware of letting your own physical discomfort determine your view of others.

Distortion: "I'm angry with you! I've always been angry with you!"

Correct thinking: Beware of assuming that how you feel this moment is how you have always felt about someone or something.

"Should" Statements

When you continually try to motivate yourself with guilt and put-downs, you will eventually have difficulty staying motivated. You need positives to give yourself enduring self-motivation and to avoid burning out. Examples of "should" statements are:

Distortion: "I should be able to handle this better than I am."

Correct thinking: Instead, say, "At least I'm working on the problem; next time I'll try to do better."

Distortion: "I should have done things differently."

Correct thinking: Maybe so, but try to learn from your mistakes without feeling that you have to punish yourself for them. "Well, I did the best I could under the circumstances. I'll learn from my mistakes and do better next time."

Labeling and Mislabeling

We lock ourselves out of possibilities when we too rigidly define ourselves, and we easily contribute to others' defensiveness when we label them. Here are some examples:

Distortion: "You are stubborn!"

Correct thinking: It's no wonder people become defensive when we label them as if that label is their enduring identity. Instead, try saying something like, "I feel you're being stubborn about this." Then they don't have to debate with you whether they are always stubborn or not. Instead they can more easily focus on the issue at hand and your concerns about it.

Distortion: "I'm a failure."

Correct thinking: Just because you haven't succeeded yet in this one aspect of your life doesn't mean that your whole life is a failure. It just means you haven't yet accomplished what you want to in that one area.

Personalization

This occurs when we mistakenly assume responsibility for a situation. Examples are:

Distortion: "I'm a jinx to these people. Every time we get together something bad seems to happen."

Correct thinking: This is superstitious thinking. Just because certain things happen together more than once doesn't mean that one causes the other.

Distortion: "God is punishing me for the bad things I've done."
Correct thinking: Many people mistakenly believe that this is a Christian viewpoint.
    Actually, from a biblical perspective, the purpose of difficulties in our lives is to
    make us stronger, not to punish us (Romans 5:3, James 1:2).

I want to be very clear that what we have been discussing is not simply positive thinking. Positive thinking can be a distortion, too. If I say to myself, "Today is going to be a great day," what happens to my great day when someone rear-ends me on the freeway? Rather, I might say to myself that I'm going to try to make this as good a day as possible.

What I'm recommending is *realistic* thinking. We generally use that word to call a person to a more sober assessment of a situation. We say, "Be realistic! You've got your head in the clouds." But realistic thinking can also mean seeing things as they are when we've been looking too much on the dark side.

There's no getting around the fact that going through a divorce is a difficult experience. It is normal to be sad and to experience grief at the loss of both the relationship and the dream of what it could have been. But sadness and grief are not the same thing as depression. Depression adds distortion to the sadness and grieving. Sadness says, "I miss him, and I am very hurt." Depression says, "I will never feel good again; I will never find anyone to love again." *Depression is never a necessity, no matter what the situation.*

COPING WITH DARK THOUGHTS ABOUT YOUR FAITH

We can distort our faith, too. These distortions can make us feel depressed, just as other distortions can. Here are some examples.

Distortion: "I have to have my act together for God to love me; and how can anyone
    going through a divorce have their act together? Therefore, God must be distant
    from me."
Correct thinking: Please remember that it is a core teaching of the Christian faith
    that *everyone* falls short of earning God's favor on their own. We all need
    forgiveness. The astoundingly good news is that we all are loved, and we
    all can be forgiven if we just ask for it! God feels your pain and loves you, no
    matter what the difficulty. Don't deny yourself the greatest resource of all for
    healing!
Distortion: "I have to have my act together for God to use me. Since things are in
    kind of a mess right now in my life, He certainly wouldn't want my services."
Correct thinking: Again, please remember that it is a basic fact of life that we *all* are
    in kind of a mess, that we all have failed God in one way or another, and that
    we all are in need of God's forgiveness—which is freely available to each of us
    if we ask for it.

Before his conversion, the apostle Paul was guilty of assisting in the death of the first Christian martyr, Stephen. Yet God saw fit to use Paul in helping the Christian faith to grow from a few thousand people in Jerusalem after Christ's death to hundreds of thousands throughout the civilized world.

Don't make the mistake of thinking that somehow you are impaired for service. If you have made a commitment of faith in Christ, you are not "damaged goods" in God's eyes! For instance, by growing through the painful experience of divorce yourself, you will probably have much more credibility than happily married people in ministering to the needs of others experiencing divorce. Seek your ministry, whatever it may be!

As I've discussed the many ways we can distort our view of our situation and become depressed, I'm sure some additional distortions have occurred to you. What are some distorted statements that you or others like you might make while coping with a divorce?

[Time is allowed for audience response.]

I have implied that this cognitive approach is relatively recent. And in terms of refined, well-researched therapy methods, it *is* recent. However, the same ideas can be found in the New Testament.

If anyone had a situation in which it would have been easy to distort reality and thereby become depressed, it was Paul when he was writing his letter to the church at Philippi. He was under house arrest in Rome, far from his homeland and most of his friends, awaiting trial for his faith, and facing the possibility of a tortured death. Yet he writes the following:

> Don't worry over anything whatever; tell God every detail of your needs in earnest and thankful prayer, and the peace of God, which transcends human understanding, will keep constant guard over your hearts and minds as they rest in Christ Jesus. . . . For I have learned to be content, whatever the circumstances may be. I know how to live when things are difficult and I know how to live when things are prosperous. In general and in particular I have learned the secret of facing either plenty or poverty. I am ready for anything through the strength of the one who lives within me. (Philippians 4:6-7,11-13, PH)

ADDITIONAL SUGGESTIONS FOR COPING

Here are other things to think about as you seek to cope with your present circumstances.

Stay Active.
If you sit around staring at the wall, you increase your chances of weaving a web of distorted thinking about your situation.

Communicate with Others.
You will probably feel better if you talk about your problems. This also gives you the benefit of getting someone else's perspective, thereby reducing the chances of your own distortion.

Every Once in a While, Make a "Good Stuff" List.
Write down everything that's going *right* in your life. This will be a helpful corrective to the natural tendency for you, as someone going through a divorce, to focus exclusively on the problems.

Don't Just Have a "To Do" List.
"To do" lists are reminders of your incompleteness. Create a "done" list that you can look at and savor what you have accomplished.

NOW IT'S UP TO YOU

We have discussed a number of different ways for you to improve your coping skills for worries, dark thoughts, and down days. I have personally found everything I've shared with you to be helpful to me in attempting to grow through my own divorce. Try it out and see if it doesn't help a lot! You don't have to be broken down by this difficult experience. For the Christian, tough times have a different purpose. This is from James:

> When all kinds of trials and temptations crowd into your lives, my brothers and sisters, don't resent them as intruders, but welcome them as friends! Realize that they come to test your faith and to produce in you the quality of endurance. But let the process go on until that endurance is fully developed, and you will find you have become men and women of mature character with the right sort of independence. And if, in the process, any of you does not know how to meet any particular problem he or she has only to ask God who gives generously to all men and women without making them feel foolish or guilty and you may be quite sure that the necessary wisdom will be given you. (James 1:2-5, PH, female gender added)

FINDING AND EXPERIENCING FORGIVENESS

In this session we are going to focus on what I believe is one of the most pivotal, crucial, and difficult areas of growing through a divorce. I would ask that you open your ears as well as your minds, and perhaps even more than that, your hearts, as you listen.

As I speak on the subject of forgiveness, I must issue a warning. Timing is critical. There's a right time and a wrong time. Yet, when the right time comes, we never feel quite ready. Even though we know we need to do some things in life, we often don't feel ready to do them. As result, many things will never get done if we wait till we feel like doing them.

It's difficult to discern proper timing. I can't discern that for you. You must work it out for yourself. However, you are probably ready to embark upon this area of forgiveness before you think you are ready, and certainly before you *feel* you are ready. What I am saying in this lecture may send shivers up your spine or create an attitude of resistance in you. Hold onto the edge of your chair, relax, think, and try to be open and pliable.

Forgiveness is absolutely crucial in order for healing to take place in the tragedy of divorce. After counseling with all kinds of people—whether or not they are spiritually oriented, Christians, or totally secular in their orientation—I am convinced that handling forgiveness is absolutely fundamental to wholeness and healing after a divorce.

It is impossible for me to separate how I understand the reality of forgiveness from how I relate to the reality of God. For me they are all wrapped together, and I cannot separate them. That's not true for everyone, but it is true for me. I don't intend to preach at you. I'm going to do everything in my power not to do that. However, I want you to know that I have a hard time separating the reality of forgiveness from the reality of God.

By nature I am not a forgiving person. Yet I have been able to forgive profoundly—not in my own power, but by the grace and strength God has given me. That's why I cannot pull the two apart. I'm not asking you to agree with everything I say. You are certainly free not to. But you do need to take good notes, so that perhaps later on you can reflect on these thoughts.

Chapter 8 in Jim's book (page 95) begins with the statement "I'm not perfect. I'm just forgiven." That is a theological statement. Jim later says that forgiveness is the experience of getting the hate out. That is a practical statement. Until you get the hate out, you can't heal.

I'm in a monthly covenant group with Jim Smoke. He tells me that this book has now sold about 400,000 copies. The chapter on forgiveness is the one that has received the most comment from those who have written or spoken to Jim as he travels around the country leading divorce recovery workshops. People are more angry or more appreciative about this chapter than any other.

The notion of forgiveness draws a divorce experience to a head. Some action needs to take place. Divorce can cause you to build walls in your life in place of bridges. In the process of going through a divorce, you can start out by hating an ex-spouse and end up hating yourself and everyone around you. You can drown yourself in a sea of negative feelings toward others and yourself. That kind of emotional bath can keep you from growing and becoming the new person you need to become. Time will diminish hatred, but it will not heal it. Experiencing forgiveness gets the hate out of your life and gets it out permanently.

It would be a lot easier to go through a divorce recovery workshop and not talk about forgiveness. Most workshops I'm aware of do not. I hope that you have come to this seminar both to take some good new ideas in and to get some bad old ideas out. I believe the intersection where the good ideas come in and the bad ideas go out is forgiveness.

All of you have come here with either a great deal of hate or a great deal of hurt locked inside you; and for many it takes a long time to deal with those feelings. It is difficult to understand them, to get them out, and to cope with them in a positive and proper manner. Forgiveness is not just words; it is also not an easy cure-all to a divorce situation. But without forgiveness you are left with only resentment and guilt. Without forgiveness you will become prisoners in prisons of your own design.

Ideally, forgiveness is a two-way street, a two-way experience. Forgiveness frees the forgiver and often the person who accepts the forgiveness. It frees you to love again. It frees you to grow again. It heals the human spirit. It takes the sting out of any memory and any pain that remains in your lives.

There is nothing sentimental or easy about forgiving. Dr. Lewis Smedes of Fuller Theological Seminary defines it this way: "Forgiveness means to give up all claim upon the one who has hurt you, including letting go of all the emotional consequences of the hurt." This is the antithesis of our selfish human nature.

Dr. Arch Hart, dean of the School of Psychology at Fuller Theological Seminary, also has a helpful definition of forgiveness: "Forgiveness is surrendering the right to hurt back." Many Jews had misinterpreted the Old Testament principle of "an eye for an eye" as mandating that they should always get even with those who had wronged them. But Jesus said something quite different in the Sermon on the Mount: "Forgive. Turn the other cheek." This is a hard teaching, but when we apply it to our lives, it sets us free.

On the other hand, as we'll see in a moment, true forgiveness involves much more than just forgetting, or excusing, or smoothing things over.

What happens to you when you do not forgive? Let me name at least ten consequences that come to mind:

1. You are controlled by your anger, pain, or hatred.
2. You are directed by negative memories.
3. You do not act freely.
4. You keep a controlling grasp on situations and people.
5. You are pressured by lives of tension and stress.
6. You probably shorten your lives.
7. Your relationships with others are strained.
8. Your relationship with God is weakened.
9. You have very little sense of self-worth.
10. You feel unrelieved guilt.

Let's try to zero in on what forgiveness is. Forgiveness is at least the following seven things. You may want to write these down.

FORGIVENESS IS A DECISION, NOT A FEELING

Yes, forgiveness is a decision. The decision to forgive is the necessary first step; what happens next depends on the individual. A lot of you will say, "I don't feel like forgiving." And that is a valid statement because forgiveness is not a feeling. It is a conscious decision to act. It is the decision to act, and not the feeling about that action, that is important. Forgiveness, first of all, is a decision.

FORGIVENESS IS SHOWING MERCY

You need to show mercy, even when the injury to you has been premeditated and deliberate. The challenge of real forgiveness is not in forgiving when there was a reason for what was done to you. Real forgiveness is forgiving when there was no excuse, when there was no reason, when there was no adequate explanation or rationale. There is a wonderful power in being able to say "I forgive you" to someone (even as your rational processes are screaming to get even) — when, instead of getting even, instead of getting the "pound of flesh" or the retribution that may be justified, mercy is shown. Forgiveness is mercy, and that is not easy.

FORGIVENESS IS ACCEPTANCE

It is a liberating experience to accept the other person as he or she is. What a gift it is to be able to forgive the child or the adult for being awkward and clumsy, to forgive a friend for being habitually late. Forgiveness is letting go of judgments and simply accepting people as they are, with all of their warts and blemishes. "I'm not perfect. I'm just forgiven." Forgiveness is acceptance.

FORGIVENESS IS RISKY

It means making yourselves vulnerable. It means some people will say, "You're a fool." They'll say that forgiveness is foolishness because it is too costly. It can hurt. But we know that surgery hurts. Why do we allow it? Why do we let somebody cut into our bodies? We do it because we know that even with the risk, even with the pain and discomfort, there is also the hope that the pain and risk will ultimately result in our healing. Forgiveness is a risk that is worth taking, not because of the short-term pain or the short-term consequences, but because of the long-term possibilities and the long-term promise of real healing.

FORGIVENESS IS ACCEPTING APOLOGY

Are you able to accept an apology? I want to share with you a personal experience. One night after speaking to a group of single folks, a woman came up to me and said, "Flan, I have to ask your forgiveness."

I barely even knew who she was and was a bit startled.

She said, "Last Sunday morning you walked by me and you said, 'Hello,' and I was in a bad mood and didn't say anything back to you. I want you to know how sorry I am for being so cold."

I didn't have the vaguest recollection of the incident, but I didn't tell her that. I simply said, "No problem. There's nothing to feel sorry about. It happens all the time." But on the way home I thought about this woman and about the way I handled her apology. I was sure she had been very upset about the incident. Apologizing was a very hard thing for her to do because she was a very shy person. And what did I do? I didn't take her seriously. I didn't listen to what she had to say. I just brushed her aside. I didn't truly accept her apology.

When I phoned her to ask her forgiveness for the way I had responded, she didn't do what I had done. She took me seriously. I learned something about forgiveness from that woman. Forgiveness is accepting an apology.

It is usually much harder to accept an apology than it is to offer it. It's very hard for me to accept either praise or an apology. I get embarrassed, flustered, and ill at ease. But as you go through divorce, it is important to grab hold of yourselves and understand how important acceptance is. Forgiveness is accepting—accepting an apology from someone else.

FORGIVENESS IS A WAY OF LIVING

It means developing in your lives a readiness to forgive. By pardoning others for little everyday hurts and annoyances, you prepare yourselves to handle the more important, significant, and painful injuries and blunders that come your way.

FORGIVENESS IS CHOOSING TO LOVE

Forgiveness and love are all wrapped up in each other. Forgiveness is not a conditional "I will forgive you if . . . ." Real forgiveness is unconditional. I will forgive you, period. There are no conditions.

Jesus tells a beautiful story about forgiveness. You may be familiar with it. It is about a father and his son. The son was a selfish adolescent who decided that he didn't want to wait for his inheritance from his father. He wanted the bucks now. He wanted to eat, drink, and be merry right now.

So, the loving father gave the son his inheritance, and off he went! He went to a city with a lot of lights, action, and exciting people. As long as the money held out, he had lots of friends, lots of action, and lots of parties. He had everything he was looking for.

Then one day the money ran out. The friends disappeared. The lights in his life went out, and he came up empty. One morning he woke up in a pig pen. He looked at the garbage the pigs were eating. It looked pretty good, so he had breakfast with the pigs. Then he came to his senses and said, "This is ridiculous."

Have you ever felt that way? Have you ever awakened in a pig pen? Maybe it was one of your own making; maybe it was not. Yet you knew that this was the pits. This was the bottom of the barrel.

So the young man made a decision. "I'm going home. I could have it better at home because my father would at least give me something better to do than slopping the hogs." So off he went again, this time headed back home. As he got about a block from the house, his father saw him coming—because he had been waiting for his wayward son. The father ran out in the front yard, jumped over the hedge, and ran down the street to greet that sweaty, stinky, undeserving kid. He threw his arms around him and said,

"Welcome home, Son. I'm so glad you're back. We're going to have a party tonight. We're going to invite all your friends. We're going to invite the whole family. I want you to have a new suit of clothes. I want you to know how glad I am to have you home."

Some folks call that the story of the prodigal son. I like to call it the story of the forgiving father. That is God's attitude toward us. It is a model for you and me—a model of choosing to love and forgive. We need to make that choice, that difficult, painful choice.

Someone has said that, if you could count all the promises in the Bible, you would come up with about 7,000 of them. That's a lot of promises. Of the 7,000 promises between Genesis and Revelation, I want to share just one of them with you. It's found toward the end of the New Testament. The apostle John, who wrote the Gospel of John, also wrote three letters. In his first letter, we read these words in the first chapter and the ninth verse: "If" (you know right off the bat that a sentence is conditional when it starts with "if") . . . "If we confess our sins, he [meaning God] is faithful and just and will forgive us our sins and purify us from all unrighteousness."

Why do I share that particular promise? I share it because it contains some tidbits of profoundly important truth. "If we confess our sins. . . ." *Sin* is a theological word loaded with all kinds of baggage. I don't know what it represents to you. It may recall a screaming evangelist you saw on television or some terribly negative experience you had. I don't know what the word *sin* conjures up in you; but the biblical idea of sin is missing the mark. It simply means to shoot at something and miss it. Sin is missing out on God's best intention for us; and it is missing out even on our best intentions for ourselves.

It would be nice if we only had to do our laundry once. But our clothes keep getting dirty over and over again. We have to buy a washing machine or keep saving quarters to wash our clothes. Somehow, the outside of us just doesn't stay clean, no matter how hard we try.

It's the same with the inside as well. God says in this promise, "If you confess the fact that you have that uncleanliness in you—if you will confess that to me, I will clean you. I will clean you up so good that you won't have to wash anymore."

If I had talked about things like this in the first lecture, many of you would have gotten up from your chairs and said, "See you later." You may even do it now, but I hope not.

Divorce is a sin. Divorce is missing the mark. Divorce is a tear in the fabric of God's divine intentions. God did not want divorce to happen. It was not a part of His plan for us. In the last book of the Old Testament, in the second chapter of the book of Malachi, God says very clearly how He feels about divorce. He says, "I hate it." Don't you feel that way, too?

Why does God hate divorce? I think there are two reasons. First, as I just said, it is a tearing asunder of something He meant to be united. The Bible says, "What God has joined together, let man not separate" (Mark 10:9). Divorce divides something that God intended to be together. The second reason God hates divorce is this: God hates divorce because of what it does to you. (You may not have thought of it this way.) I believe with all my heart that God hates to see you confused. God hates what hurts, what injures you. God takes no pleasure in your pain. He is not out to get you because you, or someone else, made a mistake in your marriage. There is no judgmental God somewhere saying, "You blew it (or he or she blew it), and now you are going to get what you deserve and suffer forever!" Some of you falsely believe in a God like that, one who right now is taking some joy in your pain. That is not the God I know. That may be your God, but it is not my God. Nor is that the God of the Bible, revealed to us in Jesus Christ. He takes no pleasure in your pain. It is absolutely crucial to remember that, while God does hate divorce, He *loves* divorced people.

One of the children in a workshop once asked me, "Who invented divorce?" I had never been asked that before. I said, "I can tell you who did *not* invent divorce. It was *not* God!" Divorce must be evaluated in terms of the cosmic intentions of God, because marriage was God's idea, not yours or mine.

But unfortunately, divorce has been around for almost as long as marriage. It has been around as long as men and women have chosen to live for themselves, to sow seeds of selfishness and discord, and to put their own needs ahead of the needs of others.

Dear friends, I'm not trying to accuse you of anything. I'm not trying to lay a heavy trip of guilt or sin upon you. I'm trying to do something that will be realistic and ultimately positive. Often, in order to deal authentically and positively with our lives, we have got to accept some reality, some responsibility, and some accountability. We have talked about that before. All of you have some accountability for the failure of your marriage. The amount of that accountability is academic. Even if you claim no responsibility in your failure with your ex-spouse, you must with your God. Somewhere along the line, in order for you to become whole again, forgiveness has to take place.

"I am sorry" are words that we either say too often or not often enough. Few of us use those three words in a balanced way. In his chapter on forgiveness, Jim offers three crucial principles.

GOD FORGIVES ME

Rather than speak theologically about this, let me tell you a story. You can read it for yourself. It's one of the most beautiful stories in the Bible. It's about a group of religious men and the woman they had caught in the act of adultery. You can find this story in the eighth chapter of John's Gospel.

The religious men in this particular story didn't care at all about this woman or even about what she was doing. They were just out to get Jesus. They wanted to paint Him into a corner, to trap him theologically so they could get rid of Him. So they created a situation in which they could accomplish that.

They followed this woman around because they knew she was in an illicit relationship with another man. One day they followed her and the man to her home. They waited for a discreet period of time until they knew the action was beginning. Then they broke into the house right in the middle of the sexual act. They dragged this woman, who was probably naked, into the presence of Jesus Christ.

The penalty for adultery was death. And it was an especially horrible kind of execution. They would put the guilty one against a wall and throw rocks at that person until he or she was dead. Stoned to death: That was the law. So they brought this woman to Jesus. They said, "Now, Jesus, you know the law says that we are supposed to stone this woman. What do *you* say?"

They were certain Jesus was inescapably trapped. If He agreed with an unforgiving law, what about all His teaching about love and mercy? He would be an inconsistent hypocrite! If He went against the law, He would be a traitor, breaking a centuries-old religious tradition that everyone accepted as God's commandment. How could Jesus go against the corporate wisdom of the true church?

The religious leaders challenged Him: "Do you want to break the law, Jesus? You know that is blasphemy!" They had Him right where they wanted Him, boxed in with no way out. Have you ever felt that way?

Finally Jesus looked up at the men and said, "Let the one of you who is without any sin throw the first stone."

There must have been a long pause. Slowly, beginning with the oldest man, they filed out and left, one by one.

Jesus didn't want to embarrass the woman, who was now standing in front of him, any further. He looked into her eyes and said, "Isn't there anyone left to condemn you?" She said, "No, they have all gone." Then Jesus said, "I do not condemn you either. Go, and do not sin anymore."

We have in this event a beautiful illustration of God's attitude toward us. We may have failed in marriage and in a lot of other ways in our lives, but Jesus says, "I do not condemn you; but I do want you to come to terms with your failure." Remember the promise: If we confess—if we admit our failure, God is just and is willing to forgive us. And not only does He forgive us, He also cleanses us from all unrighteousness. What a beautiful promise! God forgives me, and God forgives you.

I want to direct your attention to a prayer in your book on page 98:

God, I know that divorce is wrong. I know that it was not your ideal for me. I confess to you my weakness, my human failings that contributed knowingly and unknowingly to my divorce. God, I ask your forgiveness for my divorce. Help me to know and experience your love through your forgiveness. Lead me to new growth and new beginnings in my life. Amen.

I want to share with you a portion of a letter I received after I gave this lecture a few years ago.

Dear Bill:

After attending the workshop, another person who participated commented to me that the part that disturbed her most was being told she had to be sorry for some wrong she committed. She didn't feel wrong. She felt she had been the best wife she knew how to be. It was not her problem, but her husband's; and she was not being judgmental or bitter.

She was not the typical, "It's all his fault" type. She had a very understanding and very loving attitude toward her ex-husband and said that even he had told her that it was not her, but him.

There are often extenuating circumstances beyond the control of the dumped spouse. We dumpees can only accept responsibility as it relates to our sins, asking God to forgive us. We cannot be responsible for the heart condition in our spouses which causes them to give up on their commitment to God and responsibility in marriage. There may be times when the divorce was beyond the control of the dumpee. I loved my husband to the best of my ability but it was his decision to give up on the marriage, and the idea of giving up on God was his choice, not mine.

Her point is valid. Some of you feel that your divorce was not in your hands, and you are saying, "What do I have to ask forgiveness for? I was dumped on. I did the best I could. I tried with all my might to make this work."

That is true for many of you. We are not here to assess your particular situation or your blame. Some of you feel wronged and dumped on. And from a rational, human point of view, you have every right to feel exactly that way. Yet, I want to reiterate that in every broken relationship there is *always* accountability and responsibility. Remember that prayer we just shared? It covered "*my* weaknesses and failings that contributed *knowingly* and *unknowingly* to my divorce."

Is it not true that we do things we don't even know we do? In all my experience with people, I have yet to see that totally black-and-white, 100 percent/zero percent situation. We are all accountable. We are all responsible in some measure. It would be merely academic to weigh the amount.

IF GOD CAN FORGIVE ME, THEN I CAN FORGIVE ME

For a lot of you, that's harder than accepting God's forgiveness. You think, "I can accept God's forgiveness because God is God; but I am not God and I cannot forgive me." This relates more to the dumper than to the one who is the dumpee. One party knows exactly what contributed to the downfall of the marriage. That person is probably wrestling with the question, How can I ever forgive myself for what I have done?

On pages 99-100 of his book Jim shares six helpful keys to forgiving yourself.

I accept my humanity as a human being. I am not junk. Remember our first session? "I am a unique, unrepeatable, beautiful miracle of God." You can learn to accept your humanity as a human being. God made it and it is good.

I have the freedom to fail. All of us have the freedom to fail. But you do not have to be immobilized, emasculated, and destroyed by your failure. We all have the freedom to fail, to get picked up again, and to get back on our feet and not let failure ruin us forever.

I can accept responsibility for my failure. That is a sign of maturity and health. You have some responsibility in this mess. You were not perfect.

I can forgive myself for my failure. God would never forgive you and then refuse you the opportunity and strength to forgive yourself.

I accept God's forgiveness. You can have it when you take it. You can know it, even when you don't feel it.

I can begin again. Those are great affirmations. If God can do it, so can you. If God, in His perfection, can clean you up, you can say in your imperfection that you'll try to do whatever you can to make your life whole again.

I FORGIVE MY EX-SPOUSE

I know some of you are not quite ready for this final step. Some of you are. Remember what I said at the beginning of this lecture about the importance of timing.

You are probably all familiar with these words: "Forgive us our debts as we forgive our debtors" or, if you are a Methodist, ". . . those who trespass against us." I remarked earlier that forgiveness, ideally, is a two-way street. How do you make that a reality?

There are several ways. You pick up the telephone. Or sit down with a pen and paper and write a letter. Or, if you really have courage, you can do it face to face. Can any of you suggest another way? Telegram? Carrier pigeon?

After deciding the appropriate way to make contact with your ex, this is what you say: "Will you forgive me for what I did?" That is very important. That is how you start. You don't say, "I forgive *you.*" That's not the way to begin. If you have tried apologizing that way, you have probably found that it doesn't work very well. The way you begin is, "Will you forgive *me*? I apologize for whatever I did." You may want to get specific, or you may not.

After your ex-spouse gets up off the floor from a dead faint, you may hear a cynical, insensitive response like, "Well, it's about time you asked me to forgive you, but I'm not going to do it." Some of you expect that kind of reply. But that doesn't mean you don't take the risk of asking. Who knows what will happen? It may lead to what hopefully will be a two-way experience of mutual forgiveness. It may not change a thing. There are no guarantees.

Let me read a section of a testimony given publicly in a divorce recovery workshop in Colorado a few years ago. This is from a woman who walked in one day on her husband in bed with another woman—her best friend!

> I went through the process of going to my ex for what I hoped would be a happy ending. I think it threw him for a loop, because I didn't tell him that I needed to for- give him. I just asked him to forgive me.
>
> The reply was not a positive one. A part of me that is full of temper wanted to lash out and say, "I'd like you to look at these facts and what you did to me."
>
> . . . I just asked him to forgive me; but in essence I did that, not for him, but for me, and for God, because I had learned that God had forgiven me and I had forgiven myself, and I was learning to love myself again. I knew that to make the cycle whole, I had to do that for God.
>
> After the encounter was over, I got in my car to drive across town to pick up my daughter, Molly. Even though my ex had not responded positively, there was a heavy weight lifted off me. It was in the fall, and I had the car windows rolled up. I was singing at the top of my voice and was banging on the steering wheel. I was feeling great! I was singing away as I pulled up to a stoplight and someone looked over at me. I turned and looked at a guy in a truck looking back at me. I pretended I was talking to my daughter. Suddenly I realized that no one was in the car with me! It's wonderful when you feel that way about yourself. You do it for you. And you do it for God. And you hope the experience will be a mutual one; but if it is not to be that way, it is still worth doing.

There is a cleansing—maybe just partial, but enough—and God understands. God says, "My grace for you is sufficient." It doesn't have to be his or her grace, but God's grace. Some of us have to cling to that because it's all we have. It is sufficient; it is enough.

Forgiveness gets the hate out. It creates the opportunity for us to grow again. I wish that for you. You decide when the time is right. When the opportunity comes, it probably won't be a perfect situation. You'll have to make the best of what you have.

On the wall in my office is a poem, beautifully done in needlepoint. I look at it every day. You can find it on page 91 of Jim's book. It reads:

Out of my lonely place,
  I came searching.
Out of my hidden fears,
  I came searching.
Out of my need for friends,
  I came searching.
Out of my quest for God,
  I came searching.
And I found a people who care,
  And a new love to share.

That's what this experience of a forgiven community can do for all of us. The ground at the foot of the cross of Jesus Christ is absolutely level. We all stand on it. We all stand in need of that experience of forgiveness, whether we are divorced or not. We all have to be accountable for our lives; and we can all be thankful that there is a God who loves us and cares for us—in spite of ourselves.

Finally, to those who are willing to take the risk and discover the cleansing renewal of forgiveness are these words of encouragement from an anonymous author:

Risking

To laugh is to risk appearing the fool. To weep is to risk appearing sentimental. To reach out for another is to risk involvement. To expose feelings is to risk exposing your true self. To place your ideas, your dreams, before the crowd is to risk their loss. To love is to risk not being loved in return. To live is to risk dying. To hope is to risk despair. To try is to risk failure.

But risks must be taken, because the greatest hazard in life is to risk nothing. The person who risks nothing, does nothing, has nothing, and is nothing. They may avoid suffering and sorrow. But they simply cannot learn, feel, change, grow, love, live. Chained by closed-mindedness they become slaves. They have forfeited freedom. Only a person who risks is free.

THINKING ABOUT NEW RELATIONSHIPS: RELATING, DATING, AND MATING

I want to talk about relationships tonight, and I want to begin by sharing something entitled "Trying to Do the Job Alone." This is a letter written to an insurance company:

Dear Sir,

I am writing in response to your request for additional information. In block #3 of the accident report, I put "trying to do the job alone," as the cause of the accident. In your letter to me, you said that I should explain more fully and I trust that the following details will be sufficient.

I'm a bricklayer by trade. On the date of the accident, I was working alone on the roof of a new six-story building. When I completed my work, I discovered I had about five hundred pounds of brick left over. Rather than carry the bricks down by hand, I decided to lower them in a barrel by using a pulley that was fortunately attached to the side of the building at the sixth floor. Securing the rope at the ground level, I went up to the roof, swung the barrel out, and loaded the bricks into it. Then I went back to the ground, untied the rope while holding the rope tightly to ensure a slow descent of the 500 pounds.

You will note in block #2 of the accident report form that I stated I weigh 135 pounds. Due to my surprise at being jerked off the ground so suddenly, I lost my presence of mind and forgot to let go of the rope. Needless to say, I proceeded at rather a rapid rate up the side of the building. In the vicinity of the third floor, I met the barrel coming down. This explains the fractured skull and broken collarbone. Slowed only slightly, I continued my rapid ascent, not stopping until my right hand was two knuckles deep into the pulley.

Fortunately, I had regained my presence of mind and was able to hold tightly to the rope in spite of my pain. At approximately the same time, however, the barrel of bricks hit the ground and the bottom fell out of the barrel. Devoid the weight of the bricks, the barrel now weighed approximately fifty pounds. I refer you again to my weight in block #2. As you might imagine, I began a rather rapid descent down the side of the building. In the vicinity of the third floor, I met the barrel coming up. This accounts for my two fractured ankles and the lacerations of my legs and lower body.

This encounter with the barrel slowed me enough to lessen my injuries when I fell into the pile of bricks. Fortunately, only three vertebrae were cracked. I'm sorry to report however, as I lay there on the bricks in pain, unable to stand, watching the empty barrel six stories above me, I again lost my presence of mind and let go of the rope. The empty barrel weighed more than the rope so it came back down and broke both of my legs.

I hope I have furnished the information you required as to how the accident occurred because "I was trying to do the job alone!"

Trying to do the job alone. God created us not to be alone. It says so right at the beginning of the Bible. In the early verses of Genesis it says, "Humankind was not made to be alone."

Now a lot of interpreters of that passage go on and use the illustration that follows, the illustration of marriage, solely to conclude that marriage is the way you conquer loneliness. Most of you know how untrue that is. Harold Ivan Smith says, "The loneliest person in your zip code tonight is *not* a single adult.[1]

We are not made to be alone. We are social beings. We cannot be Lone Rangers for very long. We are designed for relationships. It's interesting to me, as I have worked with single people over the past twenty years, to observe the response of the rest of the community, particularly the other single people, when two people meet and develop a healthy friendship. Singles are worse than the married people. They have the new couple married off long before marriage is ever an issue. We all do that, whether married or single. We all have those hopes and dreams, for ourselves as well as for others.

As we talk about new relationships tonight, we'll be dealing with some of the most important matters of this workshop. But they're also the things you're going to forget the quickest. This is the lecture you're going to pay the least attention to.

All of you, everyone of you in this room, has the capacity to love again. I don't care how broken, how wounded, how angry, how bitter, how desperate, how despairing you are. However many of these feelings may be in you, every person in this room has the ability to love again.

One of the beautiful things about human beings is how resilient we are. In spite of the pain, in spite of the fear, in spite of all those things that want to hold us back, something in most of us pushes us forward. Why? Because we're not made to be alone. We're designed for relationships. And each of us, in our heart of hearts, wants that intimacy, wants that affection, wants that caring, wants that communication that comes in a trusting, meaningful relationship with another human being.

Now, what I say tonight applies not just to female/male relationships. That's the way you're going to take home most of the application. But I want to say that this applies just as much to female/female and male/male relationships.

I had breakfast this morning with some men here in this room. I'm in a covenant group with about fifteen guys, who meet every Thursday morning. I love those guys and they love me. We care about each other. We have a very deep and honest relationship that has been through thick and thin together. Some of us have been together for quite a few years. I value the relationship I have with my male friends. I'm not afraid to hug these guys. The world will think what it wants to think. We need to model something that is healthy and whole to the world, and we desire that for ourselves in our relationships. But most of us are slow learners.

One of my burdens in this workshop for the last fourteen years has been the frightening fact that second marriages fail at a greater rate than first marriages. That scares me. And I know it scares you. Many of you are coming to this workshop not out of the first marriage, but out of the second; and some of you are coming out of the third marriage. You are asking yourselves, "Am I doomed to failure? Can I never get this right? Am I so screwed up I can't possibly make this thing work?"

Yes, you can! If you take some wholesome principles, are patient with yourself, are patient with the world around you, and are willing to make it right and not settle for anything less, you can. But you're vulnerable. You have needs. You don't want to get hurt again, and so you're very careful. I want to encourage your carefulness. You are vulnerable right now.

Many of you are coming out of relationships where the communication was poor and sometimes nonexistent. You meet somebody, and that first date isn't so bad! You start to talk, and you start to share feelings openly and honestly. One of the things divorce forces you to do is to be honest. People who have been married before are typically honest and open. In that sense, they are really able to cut through the garbage and phony trappings that so many other people can't cut through.

So, what happens? Suddenly you begin to think, "Wow, we're really communicating. I've never had anything like this before. This is wonderful! This is great! This is fantastic! This is what I've dreamed about! Of course, I'm mature. I'm forty-plus years old. I know what I want." You run off to your pastor or somebody else and say, "This is wonderful. We've known each other for two months and now we want to get married."

I'm happy you're happy. I'm thrilled. I think it's wonderful. But wait a minute. Let me try to tell you why I'm so concerned about relationships like this. That's really what this lecture is about.

How do you develop new relationships that are healthy? Many of you play the age-game on yourselves. "I'm thirty," "I'm forty" or "fifty," or whatever you are. "I don't have much time. I'm starting to droop." "The old clock is ticking. I have to be in a hurry here." "I have to take the waning moments of my physical beauty and use it for all it's worth." You're impatient with yourselves, and you do numbers on yourselves.

You say: "I've been around life's track. I know what this is all about. I've taken my lumps. I have this incredible radar in me that is absolutely faultless in its perception." But, you see, in our old age we are capable of great maturity, but we're also capable of incredible immaturity, are we not? Fess up. Admit it. You just have to listen and be realistic with yourselves.

Let me share with you three dimensions of mature relationships, three things for you to look at as you develop a new relationship.

SPEED

When two people begin to move toward each other in this way, they begin to feel very good when that feeling is mutual. But I watch very mature adults forming new relationships that quickly die a painful death because they are exceeding the speed limit. Most of us know about exceeding the speed limit. Some of us have paid penalties for that behind the wheels of our cars, and others have paid other penalties for other kinds of speeding.

Do you remember the first time you held hands with a member of the opposite sex? Do you remember your first kiss? How many of you remember your first kiss? I remember mine. Fox Theater in Inglewood. Sixth grade. Joyce Smith. I wonder whatever happened to her? I put a plastic ring in her popcorn. I remember the feeling of a sweating hand creeping up and then . . . contact! I remember very well the electricity of that contact, of just that touch.

It's exciting and wonderful to remember. And it's great to know that, even after we've been terribly hurt and wounded, our capacity for those kinds of feelings still exists. It hasn't been beaten or bled out of you. You still have it. You may not recognize it right now, but you've still got it. It's wonderful, isn't it? It's wonderful that none of us gets so totally wiped out that we lose the capacity to love again.

A relationship that is healthy moves at the right speed. It takes time. I don't care how old you are, how mature you are, how much of life you know, how much feeling you have, how much obvious compatibility there is, how much you seem to agree on everything, and how your lifestyles, your temperaments, your backgrounds, and your interests seem to be hand in glove. You need to go through some of the crises of life together, to know some of the agony as well as some of the ecstasy. That is the anvil on which a whole, healthy relationship is forged.

Now, I'm not going to try to define how long it takes. That's academic and differs from person to person. But on the whole, when a couple comes to me and wants to get married, one of the first questions I ask is, "How long have you known each other?" If they say to me, "Less than six months," the red flag goes up. We've all heard the story of the couple who met and two weeks later got married and lived happily ever after. It's just a story. It may have happened a few times, but it is the exception rather than the rule.

Do you want to bet your life on a two-week relationship? Not me. The stakes are too high.

QUALITY

What is quality? We live in an age when things aren't quality anymore. Our family has two cars. We have a '56 Chevy and an '88 Toyota. They're really different. The Chevy is a special kind of machine. My wife, Christy, loves it. It's fire engine red. It's a very distinctive car. When you tap on the hood of my '56 Chevy and then on my '88 Toyota, you get much different sounds because the metals aren't the same. Several years back somebody in a '78 Ford careened out in front of the '56 Chevy. It was just about all over for the '78 Ford, but the Chevy just dented a fender. Quality.

We want quality in our relationships. As you begin a relationship, you need to recognize that there is no such thing as casual dating. You may have been able to do that as a teenager, but dating among single adults is a deeply serious matter. There are heavy agendas from moment one. You try to be casual, act casual, and look casual; but it isn't casual, is it? You'd like it to be, but it can't be because there are all these agendas and questions. It's serious stuff, these relationships. Whether they are verbally articulated or not, the questions are being asked from moment one. They are being asked in the minds of a couple as they try to figure out if there will be a date number two, three, or four.

And the quality has to be real. Are you dealing with each other as real persons? Dating relationships exist primarily in the arena of recreation. When we date, we do things we like to do. That's what dating is. Dating is going out and having a good time. That's how you can get to know somebody. That's the way a dating relationship begins. But a developing, mature relationship somewhere along the line crosses the bridge from recreation to responsibility. You need to take time to gauge the quality of the relationship. Is this a relationship that can only exist in the arena of recreation? Does it have any possibility of working in the arena of responsibility? That's a hard thing to discern.

While the relationship remains in the recreation stage, people can hide their true selves behind a mask and play a role. The relationship doesn't really have quality because you're afraid to risk being who you actually are. Many relationships are like that. You think, "I can just go right on bluffing my way through and hoping that maybe if I bluff long enough something meaningful will happen."

Or you may say, "I have to bluff. I'm not good enough. If somebody sees the way I really am they won't like me, so I have to play a role. I have to wear a mask." That's an esteem problem. What have we said in this workshop? "You are a beautiful, unique, unrepeatable miracle of God."

Take the mask off! The real you is not that person with the mask on, but the one with the mask off. Are you playing a role in relationships? Don't let that mask stay on. The quality of a relationship has to stand with the mask and the makeup off, or it doesn't have quality. It isn't meaningful.

DEPTH

Depth is speed and quality in the proper proportion. Have you ever watched Mr. Rogers? Mr. Rogers gets up at the end of every show, takes off his tennis shoes, puts on his leather shoes, takes off his sweater and puts on his coat, and then goes up the little steps to the little door. Right before the show ends, he usually stops and says, "You know, I like you just the way you are." That is the way God feels about us.

A relationship that has depth is a relationship that comes to the place where you say, "I hope for and dream for the perfect person, but I didn't find him or her. I've come to terms with the fact that perfect people and my dream person are in very short supply. I've got to adapt and I've got to compromise and I've got to settle for a little less than perfect." You know what? That other person had to do that for you! I'm sorry to say that, but it's the truth.

Speed, quality, and depth. Each one of you can have these qualities in your new relationships. You don't have to wallow in the pit of your despair. We said last week, "God hates divorce." We all hate it, don't we? But remember, God loves divorced people. He loves them. He loves you. He loves you enough to give you healing and wholeness and the potential for relationships that have the proper speed, quality, and depth.

Marriage? Maybe . . . in His time. Remember what we said a couple of weeks ago. We are to plan the rest of our lives as if we are never to marry again. I'm convinced that the people who do that are the people who have the greatest potential to find that marital happiness again. I believe that with all my heart.

Let me also share these five ingredients for a successful relationship. They all start with the letter C.

CONFIDENCE

Many of us lack confidence in ourselves and in our ability to have a good relationship. First of all, confidence means that we begin to trust ourselves and to trust others. That takes time. Give yourself time.

For many of us, this lack of confidence may have to do with not knowing how to manage the physical aspects of a relationship. Sex may well have been an ongoing problem area in past relationships.

One of the most helpful chapters in Jim's book has an interesting title: "Thirty-seven, Going On Seventeen." Divorcees find themselves going back to a place they never thought they'd have to go back to—and they find that the rules have changed! It's a different world. It's a scary world. People are getting hurt out there. They're getting hurt relationally. They're getting hurt emotionally. They're finding out that closeness isn't doing what they'd hoped it would do. It isn't creating the bond they were hoping to create.

There's a sexual drive in all of us, but deeper than that drive is the drive and the need for intimacy. We want intimacy. We want that closeness. Some of us think that we get intimacy through sex, and we can if that sex is healthy. But if it isn't healthy, we don't get intimacy. In fact, we find that we end up emptier, in terms of our quest for intimacy.

We can talk about sex. We can talk about intimacy, but what you're really looking for is an experience of real love. You have all had a bad relationship. Your experience of love hasn't worked out. We look all around us and we see love, love, love talked about all over the place. "I love that piece of banana cream pie I had tonight." "I love hot fudge sundaes." "I love my wife." We use the same word to talk about both relationships and much more superficial things.

I've got to be careful here because I'm a married person talking to single people about sex. I realize that there's a credibility problem here. But I'm listening to you. I have been listening to you for a long time, and I hear your pain. I hear your betrayal, your anger, and all these feelings that so many of you have. And I want to be responsive to your needs, but I still want to say, "Be careful." Develop relationships that are confident and are rooted in something that has depth and it's going to last, not something that is very transitory and superficial.

We talk about "making love." That's a fascinating phrase. Have you ever thought about that? Can you *make* love? Think about it for a minute. Can you make love? No! You can't make it. You can accept it, but you can't make it. You can share it, give it, receive it, but you can't make it. Real love is a gift. It's wonderful stuff. It's bigger than you are, and it's bigger than I am. And it's a product of the grace of God. It's something He wants to give.

We call many other things love that aren't what we're longing for deep down. The experience I had with the banana cream pie is just an erotic experience. That's *eros* in Greek. Pleasure. And there's nothing wrong with that. But that kind of love doesn't have the right stuff. It's very transitory and selfish. I gave nothing to that experience. I only took pleasure from it.

Real love is not taking. Real love is not taking for our pleasure. Real love is giving to fill the other person's need for love. That's *agape* love. That's the real stuff. It doesn't happen because we want to get something from somebody else. It is radically different from Hugh Hefner's sexual philosophy, which says "get" and "take." God's idea of love is to give. It's when you give that you receive. It's only when you pour yourself out that you can be filled up. That's a paradox. It doesn't make sense until you've really tried it.

Only when you learn to give will you have the confidence to pursue an intimate relationship with another person, knowing that you are ultimately seeking what is best for that person.

COMMUNICATION

As you try to communicate, you need to learn to look beyond the superficial. Like an iceberg that's 80 percent hidden below the surface, you need to learn to communicate with an understanding that goes beyond the obvious.

COMMITMENT

Real relationships involve commitment. Most of the commitments we make in our lives are conditional. But when you choose to get into a significant relationship, particularly one that is going to last for life, the relationship is unconditional: "For as long as you both shall live."

CRITICISM

A healthy relationship is able to endure criticism. Be careful! You have to win the right to be critical. Take your time. Don't start criticizing on the first date. That's a no-no. Better hold tight on the second one, too. You have to proceed with caution. You can't criticize until your relationship has developed some depth and some strength. You need to give the other person the option of listening to your criticism or stating that he or she doesn't want to hear it right now. Before you criticize, you need to be careful to affirm and demonstrate to your partner that you are completely and personally committed to his or her welfare and the welfare of the relationship. But a mature relationship has got to be able to withstand criticism. You have a right to be critical, as long as your criticism is constructive and guided by love.

COMMUNITY

What in the world does that mean? Speaking from twenty years' experience, I can tell you that there is an incredible rate of turnover in singles groups. I watch males and females come to a singles group with one major goal in mind. And what's the first thing that happens when they find someone? They're gone! They are out the door! They leave and, all by themselves, develop this little thing called love.

That's building a house on sand. I'm convinced that good relationships need to be built in the context of community. The relationship that is built all by itself between two people is never solidly built. It needs to be nurtured by a loving community. A relationship between two people should be *personal*. But there was never a meaningful relationship in the history of the world that was *private*, that kept entirely to itself. No relationship is going to survive purely on its own energy.

Relationships need to be nurtured by other people. That's the way redwoods grow. They grow in community. They literally hold each other up. You never see a single redwood tree. Their roots are only six feet deep, but do they ever intertwine! They live and exist in community; and that's the way we're made too.

No one person can supply all your relational needs. Yet some of you succumb to that error. You are looking for that special person who is going to make you happy. That isn't going to happen. No *one* person is going to make you happy; and no *one* person is going to meet all your needs. As you plan your life, plan it to be in the context of community. Some of our workshop participants have said, "I hate to see this end." They are mourning the loss of community. I hope you have discovered some community here in these six weeks. If you haven't, dear friends, it's your fault. I have to say that to you. You still have a little time left. There's community here. Look around you. These are good people. This is a chance for something authentic, something whole, something real. We're made for relationships.

We're made for community. So many people are settling for less, and they are not being fulfilled. They're empty.

I've been here in this workshop, as in every workshop, because it means so much to me. I'm not here just to give you some content, not just to say some neat little stuff so you can remember it. I'm trying to capture you, trying to capture you for something that's even bigger. This workshop is a transitory experience which, hopefully, will be a meaningful memory for you. Hopefully, it is a watershed, a crossroads, a threshold kind of experience in your life. But it's a transitory thing.

My desire is for you to capture something bigger than just what has happened here. There's a God who cares about you; and there's a dimension here of purpose and meaning for your life. Don't settle for less. There are people around you who really care. There are caring communities wherever you live. They're like St. Andrew's—caring, healthy places that you can plug into.

Some of you need to take some risks. Some of you need to go to extremes that are beyond what you thought you would or could do. You need to do it. You need to go for it. You need to believe in yourself. You need to connect yourself to some other faltering, hesitating, fearful, trembling people like yourself and maybe do some adventuring together.

Hopefully, you've done some of that in your small groups. If so, you'll begin to find something whole in your relationships, in your relationship with yourself, in your relationship with other people, in your relationship with God. Find wholeness. He wants that for you. People around here want that for you. It's there for you.

Let me end with the words of a poem. This is one of my favorites. It's called "The Weaver," and the author is unknown:

> My life is but a weaving,
> Between my Lord and me,
> I cannot choose the colors,
> He knows what they should be.
> For He can view the pattern
> Upon the upper side,
> While I can see it only
> On this, the under side.
> Sometimes He weaves sorrow,
> Which seems strange to me,
> But I will trust His judgment,
> And work as faithfully,
> For 'tis He who fills the shuttle,
> He knows just what is best,
> So, I shall weave in earnest,
> And leave Him with the rest.
> Not till the loom is silent,
> And the shuttle cease to fly
> Shall God unroll the canvas,
> And explain the reason why—
> Why the dark threads are as needful,
> In the weaver's skillful hand,

As the threads of gold and silver,
In the pattern He has planned;
He knows, He loves, He cares,
Nothing this truth can dim.
He gives His very best to those
Who leave the choice to Him.

Your divorce is going to leave a scar on your life. It's going to be there as long as you live. You're never going to get over it fully or work it through. I say that not to discourage you as we close. I say it because it's true. You see, a scar is a reminder of something that's healed. Scars don't hurt. They tell us that it once did, and we remember that pain and that hurt. "I'm scarred; but that scar, though it's a reminder of pain, is also a wonderful sign that it's healed. It leaves its mark, but I can be whole and I can be free."

Let's pray together:

O God, I pray for every man and every woman in this room. I pray also at the very same time for every ex-spouse and every former partner represented here. I pray for every child, young and old, of these men and women. I pray for the parents, families, and friends who also struggle with the reality of what these dear folks are going through.

Most of all, God, I pray for these men and women and for their courage and their faithfulness, their openness, their willingness to go about this process, for the way they've encouraged each other, for the way they've begun to bear one another's burdens as you've called us to do. I thank you for each of them in the process of their healing, of their coming to grips with the reality—the painful, awful reality of what is happening in their lives.

Father, I also pray for the relationships they have and that they will yet have. I pray that you will give to each of them the capacity to receive and to love and to relate and to commit along the lines that you have designed specifically for each one of them. Father, we ask for big, bold things through an experience like this. We are so inadequate. We are so weak. We are so vulnerable. Father, we need you. We need you, Lord Jesus, to be the unseen but greatly felt presence in our lives. And so I pray that as each of these people share tonight in the small groups, as they continue to grow in their lives wherever they may be, whatever they may do, that you will be with them and will bless them and use them as wounded healers in the lives of others. I pray we may even see a redemptive purpose to the pain, to the tragedy, and to the brokenness that never justifies what's happened. But, Lord, I pray that we will come from this more whole, more healthy, more real, and more molded in the image of what you want us to be.

Go with us now into this final time of sharing in the groups tonight. Be with the kids and teens in a special way as they meet tonight. And we thank you for what you've done in the midst of this process and for what you're going to do in our lives. We make our prayer in Jesus' name. Amen.

THINKING ABOUT REMARRIAGE

I no longer use the following material in the divorce recovery workshop. For several years it was the subject of the final presentation, but I began to notice that it was apparently not a significant concern to those in the traumatic initial healing period.

I include the lecture here, however, because remarriage sooner or later becomes a crucial issue for most divorcing persons. Those who are ready to deal with this material should have the opportunity to do so. You could present this as an optional session following the main workshop. Or you could present it in the larger context of your church's singles ministry.

The latter half of the lecture deals with the Bible's teaching on marriage, divorce, and remarriage. You will notice that I do not go into any great depth in analyzing specific Bible passages. Such in-depth analysis usually takes place in one-on-one consultations with interested individuals. When I was giving this lecture in the public sessions, I simply tried to present in broad terms my understanding of the overall teaching of Scripture. A print-out of the relevant Bible passages should be provided on the information table for those interested in pursuing the matter further.

As we think about remarriage tonight, we need to begin with a sober reminder of some statistics I reported to you way back in our second lecture. You'll recall I reported that, while 50 percent of first marriages fail, the failure rate for second marriages is 65 percent. And that number actually goes up to 75 percent for third marriages.

We think that we learn from our mistakes, but usually we do not. If we look honestly at ourselves we discover that we tend to repeat those mistakes again and again. We spill our milk. We have all done that more than once. When we opt for a second or third bad marriage, that's a whole lot more serious than spilled milk. I am often asked, "What is the greatest danger facing recently divorced people?" My unequivocal response is the danger of beginning a new relationship very often leads to a quick new marriage.

I have to be honest with you. For the first thirteen years of my ministry I worked mostly among young people. I listened to hundreds of junior high and senior high students as they worked through the emotional crises of their lives. But the kind of counseling I am doing today, the kind of counseling I deal with in working with adults in their twenties, thirties, forties, and fifties, is very similar to many of the things I worked through with adolescents.

I'm not trying to say that you are all immature and adolescent. Yet I have come to realize that, although we do change and grow and mature and become more sophisticated, in so many areas of our lives the child is still in us. All of us have the capacity to behave like children. If we look closely enough at ourselves, we can point to some times within the last few hours (or certainly within the last day or so) when we have behaved like children, when we have succumbed to the child within us, when we made decisions and expressed ideas that are childish.

There *is* something good about that. The wonder and innocence of childhood has not completely disappeared from our lives. We do sometimes need to cut through our own assumed sophistication.

· Yet I want to remind you that most of you are presently at a very vulnerable time in your life. When you are coping with so many negative memories from your past, you can end up making immature and superficial commitments in the present. When you hurt, you are interested in getting that hurt behind you as fast as you can; you can all too easily connect that healing to someone else who you think is going to bring new happiness into your life.

Now I know that many of you, as you think about remarriage, are saying: "If you think I'm going to go through that again, you're out of your mind! I'm going to keep others at arm's length. I'm going to do everything I can to protect myself. I'm going to crawl into my shell—and no one's going to penetrate it!"

But there are others who will say: "I can't accept the fact that I'll live the rest of my life unmarried. At the right time, at the right place, the right person will come along. Hopefully I'll be able to achieve a good marriage this time."

Yet, many folks end up marrying the same type of person they divorced. There's something comfortable about being with a particular kind of individual. And often, if you are attracted to a certain kind of personality once, it's not unusual that you would become attracted to the same kind of personality again. You may say, "But this time it's going to be different." But often it is not.

Each year I conduct about thirty weddings. Many of those are remarriages. I meet with each couple prior to the wedding at least three and most often four times. I invest a lot of time and effort in those counseling sessions. I'm still learning how to be more sensitive and how to listen perceptively. Yet, I am convinced that a lot of the premarital counseling that goes on in my office never really touches home. The couples often just go through the motions. A lot of them, no matter what they have been through, still have stars in their eyes. They're so excited about being in love, and so much looking forward to the bliss of marriage.

It's ironic that so many people, even though they didn't find much bliss in their first marriage, still look forward to their second. That's the incurable optimism, the childlike innocence in all of us. I find that many of those folks really are not truly open to grappling with some of the serious issues as to how to make a marriage successful and happy.

But, thankfully, many people I talk to do want to go deeper. I'm in the privileged position of meeting right now with five or six couples who have come to me and said, "You know, we're really thinking about remarriage. We're in love with each other. We have not set a date. We would like to have you sit down with us and help us focus on some of the real issues of what it means to commit to each other for life. We want your assistance as we explore together what it means to truly be married. We're serious enough about not making a mistake that we want to talk about some different things in our lives with someone who has been through this with a few other folks, someone who is emotionally neutral, someone who cares about us."

It's a wonderful privilege for me to do that, to grow with people, to watch a couple move into a healthy relationship with a deeper kind of commitment and a willingness to take a wide open look at the hard issues.

I have watched other couples in this process come to the conclusion that the obstacles in their situation were insurmountable. They have recognized that it would be a mistake for them to get married. They part painfully, but they part knowing they have come to a decision that is correct for them in the long run. I have unbounded respect for such people. They are the growers. They are the people who ultimately do find happiness and wholeness in their lives, whether they remain single or ultimately find the right marriage partner.

As you think about remarriage, there are many issues that need to be directly confronted, many factors that you need to consider. There are different personalities, different needs, different commitments, different lifestyles, and different pressures in a blended family. For instance, there may be four sets of grandparents. I know of a situation where there are eight sets of grandparents. It's a United Nations! Working out the rhythms of how you carry out the traditions of family life, how you operate, how you settle disagreements, how you understand your physical relationship, and how you cope with money provides you with just a few items on the vast menu of things you'll need to resolve.

PRE-REMARRIAGE CONSIDERATIONS

I refer now to the items Jim Smoke discusses beginning on page 116. The caption in the book here is wrong. It says: "Post-Remarriage Considerations." Cross out the "post" and put "*Pre*-Remarriage Considerations." It's a very important distinction. If you wait until after you're married to discuss these things, you've waited too long. These are *pre*-remarriage considerations.

How Many Children Will Be Directly Involved in the Marriage?
Who will have custody? Who will support them? Where will they live? Because I am addressing a wide variety of situations here, I will not try to answer the questions but merely ask them and let you ponder them.

Recently I was talking with a couple about an issue in their relationship, and they said, "We're working on it. We will work that out." That is admirable. I was glad they were working on it, but I posed the question: "Working on it is all well and good, but this is an issue you should not go into your marriage saying you are working on. Before you actually marry, the question will have to be, What have you decided about it? How have you actually worked it out? What conclusion have you reached?"

How Much of the New Family's Income
Will Go to Support the Ex-spouse and Children?
Here's another key issue. Solutions to financial matters are too individual for me to go into in any detail. Suffice it to say that much discussion, budget preparation, and even outside professional financial counseling may be called for if there are significant issues in the area of money matters.

Will You Live in His House, Your House, or a New House?
Smoke suggests going to a new house. There are both emotional and economic implications when you do not consider how important this is. One of you moves into the other's house and decides that the wallpaper in the den is horrible and needs to be replaced. Then the battle can begin. The other spouse says, "I happen to like that wallpaper. It has a lot of sentimental memories for me and it stays!" Suddenly, something that is of little consequence becomes an object of great consequence. Houses are filled with memories

and traditions and are decorated with certain tastes, many of which you need to leave behind you and change so that you can start over.

For many of you, your marriages probably didn't crumble and fall apart on catastrophic issues. Many of your marriages fell apart in many tiny pieces which, over a period of time, crumbled enough to wear away the whole relationship. You need to clean your house of those small reminders of the past that can come back later to haunt you.

How Will the Children Address Their New Parents?
Does a child call you daddy when the real daddy lives just a few miles away and comes to visit on the weekends? If you're a man, you now have a major responsibility for discipline and a desire to build a new home and family. How do you work that out? Can a child call two men daddy, or two women mommy? There is no easy answer, but it is a very important question. It has to be dealt with. It has to be worked out. If you do not have it worked out ahead of time, there could be trouble ahead.

Where Will the Children Who Live with Ex-spouses Stay When They Come for Weekends, Vacations, or Overnights?
Some kids will say, "Why do I have to sleep on the floor in a sleeping bag when these other kids have their own room? That's not fair." Kids need a place of their own. And yet we come back to the economics of that kind of situation. What is the resolution of that question? If you are like the proverbial ostrich with your head buried in the sand and say, "Oh, we'll work that out somehow," you may find it is just such issues that can smash a new marriage to pieces. Children need their comfort areas; they need to be a part of your decision.

What About Legal Adoptions and Name Changes for the Children?
Be careful of that! Kids can be hurt when their parents are insensitive to their needs and identity. Unless you are considering infants who have not yet developed their own identity, be very careful.

Who Is Going to Discipline Whom?
How will the discipline be handled? Will favoritism be shown to one mate's children over the others? I recall a couple that I worked with years ago. I remember Jess and Sally well. Jess had two sons by his first marriage; Sally was only about eight years older than the oldest boy, and had no children of her own. Jess was a laid-back, easygoing guy. He loved his sons and yet had not done much disciplining; the boys ran roughshod over their dad. When they got married, Sally was a very organized, disciplined person. She was a perfectionist. Jess and Sally had a good marriage, but they were very thankful when those two boys finally left home. In the two years that both sons were still in the home, their marriage was almost destroyed because of the differences between them that only showed up in reference to these two boys.

Be careful. Who is going to discipline whom? How does that work out in your relationship? When you are moving into an in-depth courtship that may lead to remarriage, you had better not only *talk* about these issues; you need to resolve them concretely.

There is a very significant paragraph on page 117 of Jim Smoke's book: "Three things that never seem to be totally resolved in most remarriages are the ongoing relationship with the former spouse, the fair and even treatment of the children on both sides, and the constant strain of stretching the family budget over two households."

So many other things also need to be worked out. I heard a woman say not long ago, "He promised that he would go to church with me."

I asked, "Did he go to church with you before you were married?"

"No, but he promised that after we were married he would." Guess what? He didn't. Remember: *What you establish in your relationship prior to marriage will be a preview of what it is going to be like afterward.* Many people seem to think that when they get married and say the vows, the problems they had before the marriage are going to go away. But in reality, what you see *is* what you get.

In the next section Jim's book discusses the fact that loyalties which have been clearly thought out may change with new circumstances. Consider these, for example:

1. If your ex-spouse were to become critically ill in another state, would you drop everything to run to his or her bedside?
2. If your new mate decides to exact severe discipline on your children, will your loyalty be to him or her or to your children?
3. If your children seem to be getting in the way and trying to wreck your new marriage, where will your loyalties be placed?

Those are very difficult questions. Many couples are afraid to face these hurdles, because secretly they know that it is these issues and the facing of them that could wipe out their marriage. So they bury them and let them go unanswered and unresolved. They desperately want to have that meaningful, loving companionship with their spouse. What actually happens is that their life together turns into a living hell. People get hurt all over again, only this time it is worse than the disaster of the previous marriage.

BIBLICAL PERSPECTIVES

I want to consider another area that Jim's book does not deal with at all. This is a subject that is important to some of you, and perhaps not so important to others. Some of you have asked me during the course of this workshop, "Are you going to talk about what the Bible has to say about marriage, divorce, and remarriage?"

There are widely varying interpretations of the Scriptures. If you read the biblical passages on marriage, divorce, and remarriage, you will find some disturbing statements. For me, this issue has been the most difficult theological struggle of my ministry. I have agonized over this, not for my own sake, but to try to have an authoritative yet sensitive and compassionate guideline for the people who come to me for counsel.

For me, the Bible is authoritative. It is trustworthy. It is the supreme guide of my life in matters of faith, ethics, and everyday living. It is the only infallible rule of faith and practice. As I come to grips with the passages that speak about marriage, divorce, and remarriage, I come up against some very weighty questions.

According to the Scriptures, divorce results when human beings, in their sinfulness, shatter and disrupt God's divine ideal for marriage. Before we look at what Scripture says about divorce and remarriage, we need to begin with its statements concerning that ideal. The Bible specifies four things that should characterize a marriage relationship.

On Marriage

Marriage is monogamous. The words of Christ confirm the original ideal of Genesis: "For this reason a man [singular] will leave his father and mother and be united to his wife [singular], and they will become one flesh." (See Genesis 2:18-25 and Matthew 19:5.)

Marriage is permanent. The familiar King James version of Genesis 2:24 is that a man should leave his father and mother and "cleave unto" his wife. The phrase "cleave unto" means to permanently hold onto. Then the apostle Paul says, in 1 Corinthians 7:39, that the woman is "bound to her husband as long as he lives." Add to such passages Scripture's overall harsh attitude toward divorce, which we'll consider in a moment, and it becomes clear that an unconditional, lifelong commitment is God's desire for our marriages.

Marriage is intimate. The relationship is designed so that two personalities find ultimate satisfaction and fulfillment in becoming one in spirit as well as one in flesh. Genesis 2:24 says, in so many words, that a husband and wife are "one flesh." And in Ephesians 5:28 Paul expresses the extent of this intimacy when he says that "he who loves his wife loves himself."

Marriage is mutual. It is a mutual understanding of that monogamy, of that permanence, and of that intimacy. Both parties hold to the same understanding and have the same commitment. We see that in Genesis 2:18-23. You can also read Paul's beautiful illustration of this in Ephesians 5.

There are eight important biblical passages that anyone seriously wanting to know what Scripture says about marriage, divorce, and remarriage needs to examine: Genesis 2:18-25; Deuteronomy 24:1-4; Malachi 2:13-16; Matthew 5:31-32, Matthew 19:3-12 (and its parallel, Mark 10:2-12); Luke 16:16-18; Romans 7:1-3; 1 Corinthians 7:1-17. A printout of these passages is available on the resource table. You are encouraged to pick it up and study the passages on your own, or with me or someone else on our church staff.

When you grapple with what the Bible has to say about divorce, you need to keep in mind five important guidelines and principles. I have tried to apply these to my own study.

On Divorce

We need a clear definition of terms. Often the Bible uses words like *adultery* or *fornication*. What do these words mean? What did they mean then? What do they mean now? In a careful study, it is important to understand what they meant then, in their proper biblical context, so you can understand what they mean to you now.

We must study each Bible passage in its proper context. I am breaking the rule by giving you a paper that has biblical passages printed by themselves. You need to go to your Bible and look at those passages in their surrounding contexts.

We need to appreciate the tension between the letter of the law and the spirit of God's grace and forgiveness. There is a real tension here. It is difficult to live in and respect both sides of that tension. God is concerned about both law and grace. Both are valid dimensions of who He is.

Law and grace are present in any loving parent. With one hand God puts His arm around us and tells us how much He loves us, how much He cares about us. That is grace. The other hand can often be raised in judgment. That is law. Yet, they are both the hands of the same God, or of the same parent. The judgment grows out of the love. We punish and we discipline our children, hopefully and ideally, because we love them. God judges us and is hard on us because He cares about us. He wants what is best for us.

We have to take into account biblical silence as well as what is clearly stated. The Bible is not an almanac that has an answer to every one of life's questions. The Bible does not have an answer to the question of wallpaper in your den. God has given you the rational faculties to make such a decision for yourself based on the best information and wisdom you can collect. The Bible does not tell us everything. It is not an exhaustive source of answers to every one of life's perplexing questions.

When we study the Scriptures from the point of view of faith, when we see it as having some binding authority on our lives, God expects us to make some appropriate response. We have to remember that God is God. God is perfect. God is all good; and God will only lay down a law that is perfect. Although He sometimes permits us to live and to operate on a sub-ideal level, God by His very nature cannot legislate less than perfection. That's why we have so much trouble with the Ten Commandments. Do all of you keep the Ten Commandments? Do you even know the Ten Commandments? You know some of them. And we know how miserably we fail to keep the ones we know. But God cannot legislate anything less than His own nature, and His own nature is perfect. Therefore, He is going to give us a perfect law.

The Word of God nowhere gives specific permission for the remarriage of a divorced person. Indeed, Jesus' words regarding the institution of marriage and Paul's words in comparing marriage to the relationship of Christ and the church may lead a Christian to believe that, if they have passed through the experience of divorce, they cannot remarry during the lifetime of the divorced partner.

On the other hand, divorce is nowhere listed in the Bible as an unforgivable sin. We are all keenly and painfully aware that God's intentions are not always realized in our marriages, just as they are not always realized in other areas of our lives. God's intention has not changed for us, nor has His judgment. Yet, the atonement of God's sinless Christ has redeemed us if we will accept that redemption. We cannot be saved, we cannot be brought to God by our obedience of the law, because none of us is good enough or strong enough to obey it. We do not have the strength fully to obey that law. We are redeemed only by God's grace.

We are not wealthy enough to purchase salvation. We are not strong enough to earn it. We are not good enough to deserve it. But God in His love is gracious enough to offer it to us as a gift. In this provision, we find complete forgiveness.

This forgiveness is appropriated or received when we express genuine sorrow for the sins we have committed, with the repentance and confession which genuine sorrow brings. That is why I make such an important issue of forgiveness. Not only does God's grace enable forgiveness, it also gives us the strength to endure pain and guilt. Grace is not just a way out of sin, but a way to bear it as well. (Look at 1 Corinthians 10:13.) The glory of the gospel, of the Christian message, is that God forgives sin and gives us a new start. Divorce is *not* the unpardonable sin.

God does not forgive us and then hold our failures over our heads. People may do that, even church people, but God never does. I need to affirm that. We talked a few weeks ago about the beautiful story in John 8 concerning the woman caught in adultery. We heard Jesus say, "The one who is without sin among you, let him throw the first stone." We discover God's attitude in that beautiful passage. We also see it in John 3:17, when we read, "God did not send his Son into the world to condemn the world, but to save the world through him." This has always been the way of God. Since the beginning, He has been a God of compassion who desires to forgive people and let them begin again.

The dissolution of a marriage is always a moral and spiritual tragedy. It is a serious transgression against the design of God in creation. It is a tear in the fabric of a community and a deep injury to everyone directly involved. The laws of God are perfect, but the people who live under them are not. And that is all of us, whether we are divorced or not.

Christians are not in bondage to the law. It is wonderful that God does not come to us and say, "Obey the law or else." I'm so glad He doesn't say that, because we would be in real trouble if He did. Scripture teaches that the penalty for breaking the law is death, or eternal separation from God. But the wonderful message of the New Testament is that Jesus Christ has come and taken upon Himself the penalty for breaking the law. Christ has paid the penalty for you and for me.

I am personally convinced that the church must sound a clear note of divine truth and judgment about sin. I have tried to do that as compassionately, as sensitively, and as clearly as I know how. We must also be as merciful and forgiving as our Lord is for people who suffer from their own sinfulness.

At the risk of spoiling its own image, the church must love the sinner and give that person a chance to begin anew. Jesus took people exactly as He found them. That is a great comfort to me. He accepts me just the way I am with all my wrinkles, all my warts, all my problems, and all my misgivings and weaknesses. None of us, in the grace of God, is disqualified or shut out from starting again. I want the church to maintain the very highest view of marriage and family that we possibly can. Yet at the same time, with sensitivity, with compassion, with understanding, I want the church to welcome those who have failed in that relationship. I want the church to welcome them in the same way that God welcomes them, saying, "I'm ready to forgive you and to help you start over again."

All of us who are thinking about remarriage must struggle with the full force of what the Bible says; and we must struggle with the full gravity of all the practical questions we have considered. Only then can we begin to set our lives on a new path according to God's plan.

Some scars will never be transformed into beauty. They will always remain scars. But people who have gone through the disruption of divorce and remarriage need the spiritual encouragement of the church once again to thrive, serve, and participate in all the fullness of what it means to stand in the Christian community as full citizens. Even divorced people can live as full inheritors of all that it means to know Christ and to stand as people in a forgiven state. What we are is full inheritors of God's grace—whether we are married, divorced, remarried, or whatever. It is my prayer that you will discover that for yourself. I do not want to offer an easy answer. I believe that when we struggle with the question at the very highest level, when we commit ourselves to doing the very best we can, we are going to find both healing and wholeness, and we are going to find that joy God has in mind for all of us. That is my prayer for you. That is my hope for you.

Let me close with a prayer written by my good friend, Ron Salsbury. Ron knows personally both the pain of a broken marriage and the joy of a happy Christian remarriage. Let us pray:

Holy God, Father of Love and Giver of Life, we pray that You will be with us in this time.

We pray that You will forgive us for our sin. And in so forgiving, keep us from other sin—

. . . the sin of putting all the blame on our ex-spouse, so that we will never learn and grow from our divorce;

. . . the sin of putting all the blame on ourselves, and in so doing, being unable to see the good in ourselves and the reasons for hope that we will be loved again;

. . . and, Father God, protect us from the sin of Christians who would be too quick to criticize, judge, and condemn, and too slow to accept, love, and affirm.

Holy God, Father of Love and Giver of Life, we pray that we, the divorced, will never forget that no sin, no failure, no loss need ever be the last word . . .

But that with You, our failure may become the soil in which the last word is grown, Your last word . . .

Your word of *wholeness*.

Amen.

BIBLIOGRAPHY

DIVORCE RECOVERY MINISTRY: MODELS AND PROGRAMS

Burns, Robert W. *A Fresh Start, A Help Seminar on Divorce*. Wayne, PA: Church of the Savior, 1984.

Cunningham, William T. *Divorce Lifeline*. Seattle, WA: University Presbyterian, 1970.

Dycus, Jim and Barbara. *Divorce Recovery Program Guide*. Chicago, IL: Support Ministries, Belmont Evangelical Church, 1983.

Fisher, Bruce F. "Identifying and Meeting Needs of Formerly Married People Through a Divorce Adjustment Seminar." Ph.D. diss., University of Northern Colorado, 1976.

Grindrod, Jim. *Divorce Recovery*. Winter Park, FL: Singles Alive Ministry – Calvary Assembly, 1984.

Haynes, John. *Divorce Mediation – A Practical Guide for Therapists and Counselors*. New York, NY: Springer Publishing Co., 1981.

Hershey, Terry. *Beginning Again: Life After a Relationship Ends*. Laguna Hills, CA: Merit Books, 1984.

Hershey, Terry, and Lisa McAfee. *How to Start a Beginning Again Ministry*. Laguna Hills, CA: Merit Books, 1984.

Owen, Guy. *Re-Entry: Discovering a New Beginning*. Dallas, TX: Northwest Bible Church, 1978.

Positive Christian Singles: Divorce Recovery Workshop. Crystal Cathedral Congregation, 1982 (includes taped lectures).

Velander, Peter L., and Larry D. Lindstrom. *Re-Singled: Building a Strategy for Surviving Separation by Death or Divorce*. Cannon Falls, MI: Shepards Staff Publications, 1982.

Wallflower, Donald R. *Divorce as a Process*. Camp Hill, PA: Master's Training Institute, 1982.

DIVORCE AS A CONTEMPORARY ISSUE

Bohannan, Paul. *Divorce and After*. Garden City, NJ: Doubleday & Co., 1971.

Epstein, Joseph. *Divorced in America: An Anatomy of Loneliness*. New York, NY: E. P. Dutton & Co., 1974.

Fisher, Esther O. *Divorce: The New Freedom*. Scranton, PA: Harper & Row, 1972.

Hallett, Kathryn. *People in Crisis*. Millbrae, CA: Celestial Arts, 1974.

Hudson, R. Lofton. *'Til Divorce Do Us Part: A Christian Looks at Divorce*. New York, NY: Thomas Nelson, Inc., 1973.

Simenauer, Jacqueline, and David Carroll. *Singles: The New Americans*. New York, NY: Simon and Schuster, 1982.

MATERIALS FOR DIVORCING PERSONS

Beason, Clyde and Colvin. *Picking up the Pieces*. New York, NY: Ballantine Books, 1982.

Chase, Elsie. *A Home to Dwell In*. New York, NY: Ballantine Books, 1989.

Colgrove, Melba. *How to Survive the Loss of a Love*. New York, NY: Bantam Books, 1976.

Galloway, Dale E. *Dream a New Dream: How to Rebuild a Broken Life*. Wheaton, IL: Tyndale House, 1975.

Hensley, J. Clark. *Coping with Being Single Again*. Nashville, TN: Abingdon Press, 1983.

Hershey, Terry. *Beginning Again: Life after a Relationship Ends*. Laguna Hills, CA: Merit Books, 1984.

Hunter, Brenda. *Beyond Divorce: A Personal Journey*. Old Tappan, NJ: Fleming H. Revell, 1978.

Klug, Ronald. *How to Keep a Spiritual Journal*. Nashville, TN: Thomas Nelson, 1982.

Krantzler, Mel. *Creative Divorce: A New Opportunity for Personal Growth*. New York, NY: Signet Books, New American Library, 1973.

Rambo, Lewis R. *The Divorcing Christian*. Nashville, TN: Abingdon Press, 1983.

Richmond, Gary. *The Divorce Decision, What It Can Mean For: Your Children, Your Finances, Your Emotions, Your Relationships, Your Future*. Waco, TX: Word Books, 1988.

Smith, Harold Ivan. *A Part of Me Is Missing*. Irvine, CA: Harvest House, 1979.

Smith, Harold Ivan. *I Wish Someone Understood My Divorce: A Practical Cope Book*. Minneapolis, MN: Augsburg, 1986.

Smith, Harold Ivan. *Single and Feeling Good*. Nashville, TN: Abingdon, 1987.

Smoke, Jim. *Growing Through Divorce*. Eugene, OR: Harvest House, 1976.

Smoke, Jim. *Living Beyond Divorce: The Possibilities of Remarriage*. Eugene, OR: Harvest House, 1984.

Smoke, Jim. *Suddenly Single*. Old Tappan, NJ: Fleming H. Revell, 1982.

Towner, Jason. *Jason Loves Jane, But They Got a Divorce*. Nashville, TN: Inpact Books, 1978.

Young, Amy Ross. *By Death or Divorce: It Hurts to Lose*. Denver, CO: Accent Publications, 1976.

DIVORCE AND REMARRIAGE

Axtell, Kent and Dru. *And They Shall Be One Flesh*. Council Bluffs, IA: Born Again Marriages, 1983.

Bustanoby, Andre. *But I Didn't Want a Divorce*. Grand Rapids, MI: Zondervan, 1978.

Ellisen, Stanley A. *Divorce and Remarriage in the Church*. Grand Rapids, MI: Zondervan, 1977.

Emerson, James G. *Divorce, The Church and Remarriage*. Philadelphia, PA: Westminster Press, 1961.

Hocking, David. *Marrying Again: A Guide for Christians*. Old Tappan, NJ: Fleming H. Revell, 1983.

Kysar, Myrna and Robert. *The Asundered: Biblical Teachings on Divorce and Remarriage.* Atlanta, GA: John Knox Press, 1978.

Laney, J. Earl. *The Divorce Myth: A Biblical Examination of Divorce and Remarriage.* Minneapolis, MN: Bethany House, 1981.

Pearson, Bud and Kathy. *Single Again: Remarrying for the Right Reasons.* Ventura, CA: Regal Books, 1985.

Richards, Larry. *Remarriage: A Healing Gift From God.* Waco, TX: Word Books, 1981.

Small, Dwight Hervey. *The Right to Remarry.* Old Tappan, NJ: Fleming H. Revell, 1977.

Small, Dwight Hervey. *Remarriage and God's Renewing Grace.* Grand Rapids, MI: Baker, 1986.

Smith, Harold Ivan. "When, If Ever, Is It Right to Counsel Someone to Remarry?" *S.A.L.T. Newsletter* (Single Adult Leadership Training), March 1984, page 1.

Smoke, Jim. *Growing in Remarriage.* Old Tappan, N. J.: Fleming H. Revell, 1990.

Woodsen, Les. *Divorce and the Gospel of Grace.* Waco, TX: Word Books, 1979.

DIVORCE: CHILDREN AND FAMILIES

Coleman, William L. *What Children Need to Know When Parents Get Divorced.* Minneapolis, MN: Bethany House, 1983.

Gardner, Richard A. *The Boys and Girls Book About Divorce.* New York, NY: Bantam Books, 1970.

Hart, Archibald D. *Children and Divorce: What to Expect, How to Help.* Waco, TX: Word Books, 1982.

Mumford, Amy Ross. *Help Me Understand: A Child's Book about Divorce.* Denver, CO: Accent Publications, 1984.

Murray, Steve, and Randy Smith. *Divorce Recovery for Teenagers.* Grand Rapids, MI: Zondervan, 1991.

Peppler, Alice S. *Single Again, This Time with Children.* Minneapolis, MN: Augsburg, 1982.

Rofes, Eric E., ed. *The Kid's Book of Divorce.* New York, NY: Vintage (Random House), 1982.

Roman, Mel, and William Hadda. *The Disposable Parent, A Case for Joint Custody.* New York, NY: Penguin Books, 1979.

Stages: Education for Families in Transition. Irvine, CA: Guidance Projects Office, Irvine Unified School District, 1982.

Wallerstein, Judith S. *Surviving the Breakup: How Children and Parents Cope with Divorce.* New York, NY: Harper and Row, 1980.

Wallerstein, Judith S., and Sandra Blakeslee. *Second Chances: Men, Women, and Children a Decade after Divorce.* New York, NY: Ticknor and Fields, 1989.

GENERAL BACKGROUND RESOURCES

Anderson, Ray S., ed. *Theological Foundations for Ministry: Selected Reading for a Theology of the Church in Ministry.* Grand Rapids, MI: Eerdmans, 1979.

Arndt, William F., and F. Wilbur Gingrich. *A Greek-English Lexicon of the New Testament and Other Early Christian Literature.* Chicago, IL: University of Chicago Press, 1957.

Berkouwer, G.C. *Man: The Image of God.* Grand Rapids, MI: Eerdmans, 1962.

Brown, Raymond. *Reach Out to Singles: A Challenge to Ministry.* Philadelphia, PA: Westminster Press, 1979.

Foster, Richard J. *Money, Sex and Power: The Challenge of the Disciplined Life.* San Francisco: Harper & Row, 1985.

Friedrich, Gerhard, and Gerhard Kittel, ed. *Theological Dictionary of the New Testament,* Vol. VI. Grand Rapids, MI: Eerdmans, 1968.

Levinson, Daniel J. *The Seasons of a Man's Life.* New York, NY: Alfred A. Knopf, 1978.

Oaks, Wayne E. *Pastoral Care and Counseling in Grief and Separation.* Philadelphia, PA: Fortress Press, 1976.

Potts, Nancy D. *Counseling with Single Adults.* Nashville, TN: Broadman Press, 1978.

Smedes, Lewis B. *Forgive and Forget: Healing the Hurts We Don't Deserve.* San Francisco, CA: Harper & Row, 1984.

Watson, David. *I Believe in Evangelism.* Grand Rapids, MI: Eerdmans, 1977.

LECTURES AND SERMONS

Burns, Robert W. "Left Off the Ark: A Biblical Mandate for Ministry to the Separated and Divorced." Wayne, PA: Church of the Savior, 1984.

DeHaan, Richard W. "Marriage, Divorce and Remarriage," Radio Bible Class, 1979.

Nicholi, Armand M. "Changes in the American Family: Their Impact on Individual Development and on Society." Lecture given at the White House, Washington D.C., October 25, 1984.

Patterson, Ben. "When Wedlock Becomes Deadlock." Irvine, CA: Irvine Presbyterian Church, January 10, 1982.

Patterson. "I Pledge You My Troth." Irvine, CA: Irvine Presbyterian Church, January 17, 1982.

Stedman, Ray C. "Caution, God at Work! – What God Says About Marriage and Divorce." Palo Alto, CA: Discovery Publishing, 1975.

Tankersly, Arthur J. "Question of Divorce." Laguna Beach, CA: Laguna Presbyterian Church, May 22, 1983.

POLICY STATEMENTS AND BIBLICAL AND THEOLOGICAL GUIDELINES FOR CHURCHES AND INSTITUTIONS

American Lutheran Church, "Teachings and Practice on Marriage, Divorce and Remarriage." Minneapolis, MN: Office of Church in Society, 1982.

Baptist General Convention of Texas, "Divorce: Christian Lifestyle for Families." Dallas, TX: Christian Life Commission, 1980.

Highlands Community Church, *Doctrinal Statement and Analysis of Divorce and Remarriage.* Renton, WA, 1984.

The University Church of Seventh Day Adventists, *Guidelines Regarding Marriage and Divorce.* Loma Linda, CA, 1984.

Young Life, *Personnel Policies and Procedures: Divorce and Remarriage.* Colorado Springs, CO, 1980.

GENERAL ARTICLES AND PAPERS (Published and Unpublished)

Alexander, Patricia C. "Pastoral Care of the Divorced Woman Who is Related to the Life of the Church." Unpublished class paper. Submitted to Princeton Theological Seminary,

May 10, 1978.

Bustanoby, Andre. "When Wedlock Becomes Deadlock—Biblical Teaching on Divorce, Parts I and II." *Christianity Today*, June 20, 1975, page 46; July 18, 1975, pages 11-14.

"Divorce and Remarriage." Editorial, *Christianity Today*, May 25, 1979, pages 8-9.

Ensworth, George. "This Marriage Cannot Be Saved: What Christians Say the Bible Says About Divorce." *Eternity*, October 1980, pages 11-12.

Fryling, Alice. "So Many Divorces." *Eternity*, October 1980, pages 83-86.

Kinnard, William M. "Divorce and Remarriage: Ministers in the Middle." *Christianity Today*, June 6, 1980, pages 24-27.

Olshewsky, Thomas M., "A Christian Understanding of Divorce." *The Journal of Religious Ethics*, Vol. 7, No. 1, Spring 1979, pages 118-138.

Peters, George W., "What God Says About Divorce—Divorce and Remarriage, Part I." *Moody Monthly*, June 1978, pages 40-42.

"Putting Asunder What God Has Joined Together." *Christian Medical Society Journal*, Vol. VII, No. 1, Winter 1976, pages 42-45.

Rambo, Lewis R. "Ministry With the Divorcing." *Pacific Theological Review*, Vol. XVII, No. 2, Winter 1984, pages 15-23.

"Requests to Remarry: The Pastor's Catch-22." *Leadership*, Summer 1983, Leadership Forum, pages 111-121.

Sinks, Robert F. "A Theology of Divorce." *The Christian Century*, April 20, 1977, pages 376-379.

"What God Says About Divorce—Divorce and Remarriage, Part II." *Moody Monthly*, July-August 1978, pages 42-45.

Small, Dwight Hervey. "Divorce and Remarriage: A Fresh Biblical Perspective." *Theology, News and Notes*, Fuller Theological Seminary, Vol. XXII, No. 1, March, 1976, pages 5-15.

Smedes, Lewis B. "Door Interview: Divorce." *The Wittenberg Door*, August-September 1979, pages 12-17.

Young, James J. "New Testament Perspectives on Divorce Ministry." *Pastoral Psychology*, Vol. 3303, Spring 1985, pages 205-216.

NOTES

CHAPTER ONE

1. Armand M. Nicholi, "Changes in the American Family: Their Impact on Individual Development and on Society," Lecture, White House, Washington, D.C., October 25, 1984, pages 3-4.
2. George Gallup, Jr., and Jim Castelli, *The People's Religion* (New York: Macmillan, 1989), 51-52.
3. Portions excerpted from: *Growing Through Divorce* by Jim Smoke. Copyright © 1976 by Harvest House Publishers, Eugene, OR 97402. Used by permission. This and all subsequent references to Smoke's book are from this source unless otherwise stated. Special permission has been granted by Smoke to use his work as a primary reference for all Divorce Recovery Workshop materials.
4. David Watson, *I Believe in Evangelism* (Grand Rapids, MI: Eerdmans, 1977), page 137.

CHAPTER TWO

1. While this book must focus on the initial workshop, the greater part of an effective divorce recovery *ministry* actually takes place in the lives of individuals in this "graduate" phase; their personal stories of struggle and victory could be the subject of many more volumes on divorce recovery.
2. Dr. Flanagan's six-part video series, "Rebuilding the Castle That Has Come Down: Divorce Recovery," is available through Gospel Films, Muskegon, MI.
3. This book, by one of my colleagues at St. Andrew's, outlines in detail our companion workshop for teens. It is an excellent resource if you are including youth in your workshop.

CHAPTER EIGHT

1. Albert Ellis, *Reason and Emotion in Psychotherapy* (New York: Lyle Stuart, 1962).
2. David Burns, *Feeling Good: The New Mood Therapy* (New York: Signet, 1980), pages 31-41.

CHAPTER TWELVE

1. I personally have found no need to use slides, films, or other visual aids. Remember that the important thing about your lectures is not how polished or high-tech they are, but how much love and concern you communicate.

CHAPTER THIRTEEN

1. All the names in this chapter have been changed.
2. George Gallup, Jr., and Jim Castelli, *The People's Religion* (New York: Macmillan, 1989), pages 51-52.

APPENDIX, SESSION ONE

1. Paul Bohannan, *Divorce and After* (Garden City, NJ: Doubleday & Co., 1971), pages 41-42.
2. Terry Hershey, *Beginning Again: Life after a Relationship Ends* (Laguna Hills, CA: Merritt Books, 1984), page 114.
3. Elizabeth Kubler-Ross, *On Death and Dying* (New York: Macmillan, 1969).

APPENDIX, SESSION FOUR (NONPARENTS)

1. Albert Ellis, *Reason and Emotion in Psychotherapy* (New York: Lyle Stuart, 1962).
2. Aaron Beck, *Depression: Causes and Treatment* (Philadelphia: University of Pennsylvania Press, 1972), pages 17-23.
3. David Burns, *Feeling Good: The New Mood Therapy* (New York: Signet, 1980), pages 31-41.

APPENDIX, SESSION SIX

1. Harold Ivan Smith, *Singles Ask: Answers to Questions About Relationships* (Minneapolis: Augsburg, 1988), page 65.

AUTHOR

Dr. Bill Flanagan is Minister with Single Adults at St. Andrew's Presbyterian Church in Newport Beach, California. Since 1977 he has conducted Divorce Recovery Workshops across the country, reaching out a hand of hope and healing to over 8,000 persons.

Bill has a B.A. degree from the University of Redlands, a masters in theology from Princeton Theological Seminary and his doctorate from Fuller Theological Seminary. He spends considerable time in personal counseling, writing, and speaking at conventions, seminars, and singles' conferences across America.

More Resources for Your Ministry with Single Adults

Contact Singles Ministry Resources
for a *free* catalog of all the best resources available
to help you build an effective ministry
with single adults in your church
and community.

Singles Ministry Resources
P.O. Box 62056
Colorado Springs, Colorado 80962-2056

Or call (800) 487-4-SAM
or (719) 488-2610